ISBN 978-1-334-93503-9
PIBN 10781689

CONTENTS.

TWENTY-SIX YEARS IN BURMAH.

CHAPTER I.

ANCESTRY AND EARLY CHILDHOOD.

1807—1817.

THE name of Binney is not an unfamiliar one, either in Great Britain or America; yet it is believed there is not an individual of that name in America whose lineage it would be difficult to trace back to one ancestor. Nor is it difficult, on unquestionable authority, to trace the lineage in England back to a period previous to 1558.

Charles J. F. Binney, Esq., of Boston, Massachusetts, has been greatly interested in the ancestry of his family. He has brought ability, leisure, and rare opportunity to the research, and has kindly furnished the writer with the result of his efforts in that direction, from which the following facts have been selected.

John Binney and wife Mercy, ancestors of all the name in America, were in Hull, Massachusetts, in 1680, with their two eldest children, John and Samuel. John, afterwards deacon of the church in Hull, was born in 1679, and died in the eighty-first year of his age. His somewhat broken grave-stone is still to be seen in the cemetery at Hull.

John Binney and his wife Mercy, with their two children
sailed from Worksop, England, for America about that
period, that is, about 1680. Their ancestors had been in
Worksop from some time previous to 1558, and had
doubtless come from Scotland with one of the early
Dukes of Norfolk, who own Worksop Manor, Worksop.

John's son, Deacon John Binney, married in Eastham,
Massachusetts, Hannah Paine, in 1704, who was con- .
nected with the pilgrim families of Hopkins, Snow, and
Shaw. One of Deacon John's sons, Captain Amos Bin-
ney, married Rebecca, daughter of Deacon Benjamin
Loring, who had with others a son Benjamin, born in
1749, who married Jane Loring, of Hull. They had two
sons, Benjamin, the father of Matthew Binney, Esq., of
Boston, and others, and Joshua, the father of Joseph
Getchell, the subject of this memoir. Another son of
Captain Amos Binney, Amos Binney, Jr., was the grandfather of Charles J. F. Binney and others of Boston.
He is still remembered in Boston as one of its merchant
princes. A brother of Captain Amos, Captain Barnabas
Binney, ship-master and merchant of Hull and Boston,
was the grandfather of the distinguished jurist, the late
Hon. Horace Binney of Philadelphia, Penn.; Deacon
John being his great-grandfather and the great-great-
grandfather of Joseph Getchell Binney and the Binneys
of the same generation in Boston.

Hon. Jonathan Binney, born in Hull and ancestor
of the Nova Scotia branch of the name, son of Thomas,
captain and merchant of Hull and Boston, who was
the son of the ancestor John and Mercy, and brother

tailor, on State Street, Boston, knew his father well.
When he had heard the lad's errand, he was quite ready
to give him a trial, only hesitating on account of his age
and size.   Could he take the place of the almost man,
who would be promoted by his coming? His duty
would be to open the store in winter at six o'clock,
make the fires and sweep the store, then to be ready to
go out on any errand required, or "wait and tend," if
needed, in the store.   Mr. Jenkins suggested, that he
would not expect the pay of a larger boy.   "Why, Mr.
Jenkins, if after trial, I cannot do what you require,
you will not want me; and, if I *can*, and do, why
should I not be paid for it just the same as if I were
larger?" Mr. Jenkins seems to have been convinced
by his logic, and there was no further objection to his
making the trial.   The mother gave her consent to this
arrangement, though with great reluctance; and the
next morning found him at his post, as he had promised.
Thus far his task was comparatively easy.   The stimulus
of the example of an older brother, the overflowing love
for his mother and little sisters, might lead to hasty
resolves and even cause a child to feel so great a sense
of responsibility, that he could not sleep the first night,
for fear his mother would fail to waken him early
enough to take a long walk, and then open the store at
six o'clock; but will he persevere?   Will the motive be
strong enough to sustain the delicate, frail boy, in the
severe cold and storms of a Boston winter, and the extreme heat of a Boston summer, in doing the work he
has undertaken? The event proved that he had not
only bent his little shoulders to the burden, with a

will, but that the young brain had been stimulated into premature activity, from which it was never really to rest, until life's work was done.

He was allowed to take the key home with him, and during the two years that he was entrusted with it, he never once forgot it. At first his mother would say, on his leaving home, "Don't forget the key, Joseph," but she soon ceased to think of it. In a short time, Mr. Jenkins began to send him to the bank with deposits, or to do other business. He not infrequently entrusted him with commissions, which legitimately belonged to others, assigning as a reason, "Joseph will be sure to be on time." Though he does not seem to have been favored, so far as work was concerned, in the store, yet the influence was good. Mr. Jenkins was one of the constituent members of the Park Street Church, and a kind as well as a just man. Mrs. Jenkins became acquainted with Joseph, and sometimes brought him to her room for a cup of hot coffee, after his long walk and work in the cold store. Then, finding he had leisure often, and was fond of reading, she stipulated with him to come to her parlor and read to her of an evening, most wisely selecting the books he read; and when he could snatch a little time to do something in arithmetic, she promised him a cent for every sum he brought her, in advance of anything he had done at school. For awhile he took the "cent a sum," as most boys of his age and circumstances would have done: he was trying to make money for others, and he did it by all honest means. But at length he began to think that Mrs. Jenkins received nothing in return for the money she gave, and that she must have only his good in view. He therefore went to her and told her that he could not take the money any longer, but would bring the sums to her just the same.

Mr. Jenkins took up his slate one day, seemed pleased with what he was doing, and suggested that he should study Book-keeping a little. He put him on the right track with some few words of encouragement; and thenceforward Joseph spent every moment of spare time in learning the way in which Mr. Jenkins kept his accounts. Thus commenced, even at that early age, that system of self-culture which after circumstances made so essential to his success.

There sprung up a strong attachment between Mrs. Jenkins and "Little Binney," as she called him. An incident may not be out of place here to show how truly the boy was "the father of the man." Mrs. Jenkins had a very pretty garden, with many choice and rare plants; and when she left for the summer, which she usually did, these often suffered from neglect or want of skill in their management. The second summer Joseph was with them, she called him to her, and showed him the selection of rare plants she had made, and proposed to leave them in his care during her absence. He hesitated to assume the responsibility, and thought a gardener would surely do better by them than he could. But she said she would leave the most minute instructions as to their treatment, and that she knew he would be faithful in obeying them. He had before expressed his sense of obligation to her; and now he had it in his power to do her a very great favor. He at once consented, made a little book and wrote down her instructions from her lips, so that he could keep them in his pocket, and never be in doubt. He has often been heard to speak of that little book as being the commencement of a habit, which he continued while he lived, of trusting nothing to memory. It was easy to carry his memorandum-book in his pocket; thus relieving the memory of a burden, which after all, it might fail to carry safely. When Mrs. Jenkins returned, she found her plants as she expected in a most flourishing state. This incident helped the lad in forming a taste for the cultivation of plants, and awakened a genuine love for them, which was a source of pleasure to him, in whatever clime he found them ever after. This friendship for Mrs. Jenkins lasted while she lived. One of his first visits paid on returning from time to time to his native city, was always to her. He often said when alluding to her; "If woman only knew her power of influencing boys, her opportunities to do so would not be so frequently neglected!"

It must not be inferred from the faithful, conscientious manner in which he performed his duties, that he was an extra quiet and good boy, in the common acceptation of these words. He loved play, and sometimes fell into boyish difficulties by it. His father used to tell the story of his having played foot-ball in front of a store in Washington Street, which was furnished with very handsome-plate-glass windows,— handsome for those days. He kicked the ball against one of the panes and broke it. Greatly alarmed and fearing some severe treatment, he yet went boldly in alone, and spoke to the head of the establishment. He told him that he was playing on the street on his way from school and had broken the pane of glass accidentally; but if he would tell him what it would cost to replace it, he would bring the money as soon as he could go home and back. He was told, and at once ran home to lay the matter before his father. His father listening to the story said, "How dare you promise the money? You have not two dollars in the world." "No, but you have, and am I not your boy?" The father acknowledged the claim, walked with him, paid for the glass, and required his son to make all due apology for the trouble he had caused, and to promise not to play foot-ball on the street again; this his father told to illustrate his early recognition of the duty of paying an honest debt; but it showed at the same time, his love for play. His grandmother used to say that "Joseph sowed a great many wild oats, but grace spared him from reaping the harvest." But what the dear grandmother called "sowing wild oats" seems never to have gone farther than the enjoyment of a good deal of fun, mostly at home or with his most intimate friends.

When about twelve years of age, he met with an irreparable loss in the sudden death of his mother. Though she never made a public profession of religion, yet she was, in all the relations of this life, most exemplary. She was a great reader, especially of history, and Joseph was accustomed to read aloud to her, while she sewed; and thus, while a mere child, acquired an unusual knowledge of history, and what was better, a taste for it, rather than for works of fiction. If he took up a story, and was told that it was fictitious, he would lay it aside at once for one of "mother's books," which were always true stories. In her was united in a remarkable degree the tender, loving mother and the strict disciplinarian. She never spake harshly or in a loud tone of voice to a child; and it was a rule with her never to bid them twice to do a thing. It was rarely necessary to punish them, though she believed in the use of the rod, according to the orthodox creed of that day. Her household was well ordered; "a place for everything and everything in its place" was the motto acted upon by herself, and so fully expected of every member of the family that it seemed natural rather than enforced. The habit of order, whether inherited or acquired, was ever a prominent trait in the character of her son. At home or abroad he rarely spent a moment looking for anything; and if by any chance anything was mislaid, the humiliation he felt in consequence was most apparent. The loss of time occasioned by carelessness, or failure to perform a duty or meet an engagement promptly, was in himself deemed a moral delinquency. The father never desired to give the children another mother.

CHAPTER II.

1821—1827.

NOT long after the mother's death, the dear grand-mother, already advanced in years, was persuaded to come to her son and supply as far as possible the place thus made vacant. As she was destined to exert so important an influence on the character of her grandson, it will not be irrelevant to notice briefly the prominent points of her life and character.

She was born in the town of Hull, Massachusetts, where in her childhood there were few educational privileges, and at a period, when they were not deemed necessary for girls, even in the " Commonwealth of Massachusetts." The late Rev. Henry Jackson, D. D., then a pastor in Charlestown, once asked her in the presence of the writer " where she was educated ? " The question was evidently called forth by the extent and accuracy of her historical knowledge. She replied, "If you mean to ask what institution I attended ; I can only say, that I went to school in the town of Hull, when nearly or quite seven years of age, just six weeks. In that time I learned to read easy readings and to write a little. As I had to walk a long way to school, my parents thought my at-

25

tainments sufficient for a girl, and took me from school. As I grew older I read everything that came in my way. I read all the English classics before I was grown. I read English Grammar pretty thoroughly and learned some arithmetic, so that when I was left a widow and had need to keep my accounts I kept them. When I needed to write my first letter, I got some old letters and studied them, and practiced on mine till it was tolerably satisfactory; and I soon learned to correspond with those to whom I deemed it necessary to write, with a good deal of ease and pleasure. I have always found the best way for me to learn do a thing was *to do it*. As to history, my personal experience of so much of the history of our own country made me anxious to read all that was written; and our early history was so identified with that of Great Britain, that the more I read, the more I wished to read. Then naturally I wished to compare the history of Great Britain with that of other countries. History seems as natural to me as my household duties. Of late years, however, I read but little except the Book. I find so much there, that I have lost my eager craving for new books. When I see ministers of the gospel getting much of their theology from other books I feel anxious. I often tell Joseph, I would rather see him more frequently at the pure fountain, and thinking less of the streams." So she told her own story.

On her, Joseph lavished all the respect and love which was due from a grateful grandchild. He was her acknowledged favorite, yet there was little demonstration in words on either side. It was not natural to them to speak much of their own emotions. It has already been mentioned that his father went away from home to find employment. He did not long remain away however. Business friends were interested, and he soon returned to Boston, and as soon as practicable his boys were placed in the public schools, where they had both thorough instruction and discipline. The latter was severe, judged even by the standard of those days; but the sons of the best families in Boston were Joseph's school-fellows, and neither he nor they would have found any relief by making complaints at home. At one time he received a very severe chastisement for a trifling offense which involved neither disobedience to rules nor moral turpitude, and he quietly told the master that he would not have the opportunity to repeat it. "What do you propose to do, Binney?" "I intend to obey the rules of the school strictly; and if I find myself in danger of a flogging, I shall leave the house; and more than that, I propose to settle this affair with you when I am a man." The master made no reply, but afterwards treated him as the relation justified. But Joseph did not forget the offense; and the purpose of settling the affair with him was cherished until his conversion, when one of the first evidences that all things had really become new to him was his unconditional forgiveness of the injury. The desire of revenge never returned; on the contrary he sought an opportunity for a kindly recognition.

When he had completed the usual course at the Boston Public Schools, he began to look about for a preparation for his life's work. About this time an Englishman, by the name of Adlam, established himself

3*

in Boston, in the business known as the " Rule, Scale, and Rod" business. It was the first attempt to introduce the business into America, and awakened a considerable interest in business circles. Young Binney was greatly pleased with it, and his father, at his request, tried to place him in the establishment as a learner; but there was only one condition on which he could be received. He must become an indentured apprentice, till twenty-one years of age, receiving board and clothing for services. With these conditions he gladly complied. He at once made friends with the foreman, and after working all day on the usual work of young apprentices, he worked often till a late hour at night on advanced parts. He preserved, while he lived, specimens of his first year's work, especially a pocket-rule, which he used with pride and almost affection.

At about the close of his second year, Mr. Adlam thought it his duty to give up business and enter upon a course of preparation for the ministry of the gospel. This released young Binney from his obligation. At his earnest request, his father bought out the business just as it stood, and placed him at the head of it. His friends generally thought it a doubtful experiment; but the father trusted him with perfect confidence, and seems to have left the business entirely with him, lending him the money required, and standing responsible for his son, who was only a minor. This money he was expected to return with moderate interest as fast as he was able to do so conveniently. He was then in his seventeenth year, slight and delicate in appearance, even younger in looks than in years. But he retained all the workmen of steady habits, together with the English foreman, and he had no trouble with the former while he remained in business. He encouraged their improve-ment, and found his own interest, as well as theirs, in so doing. Even then he had the talent of securing obedi-ence without fault-finding. He had always cheerfully rendered obedience legitimately due. He now expected it from those he employed, who had till then been his as-sociates, and they understood their relations, and gov-erned themselves accordingly. He thought he had found his vocation, and was content, having no higher ambition than to excel in it.

Two or three years before he commenced business he, with his brother Jonathan, was in the habit of attending the Park Street Congregational Church, being drawn there partly from the fact that his friends, Mr. and Mrs. Jenkins, were influential members of it, but chiefly from the fine singing Lowell Mason was then chorister of the church, and taught the choir. The two brothers joined the choir, and Joseph, having a fine alto voice, often sang that part alone, so long as his voice suited it. This brought him much into intercourse with the young people of the church, and he formed some lasting friendships. He was often deeply convicted of sin by the solemn truths which he sang, and for that reason ever after placed a high estimate upon the importance of that part of religious worship. Happily, we have a record from his own pen of the way by which the Lord led him to himself:

" My first special feelings upon my own condition and pros-pects as a sinner, so far as I can recollect, were in Baldwin Place

Church, under a funeral discourse by Dr. Baldwin, on the death of Miss Chandler, one of his singers. From that time my mind was more or less impressed, with all the vacillations of childhood and youth, until the year 1827, when I became very deeply affected under a sermon from Dr. Griffin, in Park Street Church. The leading thought was of my character as a sinner. Very soon, however, I was dreadfully alarmed at my eternal prospects. For three weeks I cannot tell which most engrossed me, my character or my prospects ; but my whole attention was given to the great question : "What shall I do to be saved ?" At about the close of that time, such was my anticipation of God's wrath, and my utter condemnation and abhorrence of myself, that it seemed to me impossible for a holy God ever to receive me into his favor. But I resolved, whether he ever forgave my past sins or not, to forsake whatever I thought offensive to him and die pleading for his blessing. The last of three nights in which I feared to sleep a moment, I sat reading in the Gospel of John the representation of Christ's love, and everything else was forgotten. Such love in such a Being for such sinners ! I melted into tears, the first I had shed during the whole time ; and adored the rich, sovereign grace of God in providing such a Saviour for guilty men. Gradually another thought equally engrossed me. "Oh, that the heathen had this Bible !" I forgot myself. I bowed down and pleaded with, God to send the tidings of this love to the perishing heathen.

After spending some time in this way I retired to bed in perfect peace, not because I thought myself pardoned or regenerated, but I felt assured that God, who had given such a Saviour for man and furnished him with such a revelation of his will, could not do wrong. I could not murmur against his will, and was satisfied that he should do with me as he thought best. Whatever disposal he might make of me, I could not help loving him. I wished to see his people and talk with them of this love, and tell them of my earnest desire that the heathen should know this God and his revealed word.

When I awoke from a little refreshing sleep the first thought was, "Am I a Christian ?" I thought I must be. I loved God and his dear Son ; and the Bible said, "the natural heart is enmity against God."

About a month after my conversion, I became a member of Park Street Church, and about the same time commenced a course of education with the design of becoming a Foreign Missionary. When I commenced my Christian course I resolved never to ask what I preferred, or I felt, but what God commanded, and his will should control my steps.

A letter from Peter Hobart, Esq., of Boston, an intimate friend of his youth, and whose heart the Lord touched about the same time, says: "I well remember that his experience was very clear, and he had a strong assurance. Even his convictions of sin were of a positive kind, and he searched the Bible diligently to see if the doctrines he heard at 'Brimstone Corner,' as Park Street Church was very much called at that time, were really true." "So," says Mr. Hobart, "we would turn it over and over, he often saying, 'We can't alter it, Hobart; we can't alter it.' "

When his mind was decided to enter upon a course of study, it was necessary for him to give up business. He told his pastor, Edward Beecher, D. D., of his desires and purposes. He thought if he sold out his business, he should be able to pay his father the money he had loaned him, and have enough left for a moderate education. He did not expect to preach at home, where, if souls were lost, it was not from necessary ignorance of the way of salvation ; and he supposed it would not take a long course to prepare him to tell the simple story of the Cross to those who had never heard it. He was persuaded, however, that even to become a foreign missionary it would be better to take a thorough course of study; that he could do better without it at home than abroad; and that a knowledge of the original languages, for a translator or a critical teacher, would be essential. A superficial education was no part of the creed of the Congregational ministry of that day.

As will, perhaps, have been anticipated, he had entered on a course involving much personal sacrifice. The bright anticipation of one day becoming a rich man, and taking his place among the respected business men of Boston had suddenly vanished. This he was prepared to give up. His friend, Mr. Hobart, says, "he was doing a good business, and men were surprised that he should abandon it for any higher calling." But his desires as well as his purposes were changed. For himself the task was easy; but how should he break it to his father? Would he consent? However, he knew nothing would be gained by delay, and he had no time to lose. It was as he anticipated. His father had "no sympathy with the wild project"—the giving up of a prosperous business rapidly increasing. It was no longer an experiment, and his future was as certain as any earthly event could be. Was his son entirely in his right mind? He had been under great religious excitement. The terrible preaching at Park Street had frightened him—had unbalanced his mind. He must have rest and a little time.

Even the grandmother, whose heart was overflowing with gratitude and joy at the marvelous change, still advised that he should wait a little, and decide deliberately; not understanding that he had settled the question with the Lord, even before he had dared to hope for himself He had early been led to recognize his Saviour in his kingly office, and he did not fail in his allegiance. The father very soon began to consider carefully the rights of conscience, and came to acquiesce in his son's purpose; he took the business from him, giving him all he had legitimately made, and thus put his mind at rest on that point. Thus the Lord cared for him and opened the way, step by step, as he needed to go forward. He had kind, sympathizing friends and counsellors. His pastor advised him to apply to the American Education Society for help. The Rev. Dr. Cornelius, Secretary of the Society, entered into his plans with an almost paternal interest; and advised him to take a thorough course of study; to save the funds he had, for special emergencies, and to receive aid from the Society for present need. He went at once to Munson Academy, a strictly denominational Institution, but one of the best of the kind then in New England. He entered upon the usual preparatory course for admission to Yale College, New Haven. He found that his thorough elementary course in the Boston schools and his business education enabled him to apply himself exclusively to the legitimate studies of the preparatory course, so that he was prepared to enter Yale one year in advance. His health, however, had become a good deal impaired, and he was advised not to do so. During the two years that he was in the Academy, he had applied himself to study too closely, allowing himself no recreation, or even social intercourse with the citizens. He denied himself this *grcat* luxury, as he deemed it, conscientiously, supposing it would hinder his preparation for the great work before him. He was known, in the town of Munson, only in connection with religious meetings and the Sunday-school. He was also exceedingly frugal in his expenses. Destined to become, as he considered himself, a Foreign Missionary, he did not expect to be able to repay the Society which was aiding him, and he was anxious to spend as little as possible. He thought, in later years, that he carried both these points too far, as he physically suffered in consequence. He had become comparatively robust while in business, but he did not bear study so well.

When he entered Yale College, if some judicious friend had advised him to rest from study for an entire year instead, he probably would have been able to complete the course; but entering as soon as he left Munson, he pursued his studies with the same earnestness. "This one thing I do," was still his motto.

When he entered College, as was customary, the furniture in the rooms of the class graduating was put up at auction and bought by the class entering. A bed was so to be disposed of, and was facetiously recommended to Mr. Binney as "though two of his name had owned it, yet it seemed not to have been slept on." When he left, and it was sold again, the same recommendation was given, that the bed had not been slept on. He certainly did not use it enough. He was in College but little more than a year. The long vacation was spent at home, but he did not rest, and soon broke down. Though in College for so brief a time, his discipline of mind and thorough preparation for it, was unusual. A distinguished educator, who in after years was in the habit of reading Greek with him, has repeatedly said that Mr. Binney was a better Greek scholar than he was when he graduated from one of the best Colleges, and better than most of the young men who had come under his instruction in our Theological Seminary.

4

CHAPTER III.

CHANGE OF VIEWS ON BAPTISM.

1830.

IN speaking of Mr. Binney's change of views on the subject of Baptism, it will be necessary to return a little in our history. While in Munson Academy, he was in the habit of walking among the surrounding hills and groves for the purpose of retirement. On one such occasion, Bible in hand, the thought came home to him forcibly, that he never had been "buried with Christ in baptism." He was greatly distressed, for a time, at his obvious neglect to obey what seemed to him from the word of God, so plainly the duty of all believers. But he finally resolved, as he was then studying Greek, to wait till he was more capable of forming an independent judgment as to the meaning, in all its shades, of the word transferred—not translated— to our English Bibles. But his mind was not at ease. He was a member of a debating club, and he was appointed to prove the duty of Christian parents to consecrate their children to the Lord in baptism. He made so bad work of it, that his opponent was quite disgusted, and declared his "foeman not worthy of his steel." He scarcely deigned a reply. Mr. Binney was

36

obliged to admit, that he "found nothing in the Bible for it, and hesitated to bring forward arguments that would suit Romanists as well." But he remained unde-cided, until, during the vacation, after his first year at Yale, he read Mrs. Judson's Memoir, by Dr. Knowles. His purpose of becoming a Foreign Missionary was not weakened, and he was greatly affected by Dr. Judson's prompt action, involving so great a trial, under the pe-culiar circumstances. He felt that he had no right to defer a decision longer. He studied the New Testa-ment, both in Greek and English, and no longer doubted or hesitated. He told his pastor, of his change of views and purpose, but was not encouraged to "hasty action." The pastor "had once been troubled in the same way, but after deliberate examination, had become satisfied." He promised to wait again. The same record, from which quotations have been made, says, "I earnestly wished to remain where I was. I most sin-cerely loved my brethren, as I had reason to do; and it was exceedingly difficult for me to leave them, especial-ly to grieve them. I therefore did my best, in reading about twenty different Pedobaptist authors, to satisfy my conscience, but in vain. The Bible required me to be baptized, and in the fall of 1830 I was dismissed by the Church in Yale College to the Baptist Church in East Cambridge, and baptized by the Rev. J. E. Wes-ton, pastor, where I was soon after licensed to preach the gospel."

In private conversation, he has been heard to give a more graphic account of what, in substance, he has thus recorded. He shut himself in a room which he had appropriated when at home for his study, a room in the attic, quite away from all interruption, and read and pondered. He had little leisure or desire either for eating or sleeping. His grandmother remonstrated, because he had come home to rest, and was applying himself as closely to study as ever. He gave no explanation; but after a time, she found a key that would open the door, and when he was out, she entered his room and learned the subject which had so engrossed him. On his return, as he was passing her room, she met him on the stairs, and told him what she had done, and the discovery she had made.

"Now," said she, "Joseph, what do you think you are doing? Are you seeking to learn what the Lord will have you to do, or trying to satisfy your troubled conscience, and have your own way too? If you think you are trying to know his will, you are certainly deceiving yourself. If you wish to know the Lord's will, why not go to his word to learn it, instead of reading all that men say about it?"

"Why, grandmother, I want to settle this question once for all now. I do not wish to have my mind disturbed by these arguments afterwards. What wiser course could I pursue?"

"I would have you lay all those books aside, and by prayer and confession bring your mind so into subjection, that if the Spirit, by the use of the word, shows you your duty, you will be ready to do it. They that will do his will shall know of the doctrine. Then take your New Testament—Greek, if you prefer, though the English will do,—and use your own common sense on so plain a matter. Then, after you have obeyed his command, if you deem it necessary, as a guide to others, to be able to meet and refute the words of men with a 'thus saith the Lord,' perhaps it would be well to read some of their leading authors."

This was all the advice he got from the Baptist side. He saw how the case stood; he was indeed deceiving himself; the Bible had been a plain book to him for a long time; he had almost no acquaintance among the Baptists. He went, however, to Mr. Weston, father of the Rev. H. G. Weston, D. D., President of Crozer Theological Seminary at Upland, Pennsylvania, pastor of the Baptist Church at East Cambridge, Massachusetts, where his father then resided, told him who he was, and asked him to baptize him, which he did. He not only brought his letter from Yale College Church, but also related his "religious experience" according to the custom of the church. The following month, October, 1830, by Mr. Weston's advice, he received from the church a license to preach. He found in Mr. Weston a safe counselor and a highly valued friend, and was sorely grieved by his sudden and untimely death by drowning a few months after. He found also in Dr. Sharp, both at this time and in after years, a warm friend, who took almost a paternal interest in his welfare, and to whom he ever turned for counsel in times of doubt and trial. By his advice he abandoned most reluctantly, any further attempt to go through the course at Yale, and went to Newton Theological Seminary. But here also his health soon failed, and with the failure he gave up all hope of entering the ministry. He had a good

4*

many business acquaintances and friends; and as he had enjoyed pretty good health while in business, he concluded that the Lord's will was that he should turn in that direction; that perhaps he might be more useful as a business man than a preacher, or rather as a Foreign Missionary, without a better preparation for the work. His heart was no less in it, but his path was hedged up. He actually entered into engagements in business, and went to Dr. Sharp to make known to him his plans. The Doctor, with other friends, was reluctant to give up the hope of his usefulness in the ministry somewhere, and suggested an agency for the Northern Baptist Education Society. This would not only be doing service to the Society, but would take him away from mental application, and keep him for a while free to enter the ministry when he might be able. He accepted the appointment, travelled much, preached and addressed congregations at different places without much study, and soon regained a comfortable degree of health.

CHAPTER IV.

FIRST PASTORATE.

1832–1834.

AS agent of the Northern Baptist Education Society, Mr. Binney visited West Boylston, Massachusetts. The church was without a pastor, and seemed in danger of so remaining. It was divided into two well-defined parties, but both were pleased with the young preacher, then twenty-three years of age, and invited him to remain with them. He was again troubled. He had not taken a thorough course of education, and he deemed such a course almost essential to success. On the other hand, this was an important field, and the prospect of bringing about a state of harmony and co-operation in the church was attractive. Would it imply giving up entirely the foreign work?

Again he laid the case before Dr. Sharp. His friend advised him to remain, and now that his health was better, to stipulate with the church that he should have much quiet time for study. He had begun to preach, and loved the employment, and thought that he might 'still, while preaching, prepare himself for the foreign work, the hope of which he had never fully relinquished. There was enough to be done in this church without extra study. They needed and desired to build a new house of worship, but their divisions made it difficult to commence. In accepting their invitation, he made the condition that they should unitedly "Arise and build;" that he must not be expected to know anything of their differences; and that all parties should so ignore the past that the wounds might heal in the natural way by rest and time. The house was soon commenced, and was completed with all possible despatch. He took the deepest interest in it, was consulted by the brethren and allowed to be the leading mind in its construction. Not that he gave much time to the details involved in carrying out the plan; but he took a daily walk to the new building, and was an inspiration to all. When it was finished, it was one of the best houses of worship in Worcester County; and even in these times of vastly increased expenditure in this line, it is considered a handsome and convenient edifice for a country church.

So soon as it was completed, and it had been dedicated to the service of the Lord, Mr. Binney was requested to be ordained and become the permanent pastor.

The fifteen months he had been with them had been prosperous times with the church. Mr. Binney had enjoyed better health than while giving himself exclusively to study, though he made great efforts for mental improvement. He had, with the best advice, selected a good library, consisting of books which he then needed, and would always need, having mostly reference to his professional requirements. Few of our best city pastors had a more complete library, and several hours each day

were given to systematic study. He told his people
from the pulpit at what hours he would be in his study,
and that at all other times he was at their service; even
then, if they really needed him. But with a consideration on their part for which he was most grateful, he
was rarely interrupted. Besides pursuing a systematic
course of study, he wrote one sermon, and often two,
every week. He was learning to extemporize, but did
so with great timidity, and his extemporaneous sermons,
as he called them, cost him more thought than those
which were written, but confined him less to his desk.

With many misgivings he was casting anchor in home
waters. He assented to the request of the church,
and a council was called, to meet on the fifteenth of
May, 1832, "to consider the expediency of setting apart
Mr. Joseph G. Binney as their pastor, and if they should
find satisfaction, to proceed to ordination." Of this
Council, Rev. Abisha Samson, the honored father of Rev.
G. W. Samson, D. D., was moderator; and Rev. Abiel
Fisher, Mr. Binney's predecessor in the pastoral office,
was clerk; Rev. Henry Jackson, D. D., then of Charlestown, gave the charge to the candidate ; and Rev. Eben-
ezer Nelson, of West Cambridge, preached the sermon.
All these, with the deacons of the church, whom he so
much revered and loved, after serving their day and
generation with rare consecration and ability, have
passed to their reward.

The relation of an amusing incident, which occurred
about this time, will perhaps hardly be considered a
digression. Mr. Jackson had been called to go by the
old-fashioned stage coach more than forty miles to per-

form his part in the ordination service for his young friend. He was pre-eminently the founder of the Charlestown Female Seminary. This was the first Baptist institution of the kind in New England, and designed to give to Baptist young ladies the advantages which Mount Holyoke was giving to Pedobaptists. His relation to the institution was such that both pupils and teachers were greatly attached to, and were on most intimate and familiar terms with, him. Miss Juliette Pattison was an associate teacher in the Seminary, and frequently a guest in his family. When Mr. Jackson returned from West Boylston, after an absence of two or three days, Miss Pattison called to welcome him home. He heard her voice at the door, and called out from the top of the stairs :

"Walk right up, Juliette; come to my study. I am glad to see you, I want to tell you all about the ordination, and all about Mr. Binney."

He then went on to describe the pretty scenery in the midst of which the little village nestled, the character of the church and people of the village and town, its new meeting-house, the history of the young pastor, of his having but recently become a Baptist, his delicate health, in consequence of which he had failed to complete his college course.

"But," he added, "he has a choice library, and will do all the more in the line of study, for his having been unable to take a regular course." "Now," said he, "Juliette, I want you to hear my charge to Mr. Binney. I want to see if you like it."

Then he playfully rose and led her across the room,

telling her to stand there, while he stood on the opposite side and delivered the charge to her. This he did with some passing comments, especially on the use he had made of Paul's advice to Timothy, to use a little wine. Said he, "I charged Mr. Binney to use but little, and that for his bodily infirmities."

He little knew the agitation of feeling he was exciting. Miss Pattison and Mr. Binney had been corresponding for several months, but on account of her connection with the Seminary, he had been asked to discontinue his visits till she returned to her brother in Providence to spend her vacation. To make her self-control still more difficult, he added as he brought her back to her seat, "I gave him a private charge also; I told him that now he was ready to be married, I hoped he would lose no time in that direction."

Miss Pattison took the opportunity to make some inquiries, which she had wished to make before, but could not without revealing her personal interest in the matter. He answered all her questions frankly, but said very decidedly, "These things do not concern you, Juliette. He does not know you; and if he did, if he dare to lay sacrilegious hands on the Seminary he will hear from me again." He was greatly surprised six months later to find that Miss Pattison had sent in her resignation as teacher; but Mr. Binney called upon him the same day to explain the special reason of her doing so. Though Mr. Jackson did not approve of Mr. Binney's interference with the Seminary, he did not allow it to break their friendship, but in a short time concluded that he loved the young pastor all the better for the "new tie" between them.　His marriage took place in 1833.

Mr. Binney had now been with the church more than two years.　They knew him well and loved him, and were glad when he told them of his purpose soon to bring his bride to dwell with them.　But would the city girl be happy in a country town, with a considerable manufacturing population, and with a church largely composed of farmers and their families?　While all received her most cordially, a few betrayed a little anxiety. A short acquaintance, however, allayed their fears. They learned that the "city girl" was the daughter of a good Baptist minister, brought up in the country, and that her being the sister of a city pastor and having had a little experience of city life, had not diminished but intensified her love of country scenery, and her sympathy with country trials and country pleasures.　It was the pastor, and not his wife, who had "to learn their country ways;" but he had shown so much tact in doing so, that they had not realized that he was not one of them.

That autumn and early winter were ever remembered by both as among the happiest of their many happy days.　With an intelligent and appreciative church and congregation, indulgent with regard to pastoral visits, yet always glad to welcome them to their homes; generous in sustaining all the interests of the church and cause generally; generous in their sympathies and encouragement, there was nothing in those respects to mar their happiness.　Then again there were fewer interruptions to study than in most city churches, and time for study was deemed, under the circumstances, a priceless boon.   Though no great revival of religion took place, yet conversions were very frequent, and the church was greatly revived and encouraged.

But this almost unmingled happiness was not long enjoyed.   On a very cold Lord's Day, in the month of February, Mr. Binney, while preaching, fainted, and was carried from the pulpit to the house of his physician near by.   After restoratives, and a little rest, he was taken to his home, which he did not leave again for several weeks.   When he did again leave, it was to be taken on a bed, in a sleigh, the last sleighing of the season, to his father's house in East Cambridge.   There with the cheerful surroundings and good nursing, he soon rallied, and returned to his grateful people.

During the next summer and autumn, he pursued his studies, with his accustomed regularity and zeal: but there was a change in his preaching and intercourse with his people, which was felt by all; and the Spirit accompanied his labors with demonstration and power. Of this more will be said hereafter.

It may be thought that so much study must be at the sacrifice of faithful pastoral duties : but it is believed that no real pastoral duty was neglected.   The sick and those in any kind of trial were promptly visited; and that he might not be ignorant of any such, he had helpers in the church, whom he asked as a personal favor to seek out and inform him of all cases requiring attention.   He spent one day every week in pastoral visits, taking neighborhoods by turns, and keeping an account of every visit made, that there might be no neglect anywhere.   He entered into his work for the wel-

fare of the church, with an interest seldom surpassed.
As the parties have now mostly passed away, there can
be no harm in giving a single example of his interest in
the social and mental, as well as the religious, improvement of his people.   It is but a specimen case.

He was accustomed to visit a farmer's family, where
both the man and his wife were members of his church,
living somewhat retired from the people generally.
The man was prospering in business, but saw little company at his house.   The wife was an intelligent, good
Christian woman, having a large family of children, but
none of an age to render her much assistance.   She
worked hard, seldom left her home, and had become
very indifferent to her personal appearance, and to that
of her household.   While the farm and barns were neat
and tidy to a degree to elicit frequent admiration, the
house, wife, and children were quite the reverse.   The
first time Mr. Binney took his wife to visit them, he prepared her for what she was to meet, but as the family
had never seemed to be conscious that all was not as it
should be, he did not give them notice of his intended
visit.   The good couple were both evidently discon-
certed.   Even the older children hesitated, and for the
first time were shy of their pastor.   The pleasure of the
visit was marred by the evident embarrassment, and the
visit shortened.

On leaving, Mr. Binney said, in a familiar way.

" Brother D——, the first time you come to the village, I would like to see you on a little matter of business, and would be obliged to you if you would come
to my study."

"I am not very busy just now, and will be very glad to serve you, pastor, at any time you will name."

The day and hour were fixed. At the appointed time, Brother D—— was in the pastor's study, where the following conversation, in substance, took place.

"Brother D——, I see your farm, and stock, and barns all show you to be prospering in your affairs. If you are not in debt,—and I am told you are not,—the world is going pretty well with you."

"Yes, pastor, I certainly have no reason to complain. I am doing as well as I have any right to expect, and am satisfied, and I hope grateful. Can I do anything for you, pastor?"

"No, Brother D——., I want to put you in a way of doing better for yourself. Will you allow me to speak freely, and believe that I only wish to help you?"

"I will, pastor; say all that is in your heart to say."

The result of the conversation soon appeared. A respectable middle-aged woman, needing a home and employment, was brought into the house; and the poor worn and weary wife and mother, thus relieved of her too many and heavy burdens, was able to attend better to her family. A new room was added to the house, and pleasantly furnished, where not only guests could be properly entertained, but where elder members of the family could gather, and spend a social evening free from domestic interruptions. A new sleigh was soon noticed taking the two tidy, happy children to church; and the whole character of the family, now rapidly growing up, was changed by the faithful pastor having dared to start them on the right course. He never revealed the secret; but as the room was always called "Mr. Binney's room," probably Brother D——, has not been entirely reticent.

The young people of the church were encouraged to use their leisure for self-improvement; and parents who were able to do so were encouraged to send their children to better schools than they had at home. An intelligent lady of the church told another in the presence of the pastor's wife, what was doubtless true, "that the people generally were aspiring to a higher plane of mental as well as religious culture."

But the next winter made it evident that the painful scenes of the preceding year would be repeated if Mr. Binney remained in West Boylston, and in December, 1834, he resigned his pastoral charge.

In an article by Rev. S. S. Cutting, D. D., published in the *Examiner and Chronicle* soon after Mr. Binney's death, the character of his labors in West Boylston and Southbridge is truthfully and vividly portrayed. We quote so much of the article as is relevant to our present purpose.

It was in December, 1835, that I went to West Boylston, where I was ordained the March following. Mr. Binney had been gone a year, but he had left an impression of his character and life which made me anxious to know him. I heard above all things of the marvels of his study, and the diligence and wisdom of his ministry. My first home in West Boylston was in the family of the late Deacon Joseph White, where Mr. Binney had his home before me. It was from Mrs. White, who still lives in extreme old age to mourn the loss of our common friend, that I had the story of Mr. Binney's habits of study, which so stimulated me. At a late day, when I came to know Mr. Binney, I learned some things about these studies, characteristic of the man and his life, which probably she had not known. Mr. Binney was very ill at West Boylston, so ill that he lingered on the confines of the eternal world. "Then," said he, "my ministry came up before me; I saw it all; I could say from my heart, 'I have preached the truth;' but I saw that I had done it under a mistaken view of my duty and my responsibility. I had thought it was my duty to unfold the truth; to lay it before my hearers and leave it there. It was their business, not mine, to apply it, I saw how utterly inadequate and mistaken was this view. I was not ready to go to my account; and I made a vow, that should it please God to spare my life, I would bring the truth home to the hearts and consciences of men. I was spared, and the first thing I did was to burn all my sermons, and to begin anew with this distinct purpose."

5*

CHAPTER V.

WINTER IN BALTIMORE.

1834—1835.

SOON after his resignation, he went to Baltimore, to escape the rigors of a New England winter. He would gladly have gone farther south, but Providence, as he thought, opened the door for his being useful in Baltimore, and he entered the open door. The Baptist interests in that city, at that time, were very low. Antinomianism had sapped the vitality of religion among the churches; they seldom had accessions, and dwindled in graces, as well as in numbers. Anti-missionary feeling prevailed, and many warm Christian hearts in other places were moved, and asking, "What can be done for Baltimore?"

William Crane had first removed there from Richmond, Virginia, where, in connection with his brother, James C. Crane, he had been a leader and prominent supporter of an important church. But the church had become strong, and had a strong man, Rev. James B. Taylor, as its pastor, and Mr. Crane was not so much needed as formerly. He made considerable pecuniary sacrifice, and greater sacrifices in social and church connections, and came to Baltimore, established himself in business, and set about the work for which he had been

52

induced to make these sacrifices. Mr. Crane, unaided, purchased the large edifice, formerly used and still owned by the Calvert Street Church, though nearly extinct; thoroughly renovated it inside and out, and fitted it up nicely. It was an attractive place, and had there been no old prejudices to contend with, would have drawn many to its interests. Its past history was against it; still Mr. Crane, with characteristic hope and confidence, thought if the right man could be found to come to his aid, it would be a success. Learning of Mr. Binney's resignation, and the cause of it, he laid the case before him, most truthfully, as it appeared to his own mind, and invited his co-operation. The invitation was accepted, without much deliberation. The missionary feature of the work, and the almost certain success which appeared to loom up before him in the not distant future, were exceedingly attractive. He entered with zeal upon his work. As yet no church was organized, but a council of two or three neighboring ministers was soon called, and a church formed, consisting, with two or three exceptions, of Mr. Crane and family. Not one person of means or influence was found willing to cast in his lot among them. The congregation was often composed of Mr. Crane and family, with a personal friend or two, and the few little children brought in from the streets to the Sunday-school; and this in spite of advertising in the papers, religious and secular. Occasionally, when there was no exercise in some of the other churches, a few of their members, out of respect to Mr. Crane and Mr. Binney, would come. It was very discouraging.

Mr. Crane naturally thought that the preaching, and the means used by the preacher, were not adapted to the need. He invited one of the most popular men then in Virginia, the Rev. John Kerr, to come for a fortnight to hold meetings every night. He did so, and people came to hear him. His sermons abounded in anecdote and apt illustrations, and often in facetious remarks, which convulsed his hearers with laughter. But he preached the truth also, and often with solemnity and power, yet it was not known that any body was converted, and when he left, and even before he left, the congregations were dwindling down to their former dimensions. Rev. James B. Taylor, Mr. Crane's old pastor, came to his aid, and with no larger result.

In the mean time, some of the other churches were being aroused, and the First Church, more generally known as the Circular Church, had called the Rev. Stephen P. Hill, of Massachusetts, to be their pastor.

Mr. Binney felt that a mistake had been made in attempting to do any thing with the Calvert Street Church. It would even be better now to abandon it, and unite in raising the tone of the other churches, especially that of the First Church. An entirely new interest might prosper, but this was a hopeless effort for him, though another and different man might possibly succeed.

This view Mr. Crane was unwilling to accept. A fair trial had not been made. If after one year, no more encouragement appeared, he would consent to the movement. Mr. Binney hesitated, lest it might seem dishonorable to abandon Mr. Crane so soon; but as he was sure he had taken the wrong road, he was reluctant to pursue it farther. Dr. Sharp was expected soon to be in Baltimore, on his way to Richmond, to attend the Baptist Triennial Convention for Foreign Missions. Both agreed to lay the case fully before him, and to abide by his decision.

Without hesitation, Dr. Sharp thought Mr. Binney at liberty to leave the interest entirely to Mr. Crane. It was better for both that he should do so. The announcement of the decision was received, not only by Mr. Crane, but by his estimable wife and every member of the family, with unfeigned regret. Mutual friendships had been formed. Mr. Crane's unreserved consecration to the cause of Christ, his self-denials in promoting it in every possible way, and his generous confidence in Mr. Binney were appreciated by him, and Mr. Binney's success in after life in the various departments of labor gave Mr. Crane sincere pleasure. His house was Mr. Binney's home ever afterward, if for any reason he had occasion to stop in Baltimore.

This apparent failure was at first very humiliating to Mr. Binney. But the winter spent in Baltimore was not a failure in the divine plan ; so far as he personally was concerned, he always believed that the Lord had a special purpose of discipline and training, and this was to him a very profitable winter. Though not in the way he had anticipated, yet in a quiet and almost unrecognized way, he really did a good work in Baltimore. Though the Lord humbled and proved him, yet he did not refuse to make him an instrument of much good to his people.

Allusion has been made to the anti-mission feeling, throughout the Baptist Churches of Baltimore. Mr. and Mrs. Binney had many opportunities socially to speak on this subject, of which they did not fail to avail themselves; and Mr. Binney was invited to preach on the Foreign Mission Work in the First Church. A good deal of interest was awakened. His manner of looking at the subject was new; and, strange to say, to many inquiring minds, the last command of the Saviour came with something of the charm of novelty. It was much spoken of wherever he met intelligent members of the various churches in social circles; and often spoken against as well.

As the time drew near for the Triennial Meeting of the American Baptist Convention, to be held in Richmond, Virginia, in April, 1835, an effort was made to interest the ladies in forming a Missionary Society, and by contributing one hundred dollars to send their pastor, the Rev. S. P. Hill, as their first delegate. Although the ladies of the First Church were asked to take the lead, others were invited to join them. Mr. and Mrs. Binney visited the leading members, and every influence drawn from the word of God and from their own observation and experience, as the consequence of disobedience to the Saviour's last legacy and command, was used. The anomalous position of the Baptists of Baltimore sending no delegate to the Convention was also argued. Finally, when all seemed ripe for action, with the approval of the pastor, a meeting was appointed in the lecture room of the church. Mr. Hill and Mr. Binney opened the meeting with prayer, and after brief addresses went away. Mrs. Binney did not dare to call for an organization and the election of officers, lest all would decline to act, but said a few words to the ladies, and called upon them to give their names. A few had promised; but they were too timid to come forward, and it seemed for a time as if the meeting would have to be dismissed and nothing accomplished. At length one lady, of a good deal of influence, responded cheerfully; another and another gave their names, the hundred dollars and more were given, and officers for the year chosen.

Such was the reaction of feeling when this was accomplished that Mrs. Binney, whose voice had never before been heard except "where two or three were gathered together," said "Let us pray." In the midst of intense excitement, yet most profound feeling, she mingled with a brief supplication for a blessing upon the new organization, words of joyful thanksgiving and praise. On hastening from the church to report to her husband, she had to go but a few steps before she met him walking back and forth, lingering near, in order to learn the result; and when with enlivened step they walked homeward together, Mr. Crane met them with eager congratulations. Others too were waiting.

And what was there in this simple gathering of a few ladies in a large city that should have caused such intense feeling? There was this: Christ was so dishonored by his churches living in utter neglect of the command and example of him who had suffered unto death, in order to save the lost and perishing, that it was feared other candlesticks would be removed out of their places;

and this looked like remembering "from whence they had fallen" and returning to their first love.　Angels too were doubtless hovering near to carry the news of the first evidences of repentance to the shining realms above.

Thus was formed the first Baptist Missionary Society in the city of Baltimore.　This narrative presents so striking a contrast to the present condition of the churches in one of the foremost of our cities, in every good word and work, that it must seem almost incredible to this generation.　A few only linger, to whom this account will be no surprise.

The following April, Mr. Binney attended the meeting of the American Baptist Convention held at Richmond, to which reference has already been made.　It was in many respects a most extraordinary meeting.　For the first time England sent delegates to greet their brethren west of the Atlantic.　All the leading men, north and south met together.　Rev. Spencer H. Cone, D. D., of New York, presided with grace and dignity rarely equalled.　All who came were entertained with hospitality unlimited.

Mr. Binney had most earnestly desired to attend this meeting, not only that he had anticipated in it a rich opportunity for enjoyment; but his heart was thoroughly in the work to be promoted by it, and he greatly wished to become better acquainted with the Baptist ministry.　He wished, however, to attend as a delegate, that he might the more freely mingle in its councils and learn its methods of work; but he had no church or other body to represent.　He spoke of this to no one.

The ladies of the new organization, however, began to think and talk about it. "Mr. Binney had made it possible for them to send their pastor, and now it would be pleasant for them to raise another hundred dollars and add Mr. Binney's name as one of their delegates." This, for obvious reasons, he discouraged. The time drew near; delegates from the North were arriving in Baltimore *en route* for Richmond, and he was still doubtful whether he should be able to go in a satisfactory way, and therefore thinking it would be better for him not to go at all, when he received credentials from the Worcester County Association, of which he had been a member, as one of their delegates, with the necessary funds for meeting all expenses. This unexpected kindness and courtesy enabled him to go cheerfully. He was young, and a stranger to the body generally; and, as was fitting, he was for the most part a quiet listener; but wherever present, whether in the social gathering or public meetings, it was most apparent that his convictions, as well as his sympathies, were strongly enlisted in Foreign Missions.

When he was heard it was very evident that he neither spoke nor prayed in behalf of missions because it afforded a fine theme for the display of rhetoric. So thoroughly informed was he with regard to all that had been accomplished on the foreign field, both by the American Board and by the Baptists, that information was repeatedly sought of him, as if he had actually been on the field himself. On his return to Baltimore he said to his wife, "I do not think I shall ever attend another meeting of that kind. 'What doest thou here,

6

Elijah?' is almost constantly sounding in my ears."
But in his delicate state of health the Mission Board
would probably not then have sent him abroad.

He went from Richmond directly to his father's house
in East Cambridge, near Boston, to spend the summer
and await the leadings of Providence. He had abandoned the hope of going abroad, and well nigh the
hope of being able to preach in New England, but was
cheerful and trustful. He gathered his books about him
again, and lost no time in idle waiting.

CHAPTER VI.

SOUTHBRIDGE PASTORATE.

1835—1837.

IN the latter part of July, 1835, while quietly pursuing his studies, and each Lord's Day supplying some vacant pulpit in Boston or its environs, he received an invitation to spend a Sunday in Southbridge, Massachusetts. This he at once accepted, for he had no other engagement, and he loved to preach, and never lost an opportunity. He knew nothing of the church or people, but took pains to learn something of both. He ascertained on the Saturday of his arrival that there was in the congregation a variety of tastes as well as of beliefs. There was a good, intelligent, prosperous farming population, of which the church was largely composed; but a respectable minority of artisans, successful business men, with a small number of professional men. The feeling of class in the place was as strong as in any of our large cities, and perhaps stronger, from the necessity of asserting itself if recognized at all. The pew-holders were not all Baptists, but Unitarians and Universalists were influential members of the society; and, though not actually having a voice in the calling of a pastor, yet their influence was none the less felt. It was suggested that it would be

61

well "not to hurt feelings unnecessarily." This Mr. Binney would have been most unwilling to do, but he thought it very necessary that to such the gospel should be plainly preached, and he aimed to do so. He preached twice in the day, and attended a meeting for conference and prayer in the evening, according to the custom of the church. After a short evening service the church and society were invited to remain a few moments. The object of their remaining was made known to Mr. Binney the next day, by a paper handed him by a delegate appointed for the purpose. He was unanimously invited to become the pastor of the Southbridge Baptist Church. Those who could not concur in his doctrinal views believed him to be an able, honest man, and wished to unite in the call.

This paper was handed him just as he was stepping into the stage coach to leave for Boston. He was taken by surprise, and could give no reply then. He said, however, that he would go home and after consultation with his wife, and further prayerful consideration, write them, or as he hoped to be with them the following Lord's Day, he might then be able to give them a definite answer. So he left them. A young gentleman, a friend of the family, chanced to be spending the Sunday in Southbridge, and preceded Mr. Binney a few hours in his arrival in Boston. He at once called on Mrs. Binney, and made known that her husband had received a call to the pastorate of the church at Southbridge.

"And what did he say to that?"

"Well, he said he could give them no answer unt'l he had consulted his wife." This was said with a curl of the lip, which showed very plainly what he thought of the reply.

The observant eye of the grandmother saw it; she saw, too, that the wife looked troubled, and instantly relieved the case by saying:

"That, probably was not the entire reply; he must have been unprepared, as he could not have anticipated the invitation; and as, if he should accept it, he would not go to Southbridge alone, it was but right and natural that he should consult her, whose happiness is as much involved in the decision as his own; and it would not be like Joseph to be ashamed to declare his purpose of doing what he knew he ought to do."

There was nothing more said on the subject, and the young gentleman soon took leave.

The next Sunday Mr. Binney spent in Southbridge, when he gave a favorable response to the call. He stated frankly his fear that his stay with them would be short, but he was anxious to make one more trial of a New England pastorate. The providence of God had seemed to point in that direction, and as they knew all the history of his ministry he would not hesitate to accept.

The week following his furniture was purchased in Boston, and preceded by a few days the arrival of the pastor and his wife. When they reached Southbridge they were escorted by several of the brethren directly to the parsonage, where a company of ladies were engaged in laying down carpets, arranging furniture, furnishing the store-room, and attending to other requisites. Even the books were unpacked and arranged upon the shelves. A warm dinner was soon prepared

6*

for a large company in their own dining-room, and before the evening closed they were quite settled at housekeeping. This reception was very cheering. Recognition services were held in the church the September following. A little delay had been caused, in order that the repairs which they were making on the church edifice when he was invited to become their pastor might be completed. The church building was an old one, but capacious, and had just been considerably modernized and newly painted and furnished, so that it was quite attractive as well as comfortable.

With regard to the impression made upon the people of Southbridge by Mr. Binney on his first arrival among them, and of his labors and success as their pastor, an extract from an article of great interest, written by D. B. Cheney, D. D., and published in the *Standard*, Chicago, soon after his decease, will best tell the story. Only so much of the article is taken as relates to the present purpose:

Later in that year (1835), his health being partially restored, he settled in Southbridge, Massachusetts. Here I first knew him, and his wife, who was a sister of the late Robert E. Pattison, D. D. I remember well their appearance at that time. They were both very frail. While dignified in his bearing, to an extent now seldom seen in young pastors, he yet always greeted his people with genial warmth, and soon made them at ease in his presence.

During his first winter in Southbridge a precious revival occurred in one of the public schools of the town. The converts connected with his congregation he taught with great painstaking and care. In the ensuing spring he baptized in one day twenty-two, mostly children and youth, in the river that runs past the town, when cakes of ice were floating around him. The public interest was very great. Never before had such a company of young people been baptized there. Some blamed the pastor, and thought it would cost him his life, in view of the feeble state of his health. A great crowd witnessed the scene. No harm, however, came to pastor or candidates, and a more steadfast company of Christians a pastor seldom welcomes to a church than those young people proved themselves to be by their later lives.

But Mr. Binney's stay in Southbridge also was short. He became satisfied that he could not live in New England. Indeed, many of his friends thought he would fill an early grave. Hence he tore himself away from a people by whom he was almost idolized, and soon after settled in Savannah, Georgia.

In this connection may be mentioned some of the more marked characteristics of his ministry. As already stated, he was a close student. His sermons bore the marks of careful preparation. He possessed a wonderful power of analysis. He could open a subject before his people so that they could look at it in almost every possible light, and in this way he caused the truth to make impressions not easily effaced. He ordinarily covered but little ground in a single sermon. He seized rather upon a single point, and drove that home with all his power.

As a pastor, Mr. Binney was emphatically the *overseer* of his church. He was a born leader; but he knew how to lead so as to make the people feel that they were leading themselves. He maintained a very high standard of discipline in his churches. He sought to make

them in the best sense training schools for Christian
labor.   He possessed great tact in working through
others, and reaching important results where his own
hand would not appear.   While he always was gentle
and kind, in an eminent degree, in his relations to his
people, he was also one of the most inflexible men in
the maintenance of right.   His persistency of purpose
was one of the most marked characteristics of his life
None could know him without soon learning that he
had a mind of his own, and that he was governed by
his own clearly defined convictions of truth and duty.
That he possessed rare talents for the pastorate would
doubtless be the testimony of all who knew him in that
relation; yet God, in his providence, was arranging that
he should do his great work on a widely different field
of labor.

During the two years of Mr. Binney's ministry in
Southbridge, he had the privilege of baptizing some
very choice young persons, whom while he lived he
loved to call his "Southbridge children."   Amongst these
was Miss Catherine B. Morse.   He baptized, and married
her to the Rev. Levi Hall, and publicly consecrated her
to her chosen work.   In July, 1836, just two months after
reaching the shores of Arracan, she was called to enter
upon her reward.   Who shall say that the sacrifice was
too costly?   She did not so deem it, when, in vivid remembrance of the terrible sea-sickness and other sufferings caused by sailing in an unseaworthy vessel, and now
suffering from a raging fever, and in anticipation of a
speedy death, she sent back her dying message to her almost idolized, stricken parents—" I am not sorry for the

offering I have laid upon the altar, and you must not be sorry; do not in your hearts take it back." The husband died two months later. This, in a worldly sense, untoward termination of many hopes did not diminish, but quickened greatly the missionary zeal of the church. The writer of the article from which the above extract is taken was also "one of his Southbridge boys." It always gave him great pleasure to follow their course in life, and to observe how loyally most of them have borne themselves through life's struggles and temptations. He has often been heard to say that "wherever he found one of his Southbridge or West Boylston children, there he was pretty sure to find an active worker for the foreign mission cause.' This was to him the touch-stone as to their fidelity in other labor for Christ. He used to say, "People do not work and pray for the salvation of the heathen, and stand indifferent as to the salvation of their kindred and neighbors."

Those were pleasant years for the young pastor in Southbridge. Two nobler men than the two senior deacons are seldom found in any church, and to them, as has been said in relation to the deacons in West Boylston, he was greatly indebted for his success as pastor. The younger of the two was an elder brother of the Rev. David B. Cheney, D. D., a man capable of appreciating the labors of the pastor, and who co-operated with him in every possible way, and whose work the Master blessed and honored in a wonderful manner.

Deacon Cole, the senior deacon, was like a loving father to both the pastor and his wife. Indeed, the church generally seemed to have a paternal as well as a fraternal feeling towards them.

A reminiscence of the manner in which the deacon received his new pastor will show something of the spirit of the man on whom Mr. Binney so much relied. The parsonage was an old-fashioned cottage, painted white, with green blinds, sufficiently roomy, and with pleasant surroundings. Though the interval between Mr. Binney's acceptance of their invitation and his coming to them was very short, yet, with a promptness which was characteristic of that church, they had put the house in perfect order; and even the "picket fence" which enclosed the grounds, had received a new coat of paint. The inside had also been freshly painted and papered, and mostly in excellent taste; but the dining-room and kitchen had always been painted a dark, sombre hue, and the new coat of paint was not unlike its predecessors. On first entering these rooms with only her husband, Mrs. Binney exclaimed,

"These rooms are dark and gloomy."

"Yes, I see they are, but this must not be said aloud. A very little expense would put on a light coat of paint and greatly change their appearance; but, though I would not mind doing it to make them more cheerful for you, yet I fear it might be very unwise."

There, as Mrs. Binney supposed, the matter ended. The next morning, however, the deacon called, and in speaking of what had been done to the parsonage, inquired how Mrs. Binney liked the dining-room.

"Well, Deacon Cole, to be candid with you, my wife is a little sensitive in matters of taste, and I dare say would be positively happier if this dining-room had been painted of a lighter color, but she is too sensible a woman to allow so small a matter to affect any one else. Besides, she is also sensitive to the kindly feelings others may entertain toward her; and I think she would rather I had said nothing about it.'

"Ah, I see," replied the deacon, "but we shall not allow Mrs. Binney to be selfish in the matter. There is another side to the question. If she is anxious to stand well with us, we are equally anxious to stand well with her; and if a little white paint will help us to do so, I for one claim the right to send the painter here at once." This was no sooner said than done; and the rooms were made decidedly more pleasant.

As has been stated, there was a great diversity of tastes, as well as of doctrinal opinions, among the people; and at first it seemed as if it might be difficult to so please all, that all might be profited by his ministry; but Mr. Binney had unusual tact in adapting himself to such diversity. An incident which occurred the next June after his settlement may serve as an illustration.

A fine, venerable rose-bush, planted by the side of the front door, had climbed up by a pillar of the small porch, and was covered with roses and numberless buds of promise. It was perceived, however, that this beautiful creeper was infested with a small insect which threatened to destroy its beauty for the season. The result of a council held on the case, appeared the following day, when the pastor and his wife mounted a set of steps, armed with small brushes and strong soap-suds, bent on a war of extermination. While engaged in this humble yet exalted employment, two ladies, mother and daughter, members of the congregation, drove past. Though recognized, it was rather inconvenient speaking to them, but while yet near enough to be overheard, the following colloquy took place between them.

"Well now, that is what I call folly. Can there be any real religion where there is so much pride?"

"It does not look like it."

. The next afternoon the horse and chaise were brought to the door, and the wife invited to take a drive, to visit some farmers' families, and especially to call on the lady who had thought the love of roses and the love of Jesus could not dwell together. This family was called upon first, and an appointment made to return to tea. During the evening, which was spent in a very pleasant manner, allusion was made to the beautiful rose-bush, planted and cherished by their former pastor, of the efforts made to preserve its beauty, and of the apparent success of these efforts. This touched the right chord. The hostess loved her old pastor; and her interest was also awakened in behalf of the handsome rose-bush; and when she knew her new pastor and his wife better she became their friend. She would often come two or three miles of a stormy evening, to the Monday evening Monthly Concert, "for prayer for Foreign Missions," giving as a reason that Mr. Binney would miss her so if she failed to be present. This might have been said of every other member who failed to be present at the Monthly Concert. They were not only missed, but inquired after; and they were made to feel that they too had missed something which would be a real loss to them.

On one or two occasions, when the weather was so inclement that few were able to go out, the pastor was requested to repeat the subject on the following month. There was usually a connection with the preceding subject, and the hour was always too short. The next meeting was generally looked forward to with the kind of interest felt in the serials now-a-days. A history of some particular mission often formed the subject of the meetings for several months, and prayers would be offered especially for that mission, its state at the time being also brought to notice. There was seldom a word read, though the topics of special interest in the last Missionary Magazine were always referred to. Every family had the Magazine. If any declined taking it, because of inability, a fund was raised at · once for such, and the Magazine sent them free. There were few such cases.

Numerous analyses of subjects, presented from time to time at monthly concerts, are among his papers, prepared with as much care as his sermons, and marked West Boylston, Southbridge, Savannah, Elmira, Augusta, with the various dates, and a fresh bit of paper attached, containing items of interest of more recent date. The Monthly Concert, when he was pastor, was never deemed an uninteresting or an unimportant meeting, yet the much larger part of the time was spent in prayer.

Another extract from the article by Dr. Cutting's graphic pen, from which we have already quoted, will throw still further light upon the character of his Southbridge pastorate.

In November, 1836, I was sent to relieve Mr. Binney, by taking his pulpit for a Sunday. It was then that I first met him, and then commenced, unconsciously to him, his great influence upon my life. I was but a youth of twenty-three years of age; he was twenty-eight, with experience of four years in the ministry. On Monday a furious storm was raging, which detained me at his house till the next day. These were busy hours of converse, which led me to the secret of his power. In June, 1837, I was sent for in a similar emergency, with other like opportunities of intercourse; and in August of that year, I was called to succeed him at Southbridge. I purchased his furniture, and took possession of the parsonage, and it would have been difficult to tell who were hosts and who were guests. Faithful pastor and friend, he had the large " standing committee " of the church in the study to a late hour the night before he left, that he might, if possible, leave a protracted case of discipline in such form as to do no harm to his youthful successor. Pale, slender, fragile, he kissed me as if I had been a brother, when he departed on the morrow, in hope that a sunnier clime would give the power to work. His great life shows how wisely and under what divine guidance that step was taken.

I shall not forget the day, when at the Southbridge parsonage in one of my instructive conversations with him, I wept that I could not approach the standard to which he had attained in faith, in the methods and achievements of study, in power to unfold and send to the heart the truths of the gospel; he seemed so far above me that, though I felt the powerful stimulus of intercourse with him, I could see no hope that I should be able to copy his example.

Mr. Binney undervalued nothing that belonged to the duties of a Christian pastor. Knowledge of the spiritual condition of the congregation, attained by personal intercourse only; faithful dealing with individual souls in their struggles; support for the weak, and sympathy for all who were in sorrow; method in all pastoral work, in order to accomplish much of it,—all this he understood, and I never heard a lisp of deficiency in what we call pastoral labors. But he believed the great function of the

Christian ministry to be to teach; and hence preaching was with him the first care. I was to be his successor in a country congregation of considerable size, and at that time, somewhat singularly composed. "Take care of your pulpit," said he, "before all things. Bring to it every Sunday the product of a hard week's work. Your congregation will never fail to recognize a week's industry devoted to their instruction. If you exchange pulpits with your brethren, make the best exchange in your power. If you are absent and seek a supply, procure the best. Let it be understood in Southbridge that the Baptist pulpit never declines."

Under the impulse of such an example and such instructions, I succeeded this remarkable man. My books passed to the same shelves which his had occupied. I prepared my sermons at the same desk. It was not in me to repeat his ministry, but if I sat at that desk, and held myself to distinct and practical aims, in my preparations for preaching, and stated to myself, week after week, in distinct terms the exhortation—"do your best or die"—it was at least in part, that he still lingered with me, a vital presence stimulating the best purposes of my life.

The picture of Mr. Binney's pleasant relations, both in West Boylston and in Southbridge, would not be complete without the beautiful background which legitimately belongs to them both,—the character of the ministry in the neighborhood. He always deemed it one of his greatest blessings, and one to be remembered with unmixed pleasure, to have been in so intimate relations with such men. In a small circle of neighboring towns there were pastors of culture, of talent, and of fraternal spirit; men with whom it was pleasant and profitable to exchange pulpits and to hold frequent social intercourse; men who so obeyed the apostolic injunction, "in honor preferring one another," that, to use his favorite expression, "it was at all times possible to be courteous to them." Nothing was more common than for some one of the neighboring ministers to drive in at the open gate, which led to a well stored barn, and feed his horse, before making his appearance at the front door. He would perhaps receive an approving word from the study window, where the pastor was hard at work and would not be interrupted, till footsteps were heard upon the stairs leading to the study, when a warm reception and a good time were pretty sure to follow. A mid-day dinner, according to the custom of the times and place, and the good-byes did not long linger. These were usually pleasant times, such as only ministering brethren on brotherly terms can enjoy.

But sometimes a different motive brought the dear brother to the parsonage. Some trial in his own personal experience, or some trial in his church would closet them quietly in the study, when Mr. Binney always had leisure to make the case his own, and advise as he might be able, usually adding, "that would be my way, and it may suggest your best way." Sometimes it would be in his power to help directly, by an exchange of pulpits or in some other way seeking an interview with the disaffected member or "troublesome deacon," a class of men with whom, he was accustomed to say, it was his good fortune never to have had personal relations.

Then again, the parsonage was at the junction of two important stage routes, so that it was a convenient place at which to stop for refreshments, and a social interview of an hour or more. The stage running between Boston and Hartford, stopped so frequently at the parsonage at half past twelve o'clock, that it was not considered safe to sit down to dinner, till it had passed. This might not be always so pleasant, but the cases in which it was otherwise were few, and abundantly compensated for by the pleasant interviews thus enjoyed. A single instance, as a specimen of the way in which those things were done, will perhaps bring to mind to some the fashion of the times, which changed circumstances have rendered in our country quite obsolete.

On a pleasant day, late in October, as the stage-coach was driven into town with the usual flourish of trumpet, two pairs of eyes were peering out of the parsonage windows, to see if it would stop at the gate. It did stop; and before Mr. Binney could get to it, Dr. Sharp's venerable head appeared at the stage door calling out:

"Brother Binney, can you give three hungry men a dinner for the sake of an hour's visit, which they are desirous to have with you?"

"Yes, Dr. Sharp, my wife will be sure to manage that somehow. Come up stairs, refresh yourselves a little and look at my library for a few minutes."

While this was going on up stairs an additional leaf lengthened the table, plates were added, and thoughts were busy as to ways and means of so suddenly providing double rations, when it appeared that another pair of eyes had been watching the stage coach. A near neighbor, an active member of the church, had seen the gentlemen alight, and had sent her two sons, bright lads of ten and twelve years, with all possible dispatch, bearing a large roast fowl, a dish of vegetables, and two large pies of the New England style, all smoking hot and savory.

7*

On entering the dining-room with his guests, the anxious look of the host was quickly changed to one of relief and pleasure; and conversation kept pace with the progress of the dinner. Dear Dr. Sharp had many inquiries to make of the success and prospects of his young friend, while Mr. Binney, in turn, plied Dr. Bolles, the venerable Secretary of the Mission Board, with questions as to the prospects of the work in which he was engaged.

The nice and plenteous dinner was thoroughly enjoyed by the travelers, and when their hosts told by what means such ample provision was made for them so promptly, it afforded a good opportunity to expatiate on the kindness of their Southbridge friends, which often saved them for several days the necessity of going to market. Six weeks even, at one time, had so passed, so amply had the table been provided for by thoughtful friends. On leaving, with the good-byes and God bless yous, almost in concert was the wish repeated, "Long may you live in Southbridge."

Early in the month of July, Mr. and Mrs Binney went to Boston to visit friends, and for a rest and change. They took a private conveyance, and performed the journey of seventy miles in a single day. The fine horse seemed to enjoy the journey to the end, showing no signs of fatigue. The day was fine and the scenery charming. Mr. Binney seldom indulged in either rest or recreation; this journey was both. Mrs. Binney seldom had her husband "all to herself." There were rare sweet communings of the past, present, and future. Not a cloud was visible on their horizon.

After spending a pleasant day or two with relatives and friends, Mr. Binney thought it well, before returning, to call on his Boston physician, Dr. Jackson, and see what he thought of the state of his throat. Two years before, when hesitating as to the safety of trying another pastorate in New England, he had assured him that the trouble was merely bronchial. Yet, he had a little persistent cough, which did not give him much anxiety: "but it might be well to see the Doctor." On his return to the family, visitors were present, and little or nothing was said of the Doctor's opinion, until well on the way home, when he was asked if his visit to him had been satisfactory; he answered promptly and cheerfully, in the affirmative. It had been their plan to divide the journey and spend a night with a ministering brother, and secure an exchange of pulpits, that he might have a little longer rest. Just before reaching his friend's house he suggested that they should stop at the little tavern to rest and refresh themselves and the horse, and then drive home by the bright moonlight. He did not feel like talking with anybody else. The wife then perceived that her husband had not been so cheery as on the journey to Boston, but she had been so happy herself, that she had before failed to detect the change in him. Indeed, he had up to that point, taken great pains not to mar her enjoyment; but the facts must be told: the doctor had pronounced his lungs to be in imminent danger. He must go South as far as Florida, or Georgia at least; and that, not for a winter, but to remain for several years; and it would be better that he should refrain from preaching altogether. Teaching would be better than preaching, but in either case he must "flee for his life."

This was a terrible announcement. Both were naturally timid, and neither used to, nor fond of, adventure. Georgia and Florida were farther off to their minds than Asia and Africa were, a few years later. His means were small, though, for a young New England pastor, they were comfortable. His household furniture, a good library, and a few hundred dollars in the bank, were all that he possessed. But he owed no man or society of men anything but love. His debts to the Education Societies had been paid as soon as he had the ability, though his Congregational friends were reluctant to accept the money. Mr. and Mrs. Binney had never spent for themselves anything like the amount of his salary; and, so far as means were concerned, this was the first time they had ever felt themselves poor. But now the prospect in that respect looked dark; and the probability of having to give up preaching was a thought he would not yet allow. As they drove home that moonlight evening, and the pretty white parsonage, with its pleasant surroundings, appeared in sight, they dared not trust themselves to speak, but both inwardly exclaimed, "Can we leave thee?"

The people were soon informed of the stern necessity. The sorrow was general, but on their part the sad tidings was not entirely unexpected. Nothing, however, could exceed their kindness in this hour of trial. When the time to leave arrived, his farewell sermon was literally preached among the tears and sobs of the large congregation. He was never a "sensational" preacher, but with unaffected truthfulness and simplicity he expressed the deep emotions of his heart. He told them of his love for his flock, especially for the dear lambs that had been born into the fold during his short ministry among them, and that he had buried with Christ in baptism, and raised up to walk in newness of life. He told them too, of his longing, agonizing desire for the salvation of those of his hearers who were still unconverted, especially of those who were resting on the sandy foundation of false views, alike of the justice and mercy of God; and appealed to them to bear witness, that he had not failed to declare to them from the first, "the whole counsel of God."

Few eyes were dry but his own, as he came down from the pulpit, and silently walked to his study, where he remained some time alone. When he did appear, it was very evident, that though he had restrained himself in their presence, yet he "had entered into his chamber and wept there."

The next day one of his parishioners took the pastor and his wife in a private carriage as far as Worcester, and left them with friends. Just before leaving, Deacon Cheney called to say farewell. On taking his hand, the pastor's wife, who, though herself in extremely delicate health, had kept up helpfully and cheerfully till the last, quite broke down, and was only able to sob out,

"We shall never meet another Deacon Cheney."

"Well, well, I am surprised! You should not be depressed, you have a very strong arm to lean upon."

"Yes, I know that," she replied, supposing he meant

the strong arm; "but we are such creatures of sense, we like to see and feel the strong arm encircling us."

"And you can do both; I mean the strong arm of your husband. He is leaning on the Lord, and you can just lean on him. You are all right."

A little laugh all around relieved the sadness of the trying moments wonderfully, and was ever afterward remembered with sincere pleasure.

CHAPTER VII.

SAVANNAH PASTORATE.

1837—1843.

ABOUT the time of Mr. Binney's resignation at Southbridge, Rev. Jonathan Going, D.D., had just returned from a Western tour, made in behalf of the American Baptist Home Mission Society. He had engaged in this work from a deep conviction of its importance, and labored in it with his accustomed energy and zeal. He was a pastor in Worcester, when Mr. Binney was in West Boylston, only six miles apart; they knew each other well. He had heard of Mr. Binney's resignation. The Baptists of the West were just establishing a College or Theological School, or both, at Alton, Illinois, to be named in honor of its largest donor, Shurtleff. Dr. Going was delegated to procure them a President. He did not write to Mr. Binney, but came at once to see him. It seemed to him most providential that Mr. Binney should now be compelled to abandon the pulpit for a season, and that this vacancy should need to be filled at the same time. He had thought of applying to him before, but did not like to disturb his pleasant relations at Southbridge. He thought Mr. Binney could be more useful at Alton than in any New

England pulpit. The latter could and would be filled by another, but Alton needed him, and now the need was mutual. All night, till the day dawned upon them, did these men discuss the claims of the West in general, and of Alton in particular. The result was that Mr. Binney promised to accept an invitation to Alton should one be tendered him, if nothing should occur in the meantime to render it possible for him to resume pastoral labor. Such an invitation was tendered, and he, as good as his word, wrote his acceptance promptly.

But in the meantime, unknown to him, other events were transpiring, which led him to change his plans. Holmes Tupper, Esq., a wealthy merchant, and a prominent Deacon of the Baptist Church in Savannah, Georgia, had been spending the summer, as was his wont, in Maine. He had been requested by the Savannah Church, then without a pastor, to make inquiries, and if possible procure them one. He had not been able to learn of any suitable man not engaged, and began his return with no prospect of aiding them in that respect. On his journey, however, he made some inquiries which led to important results.

Mr. Tupper reached Savannah toward evening, and on landing, learned that there was a meeting in session in the Baptist Church for the purpose of electing a pastor. He hastened thither at once. The names of three candidates, all Southern men, were before them. After several ballotings, it appeared that it would not be possible for any one to be elected unanimously, or even by a large majority. Just at this point, Mr. Tupper asked

permission to add a new name to the candidates before
further balloting.   He told them, that although he had
left Maine with no hope of being able to aid them in
procuring a pastor, yet in the stage coach between Boston and Providence he had for a fellow passenger, the
Rev. Dr. Pattison, pastor of the First Baptist Church in
the latter city, of whom he had made inquiries concerning a suitable man for Savannah.   He had described the
man they needed as well as he was able, and Dr. Pattison had told him in reply, that he thought he knew the
right one for them, and that he could be obtained.   He
hesitated, however, to urge any active measures to procure him for two reasons: because, from the extreme
delicacy of his health, he feared he could not meet the
wants of a city church; and also, because he was his
brother-in-law.   He recommended him to call on Dr.
Wayland, or any of the leading Baptists in Providence,
or to write to Dr. Sharp, of Boston, all of whom would
be able to give needed information.   He was willing to
say, however, that he had been pastor of two good country churches in Massachusetts, and that not only the
churches, but the Associations with which he had been
connected, considered his being obliged to leave them a
great loss.   Finding the church in its present divided
state, Mr. Tupper said that he for one would like to use
Mr. Binney's name without delay.   They all knew Dr.
Pattison by reputation, and all would be willing to trust
him.   Mr. Binney's name was added, and the first balloting gave him a large majority.   One of the deacons
who had been very active in presenting one of the
former candidates, rose and said,

8

"Brethren, this seems a very providential interposition in our behalf: let us make the call unanimous!"

This they did at the next balloting.   Every vote cast
was for Mr. Binney; but two brethren, both South Car-
olinians, explained that they had not voted at all, because,
in their haste, they had declared their purpose never to
vote for a Northern man; they would be glad, however,
to see Mr. Binney pastor of the church; they had no
doubt the Lord had interposed for them.

Our narrative leaves Mr. Binney in Worcester, Massachusetts, with the letter of acceptance of the Presidency of Shurtleff College written.   This letter he took
to the office, but, before dropping it into the letter-box,
he thought he would first see what the mail, just in, had
brought him.   He took from his friend's box, the letter
from the church in Savannah, a unanimous and unconditional call to become its pastor.   He well might be
surprised.   There had been no previous intimation from
any quarter of its probability.   He received at the same
time a letter from Mr. Tupper, explaining the circumstances which had brought about so unexpected an event.

It was a kind letter, characteristic of the man—though
one of the very smallest of men in physical stature, yet
possessing a heart equally remarkable for breadth of
comprehension and fervor of emotion and sympathy.
He urged Mr. Binney's acceptance, assuring him that
even if his health should prove inadequate to the task,
he would unite the church for the present, and thus do
a good work; he added, that they knew the doctor's
opinion of his case, and that he would not be blamed if
he failed; he would be *among friends, sick or well.*

Mr. Binney burned the Alton letter, and the next day despatched another which made him pastor elect of the Savannah Baptist Church. He told them, he was quite aware that it was largely because he was a stranger to them, that he had been unanimously invited; that he was, however, in the habit of studying God's providences; that they had seemed clearly to define his duty in the case; but that he was fallible, and if he had misinterpreted them, future providences would make it known. He fixed the time, as definitely as the arrival of sailing vessels would permit, when he would be with them.

This seems in the narrative a very simple and easy thing to have done, but it was in fact far otherwise. The Baltimore experiment of entering into new relations, but partially understood, made him cautious of repeating the mistake. But the chief reason for his hesitation was the existence of slavery in the Southern States. He had previously studied the subject thoroughly, but with his usual calm deliberation, and had formed his own judgment in regard to it. The question which now was presented to his mind was, whether in assuming the pastoral office where slavery existed, he could, with any justice, be regarded as giving his approval to the system. He also questioned as to whether he could do justice to his own convictions, and at the same time do his full duty to masters and slaves. These questions had to be met and answered, as in the sight of God, and as his servant, seeking above all things to know his will, and to please and glorify him. That night was mostly spent in a prayerful consideration of the matter. The facts were all before him, and before the morning dawned he decided to accept the pastoral charge of the church; and the blessing which God bestowed upon his labors in Savannah was such as to leave little room afterward to question the correctness of his decision.

After writing his letter of acceptance, he read it to his wife, assuring her, at the same time, that if a doubt remained in her mind as to this step being the right one to take, the letter would not be sent. It was sent, and two weeks later he entered upon his new duties, re-solved to give such teaching as the Bible presented, as arising from existing relations, and to strive, so far as lay in his power, to make both masters and servants better and happier.

He reached Savannah in October, 1837. There had as yet been no frosts, and it was considered early for strangers to come to the city, but the season was healthy, and with care it was not deemed particularly unsafe, The evening of his arrival was the usual Wednesday evening lecture. With true Southern hospitality, the church was largely represented to greet their new pastor. After a rough sea voyage they did not expect to hear him say much, but they came to welcome him. He took in the situation at once. The sea had not fatigued, but rested and invigorated him. He would like to address them, and he could speak better from a text. and chose the words, "Not as pleasing men but God."

The refinement in manner, the gentle, tender consid-eration manifested in the hearty welcome he received, took him by surprise. The citadel of his heart was taken; he surrendered that at discretion, but saw before him the temptation to be "time-serving," and he resolved at once to put it out of his power to be a time-server, at least to be so consistently.

His fine address and manly bearing were united with an appearance of delicacy, of frailty even, which made all feel as if he had come to them on a special mission, and that when it was done he would be taken up ere long from their midst. They were satisfied. The two gentlemen who had refused to vote, walked home with him to his boarding-house. They told him that they had refused to vote for him, because he was a Northern man: but they did not know him. They were sure he would be an honest, able preacher and pastor, and he might rely upon their hearty sympathy and support. They were true to their pledge.

A few days after their arrival, before the first visits of ceremony were fully exchanged, Mrs. Binney was laid aside with a fever, which so prostrated her, that her recovery was considered doubtful. She did not leave her room for thirty days, but under most judicious medical treatment soon after found herself better and stronger than she had ever been before, so that she was enabled to nurse her husband for more than three months without intermission. She had been able to hear his voice from the pulpit but once, after an absence of six weeks from the house of God, when he was prostrated, and kept his room and bed for twelve successive weeks, never once being able to be moved further than from one side of it to the other. On the fourteenth day the doctor was hopeful of a change for the better; but, instead of abating, the

8*

fever went to the brain, and for fourteen days afterward he recognized no one, and was unconscious apparently of pain or pleasure. A good, skillful nurse watched him during the nights, from ten o'clock till five in the morning, and Mrs. Binney took sole care of him by day, with only occasional assistance from the nurse. The doctor said his life depended upon the most perfect freedom from all excitement. For weeks after he began to recover, his mind was in a critical state, and regained its balance only as his physical strength was restored. Both, however, were not only restored, but their vigor was greatly increased. He arose a new man. He had often said, that with his constitution, he needed a task master to keep him at hard work; but now work was a pleasure; for the next five years he scarcely knew fatigue. After long walks in the sandy streets and hot sun of Savannah, he never complained of fatigue. He would sometimes say: "The word sounds strangely now, though we used to be bosom friends." It may be well to mention that for a period of about five years after his recovery, he preached every Lord's Day, with no exception, twice and often three times. He was so strengthened that he emphatically abounded in labors.

The severe illness through which Mrs. and Mr. Binney were called to pass, especially the illness of the latter, brought the church and their new pastor into intimate and tender relations, and created a stronger tie than many years of prosperity could have done. The kindness of the church, and of the community even, should not be passed over in silence. The large bills for medical attendance, for medicines, and for an expensive professional nurse were all met by the church; while the pulpit was supplied, and the salary allowed to go on as if he were at work himself.

Of all this Mrs. Binney was kindly informed while her husband was too low to care about it, so that she was freed from anxiety on that point. Mr. Tupper's assurance, in his first letter to Mr. Binney, that "sick or well he would be among friends," was often brought to mind. The many nameless attentions, kind words of sympathy, and strong desires expressed for her husband's recovery, sustained her during many an anxious night and many a weary day, in the darkened room where no other foot was allowed to enter, except for temporary assistance.

When Mr. Binney resumed preaching, after that illness, his sermons had a "fresh unction." It seemed as if the prayer of the rich man in the parable had been answered, and that he had been raised from the dead to warn men to flee from the wrath to come. The church was quickened; backsliders returned to their first love; and sinners were "pricked in their hearts:" but many months passed before conversions took place in any considerable numbers. It would seem, at times, as if the dense clouds must burst in refreshing showers; but again and again they passed by. The church was aroused, became restless, and wanted "some evangelist to come in and assist their pastor." Dr. Richard Fuller, though not an evangelist in the ordinary sense, was exceedingly popular in Savannah. He was pastor of a small church in Beaufort, his native city, and yet a young man. But he preached the truth in the demonstration of the Spirit, and with power. Mr. Binney knew all this, and entertained for him a very high regard : but he invited even him with reluctance, as he feared a diversion of feeling. Dr. Fuller came however. Crowds of eager listeners attended upon his preaching night after night. The pastor heartily worked with him, but it was as he feared; the solemnity diminished, and again the church was disappointed. It did not at that time see the expected " powerful revival."

But from the time of his recovery the regular congregation had greatly increased, so that there were no more pews to be let, and no seats even for strangers. It was with much persuasion that he brought the church to see that their almost new edifice, yet scarcely paid for, needed to be enlarged. He brought an architect to see it, who gave his opinion that the rear end could be knocked out and the building thus made to accommodate about one-third more, to the advantage both of its acoustic qualities and its appearance. A subscription was raised by the almost unaided exertions of the pastor, sufficient to pay the small debt still remaining on the building, and meet the expense of the proposed enlargement.

The work was commenced early in the summer, when many of the inhabitants were accustomed to leave the city, and in consequence several of the churches were usually closed. Simultaneously with its commencement the long-looked for shower of divine grace descended. Souls were converted daily. The large, fine Presbyterian Church was about to be closed, as their pastor needed a "summer's vacation." It was offered to the Baptists while their improvements were in progress. They said that it would hold both congregations, and desired "that Mr. Binney should use it as his own." Mr. Binney fully appreciated the kindness, but thought the Baptist Church must not be abandoned. The Lord had set his seal of approval by the conversion of souls, and the young converts must be made to feel at home. The baptistery also must be used from time to time, and, as many people were out of town, he thought the building would hold all who wished to come. So amid brick and mortar, the church well swept and dusted on Saturday afternoons, the old pulpit undisturbed, the people met and worshipped all summer, only closing the building for two or three weeks, while painters and upholsterers were at work, when the Presbyterian Church was used. On Dr. Preston's return a vote of thanks was passed by his church for the courtesy received from the Baptist Church during his absence.

During all that summer there were no extra meetings, except the pastor's multiplied inquiry meetings. He had for a long time, perhaps from the first, given notice of an evening at home, when he would gladly see any one wishing to converse on the subject of religion, but seldom any except members of the church came. There was a great deal of feeling among a class of young men, regular attendants at church services, but this only showed itself by their manner. They had been invited, urged, to come for personal conversation, but there had been no response. The first Monday evening after the work had fairly commenced in the church, the pastor,

from his study window, saw a young man pass the
house, whom he knew to have been for some time
anxious for his soul.   He soon returned, almost passed
again, but turned and timidly came up the front steps.
Before he could have time either to ring the bell or retrace his steps, the pastor met him, drew his arm within
his, and said, while taking him up stairs:

"Come in, my dear young friend, I know all about
it, and so does the Lord.   What is the use of keeping
up this contest any longer?   Either you or God must
yield.   He will never relinquish his claims upon you,
but may withdraw his Spirit, now striving with you, let
you have your own way, and leave you to the consequences.   Let us kneel together, and ask God to
help you, and do not rise till this strife is ended.
Hasten to make an entire surrender to him."

Before he arose from his knees, praise was mingled
with entreaty.   The next evening he brought others,
and it seemed as if no one entered the room, however
depressed, but left it rejoicing.

In the midst of the revival, after several had been
baptized, and others had exercised faith in Christ, a
young man of another congregation came in with a
friend, who was rejoicing in a newly found Saviour.
After some conversation with others, Mr. Binney turned
to this young man, whose whole appearance indicated
but little interest, saying,

"I am glad to see you here, M———, I suppose you
would not have come, except to seek counsel.   Yet in
order to help you I must know your difficulty, and on
what particular point you desire help."

"Why," said he, "Mr. Binney, I did not mean to insult you by coming here to-night; but I really have no feeling on the subject of religion. My friends here are all in earnest, and have urged me to come and talk with you; but I cannot say that I am anxious enough to care much whether I am saved or lost. I know this is a fearful state, and I suppose I ought to feel alarmed about it."

Mr. Binney reminded him that he had been a constant attendant on his ministry since the revival commenced, and that he surely knew all that was necessary for him to know. If he was indifferent now, it could be neither from ignorance of his danger, nor of the way of escape. If he was now indifferent, it was probably judicial punishment, for not heeding the monitions of the Spirit. He must not expect sympathy from him, or that he would take his side against God, for not forcing him to feel as his associates were feeling. On the contrary, he could only vindicate the justice of God in so leaving him in this state of indifference. There was nothing more to be done on God's part; it only remained for him to say whether he would cling to his sins and serve the devil, or whether he would abandon them with loathing, and turn to the Lord with full purpose of heart, and leave himself in his hands to dispose of as he saw fit. By his neglect he was making the former decision; if he ever became a Christian, the latter decision must be made, and this might be the last opportunity.

The young man's face showed the change that had come over him, and the intensity of his emotions. Silence ensued. Every heart seemed going up in prayer for him.   After a few moments, in which not a muscle of his face moved, but it seemed as if the blood must burst forth, he broke the silence, saying,

"It is done, Mr. Binney.   I have given myself to him unconditionally; saved or lost, I wish to have nothing more to do with the devil and his works; and Christ will receive me.   He has."

His subsequent life proved the sincerity of his consecration.   This case has been mentioned to show his way, or one of his ways, of dealing with the impenitent.   From that time few months passed when the baptismal waters were not moved.

An extract from an article written by W. T. Brantly, D. D., of Baltimore, and published in the *New York Examiner*, soon after Dr. Binney's death, will show the character of his preaching, and the estimation in which he was held in Savannah.

My acquaintance with our departed friend runs back through a period of thirty-five years, when we were fellow-pastors in the State of Georgia, he in Savannah, I in Augusta.   Six years previously the church in Savannah, needing a pastor, extended a call to young Binney, then unknown to fame, but well known to a member of the church which called him.   The eloquent and devoted H. O. Wyer, his predecessor, had been in feeble health for some years, so that when Dr. Binney became pastor, in 1837, the church was far from flourishing,   But through the faithful labors of the young pastor the former prosperity was soon regained.   After a year or two, it became necessary to enlarge the house to accommodate the increasing congregations, and though the enlarged building afforded as many sittings as are found in your Tabernacle Church on Second Avenue, it was soon filled. Dr. Binney attracted many of the most gifted and cultivated minds in the city.

It was his custom to preach in the afternoon, when other houses in the city were closed. On these occasions the spacious edifice would be largely attended by members of other churches, though they had the privilege, morning and evening, of listening to such men as Bishop Elliott, Dr. Preston and Dr. Pierce, who were his contemporaries in the city. Yet Dr. Binney was not a popular preacher, as the phrase is commonly understood.

His presence at that day was interesting. His handsome, intellectual face and beaming eye attracted attention. His extempore delivery and agreeable manner impressed you. But he was a close thinker, and it required both mind and attention to follow his well-digested trains of thought and appreciate their significance. But there were some persons equal to the exercise, in his congregation. They were enthusiastic in their commendations; and whilst his sermons were marked by profound thought for the strong, he would, from time to time, supply milk for the babes, so that each might receive his portion. As an evidence of their appreciation, when the enlarged house was completed, the pastor was tendered such an increase of salary as he might deem sufficient. "I told them," he remarked to me afterward, "that I should need $1,500 for my support; and that besides this I wanted something to give away; and I should be glad also to put by a little every year. So they fixed my salary at $2,500 a year." I do not suppose that any Baptist minister in all the land was at this time in receipt of so large a salary.

It was when he had obtained this great success in Savannah, a large and devoted church, an increasing congregation, an ample salary, the blessing of God following his labors in the conversion of souls, that the call came to him to go to Burmah.

The above extract shows Mr. Binney as a preacher at that time. As a pastor in Savannah his labors were arduous, and, though somewhat peculiar, were very successful, not only in harmonizing conflicting elements, but especially in organizing the whole church into a well trained band of workers. In speaking of his system

9

to other pastors, as they sometimes inquired of him concerning it, he would say, "this works well with me, but no two work exactly alike. I would not present it as a model."

He had a large standing committee of the church, chosen from the various stations and positions of life, and of different ages, mostly composed, however, of men of middle life and past. This committee he met at stated periods in his library, when everything pertaining to their duties was freely discussed. It was understood that the subjects there considered were not to be discussed elsewhere. In that room most cases of discipline were settled, and never brought before the church, to be the cause of party feeling, or of reproach to the offender in the community. If the offender could not be saved by the united efforts of the pastor and a good sub-committee, the case would probably be so clear, that there could be but one opinion of it when brought before the church.

A plan for aiding the needy sick of Savannah, was introduced by him, and found from several years trial to be admirably adapted to the wants of the city. The plan devolved on him a large amount of labor in carrying it out. While others were heavily taxed, yet in superintending this work he was called upon to visit the needy sick, most of whom belonged to no church whatever, and to bury those who died among them. He thus performed an amount of work which would at any other period of his life have been quite impossible. Benevolent persons not of his own church often sent funds, unsolicited, to him, sometimes to the amount of fifty dollars or more, wishing to give to the suffering and worthy poor, but not knowing where it was wise and safe to do so.

There was a feature in his work in Savannah that was not easily accounted for. That he should attend so large a number of funerals among the poor and unfixed population always found in every city seemed to rise naturally from his special attention to that class; but he married as well as buried a larger number of persons than any other pastor, more even than all the others combined. His congregation contained a fair proportion of young people, but not so large a number as to account for this fact. All persons wishing to marry were obliged to obtain a marriage certificate from the proper authorities. These were numbered and, when presented to the minister, were his authority for performing the ceremony. It was very easy for the officiating minister to see how many had been issued between those presented to him; and in that way he learned, that for two or three years before leaving Savannah more than half the marriage certificates issued in Chatham County had come to himself.

He also had a small band of lay preachers from the business men of the city, who went out to the destitute places in the suburbs, chiefly the plantations on the Savannah River, and preached to the destitute colored people, masters and their families often being among their most interested hearers. These preachers reported to Mr. Binney, and received counsel as they needed, often involving cases of great delicacy and requiring patient thought. When possible they would go out in the morning, and return in time to hear the afternoon sermon, as they would sometimes playfully say, "to lay in a stock for retailing the next week." They had little time for study, and their pastor often had their need in view in preparing his afternoon sermons. This may have served to give them a somewhat didactic character, but they were equally characterized by a fervor and eloquence that fastened every eye upon him, and which "Silence failed not to honor."

It was Mr. Binney's decided conviction that no church could prosper, that did not give liberally for the general interests of the Redeemer's kingdom. He was not satisfied with simply confining his efforts to domestic missions; foreign missions also had claims which could not be ignored. He found the church with "so much to do at home" as to attempt little foreign work. The first year he was there, less than ten dollars was given to the Foreign Board, but in the last year donations had increased more than a hundred-fold. His monthly concerts were among his most interesting meetings. On one occasion, while in the midst of a remarkable interest and at every meeting for conference and prayer some new convert was coming forward to tell what the Lord had done for his soul, a deputation from the standing committee of the church called upon him to inquire if it would not be well to omit the monthly concert for once, lest it might interfere with the revival, and the special attention to the salvation of souls.

"No! No!" was the prompt reply; "if we have any excitement in our church that can be checked or diverted by prayer for the salvation of souls in the darkness of heathenism, the sooner it is checked the better. I want no such revival as that. We want the Spirit of him 'who though rich, for our sakes became poor,' revived among us. Any other excitement is spurious."

That monthly concert, as Dr. Binney stated afterwards, not only did not interfere with the prevailing religious interest, but seemed to give it a most unmistakable impulse. It is doubtless still remembered in Savannah by a few. It is known to have given character to the Christian labors of one young convert at least, who though a business man, has been eminently useful in both home and foreign work.

Mr. Binney's plan for raising money for mission purposes was simple, and took less time than the results might lead one to suppose. A collection was always taken at the close of the monthly concerts, which not only included the usual contributions from the regular attendants, but those of strangers present, amounting to a considerable sum. About three months before the stated period for sending their contributions to the Home and Foreign Mission treasurers, he would preach a sermon on the claims of each, of which sermon due notice was always given. At the close of this, he would say to the congregation, that he had a little book prepared for each object, and after the services it would be brought to the table, that those who wished might give their names and residences with subscriptions, or the money might then be given: that he should carry these little books in his pocket and be prepared to receive their names or the money for at least a month longer; and when these opportunities were exhausted, if he did

9*

not hear from them, he would call upon them at their homes. This was seldom necessary. Every member had an opportunity to give. Several old ladies were supported entirely by the church, but they were usually among the first to bring their thank-offerings to the Lord; one said, when remonstrated with, "Why cannot I afford to give. If Mr. Binney preaches the truth, and he seems to be sustained by the word of God, the poor cannot afford to withhold. I shall leave it for the rich people to try the experiment." The Lord made the rich deacon, who remonstrated with her, the instrument of "rewarding her double."

Mr. Binney was accustomed to head the list, with such a sum as he thought the Lord required of him, and as he was willing to take from men of similar pecuniary ability. At one time a leading member put his name under the pastor's with the same sum as his annexed.

"Why is this, Brother C——?" said Mr. Binney. "Do you think I have given too much?"

"Oh, no! I do not judge for you, and I suppose you will not wish to judge for me!"

"No. I must leave it with your own conscience what you will give, but unless you add a cypher to that sum, I shall have to make a new book. You can certainly afford to give more than ten times the sum that I can, and you will be so judged. Your example will be bad. I will make a new book, and take your name later."

He made a new book and went on with his work. Some days afterward Brother C—— came to him saying,

"My wife thinks I should double that subscription for Foreign Missions, and I will hand you the money now."

"Wait a little, Brother C——, I want a few names first; and if you are asking the Lord as well as your wife about it, I can afford to wait."

Not many days later his name stood under the pastor's with the cypher annexed, and with emotion he said,

"I do believe I shall pray more for the heathen now I have made a little investment in the enterprise myself." The next year there was nothing said on the subject; but a larger sum was freely given.

As their "Domestic Mission" was so largely for the colored people, he did not fail to press their claims to special religious instruction, and to urge the supporting of missionaries among them for this purpose, on the ground that the laws of Georgia made it a penal offence to teach them to read. Standing at the Lord's Table, he once said with a tenderness and pathos which showed how deeply he felt on the subject:

"I do not stand here, brethren, either to vindicate the necessity of these laws in sustaining slavery, or to denounce their injustice and sinfulness in keeping these people—who if saved at all, must be saved by this truth which the Bible reveals—from being able to read for themselves; but I could not be faithful to my duty to you as your pastor, without bringing to your notice the existence of such laws, and the obligation resting upon us from the fact. I could not hope to meet either you or them in peace at that great day, when master and servant, people and pastor, shall stand before the judgment seat, when he who died for us all alike, will alike be the judge of us all."

The confidence which these poor bond-people generally placed in Mr. Binney made it harder for him to leave the church when the time came, although they had many true friends in it beside him; men who were glad to spend and be spent for their spiritual welfare.

In all objects of simple benevolence in the city the pastor of the Baptist Church was a prominent leader. In efforts for the promotion of intellectual culture, his friends ever placed him in the foremost rank. On the formation of the Georgia Historical Society, Dr. Stevens, now Bishop of the Protestant Episcopal Church of Pennsylvania, was most active and efficient in organizing it, and looked at once to Mr. Binney for assistance in so doing. Judge Law, then very popular in Savannah, and one of its ablest men, gave the first address before the Society, and Mr. Binney was invited to give the third lecture in course, and the subject was suggested, as one desirable in itself and as "especially in harmony with the sympathies and character of the speaker," " Whitefield in America."

The lecture was more than an hour in length, but was listened to with almost breathless attention to the close. The Press, in commenting upon it the next day, spoke in terms of the highest praise. The editor of a leading paper said, " Never, since the days of Whitefield, has Georgia been favored with so eloquent a speaker and preacher as now, in the young pastor of the Baptist Church."

Rev. Dr. Preston, for so many years the able and revered pastor of the Independent Presbyterian Church, not only frequently exchanged pulpits with Mr. Binney, but they were so often seen in the streets of Savannah, walking side by side to or from the burial of prominent citizens, and on missions of love and benevolence, that it ceased to attract notice or cause remark. The relation often seemed like that of a father and son, such was the difference of their ages and periods of labor in Savannah. Dr. Preston's young people not infrequently attended Mr. Binney's inquiry meetings, held in his study, to which the Doctor never objected, but which, in one instance at least, he was known to encourage

Bishop Elliot also sustained very kindly relations with him. At one time, in consequence of a sermon on Baptism and the Lord's Supper, some sectarians raised the cry of "bigotry," and succeeded in producing considerable excitement, and, of course in passing, much misrepresentation. The bishop was consulted as to the best course to pursue in the matter. Several sermons had been preached in the Methodist Church in answer to the arguments, but this had apparently only caused a greater rush to the Baptist Church.

"Where did Mr. Binney preach that mischievous sermon?" inquired the bishop.

"Why in the Baptist Church, of course."

"Ah! I see! he was instructing his people, his own charge, in what he honestly believed to be the truth of God's word, and you question his right to do so;—his right to do what your own ministers are doing, and what you expect them to do; a right which I exercise throughout the State of Georgia. It strikes me that the charge of bigotry would more justly apply to those who meddle with the matter.   Mr. Binney seems to me to be a man of a most liberal, catholic spirit, and courteous to all who differ from him, at the same time that he preaches what he deems the truth fearlessly.   Let us imitate his example."

This was a quietus, especially as about the same time Mr. Binney at the close of a Sunday afternoon service said:

"As I understand that a statement which I made from this pulpit a few weeks since—that John Wesley, the founder of Methodism, believed, and sometimes acted on the belief that immersion was the primitive mode of baptism—has been denied from a neighboring pulpit, I beg the privilege to read from this ' Life of Wesley," a standard work in the Methodist denomination, the authority I had for the statement."

He named the work with the page, and reading without further comments placed the book on the table for examination by any one who cared to make it.

The ministering brethren in the Association whom he often met, were brethren indeed, and hailed his labors among them with joy.   As his church was the leading church, they delighted in giving him a leading position among them.   He ever loved the mention of the names of such men as Josiah Low, Wm. H. Mackintosh, and others.   Dr. Richard Fuller, then of Beaufort, S. C., was in the habit of spending a week or two, once a year, with him, helping him in his work, and sometimes Mr. Binney would go to Beaufort for a Sunday or two.   No more fraternal intercourse ever existed, even in Massachusetts, his native State, than he enjoyed in Georgia.

CHAPTER VIII.

CALL TO BURMAH.

1843.

ON a lovely afternoon in January, 1843, such a January day as few cities but Savannah ever witness, Mrs. Binney sat at an open window of her husband's study looking down the street for his return from some pastoral duties. He did not fail to meet her expectations, but instead of his usual elastic step, he walked slowly and abstractedly toward his home. Failing to receive the usual recognition from the window, she hastened down to meet him at the door, when an open letter was put into her hand, with the simple remark, "I have just taken this from the office." As soon as her eye enabled her to take in its contents, she joined him in his study, where they unitedly asked guidance and strength. The latter seemed to the wife to be more needed than the former, for as to the result of an invitation from the Executive Committee of the Board of the American Baptist Missionary Convention, to become their "agent in training up a native ministry among the Karens of Burmah," she had little doubt. She saw at once that her husband would deem the path of duty made very plain, and he would not decline to do what he had from the moment of his conversion so earnestly desired, "make known the revelation of God's will as found in his word to those who knew it not." "Oh, that the heathen had this Bible," was the instinctive cry of the new-born soul; and the longing desire had grown with the growth and strengthened with the strength of his spiritual nature. Still, little was said to each other for a time, but much was "told to Jesus." The "proceedings of the Savannah Baptist Church," with regard to this matter are here inserted entire, as in no other way could the history be so well given.

SAVANNAH, June 6, 1843.

Rev. J. G. BINNEY; DEAR SIR :—Knowing your feelings upon the subject, we feel much delicacy in requesting your consent to publish our recent church proceedings respecting your removal from us, which, of course, includes your letter to the church. But fully believing that it will benefit us ; and that your letter, which we highly approve, will serve to advance our Redeemer's cause, we hope that you will comply with our request.

We are very truly your brethren,

THOMAS CLARK,   W. W. WASH.

A. HARMON,   JNO. PASSELL.

SAVANNAH, June 9, 1843.

MESSRS. J. CLARK, A. HARMON, W.W.WASH, and JOHN PASSELL.

DEAR BRETHREN :—When I addressed you my letter I had not the most remote expectation that it would be presented to any others than the church and pew-holders. I knew you would appreciate the statements and arguments there presented, and my sole object was to convince the dear people of my charge of the propriety of my decision. Hence the unreservedness of that communication. But if it will gratify you or advance the Redeemer's kingdom, I cheerfully comply with your request.

Most affectionately, your Pastor,

J. G. BINNEY.

EXTRACT FROM THE MINUTES OF THE CHURCH.

SAVANNAH, Jan. 29, 1843.

After Divine Service this morning a special meeting of the church was held, when our Pastor informed the church that he had received communications from the American Baptist Board of Foreign Missions, in accordance with a resolution adopted at the late "Missionary Convention at Worcester," which encouraged the Board to invite pastors from this country to enter the foreign field. These communications state the pressing demands of the missionary cause for men, and say, "We have reached a point in several of our stations, where neglect to strengthen is equivalent to desertion. But we have none to send." They therefore ask him to examine the question of duty as to his personal consecration to this work; and invite him particularly to engage in the training up of a Karen Native Ministry, etc.

He stated that this subject was brought to the notice of the Church Committee when first submitted to him, but at his request it was not repeated out of the Committee till more mature reflection on his part; that having prayed over and considered the subject to the extent of his present opportunities, he now wishes to ask the prayers and counsel of the church respecting it, leaving it for God to direct him in the path of duty.

After a few remarks from brethren, it was voted to observe the next Thursday as a day of special "Fasting and Prayer," that our Pastor may know the will of God in this matter, and that the church may be rightly directed. It was also voted, that this subject be referred to the Standing Committee of the church, to report at their earliest convenience, and that Rev. H. O. Wyer act as chairman pro tem.

Thursday, February 20, was observed as a day of Fasting and Prayer, agreeably to a vote of the last meeting. At a full meeting of the church in the evening Rev. Mr. Wyer, in behalf of the Committee, presented the following report:

"The Committee, to whom was referred the subject laid before the church by your Pastor on Sunday last, relative to his

10

removal from his present field of labor to become a Foreign Missionary, having bestowed a deliberate and prayerful consideration on this important matter, desire to express the following sentiments:

" We cannot but feel that the subject is one of great delicacy and importance, a subject so obviously dependent for its solution upon the leadings and teachings of Divine Providence, that it becomes us to approach it with fear and trembling, lest by our selfish feelings and partialities we should make up a rash decision, and be found fighting against God. It is an undoubted truth, that God's claim upon all and every one of his servants is paramount to all other considerations. It is his prerogative to say to this man, 'Go, and he goeth,' and to another, 'Come, and he cometh,' and to his servant, 'Do this, and he doeth it.' Hence we freely acknowledge that it is alike our duty and our blessed privilege to bow with unmurmuring submission to the known will of the Supreme Master, though it may involve heavy sacrifices, and sunder some of our dearest ties. In our contemplations upon this interesting subject, we have not overlooked the important fact, that the claims of Foreign Missions call loudly upon our American churches for immediate and essential aid. Perhaps the demand for men and money was never more imperatively urgent than at the present moment. The voice of perishing millions who cry, 'Send us missionaries,' is echoed through our wide-spread land; and by all the compassions of humanity, by all the endearments of heavenly love, by all the authority of the ascending Saviour, we are bound to hear and obey that imploring voice. Said the Master to his disciples, 'Freely ye have received, freely give.'

" In resolving to induce, if possible, some of our pastors to enter the Foreign Missionary field, we are inclined to the belief, that the Board of Foreign Missions have acted wisely and in accordance with the pressing exigencies of our Foreign Mission stations. The execution of this plan must, however, necessarily involve great sacrifices, both with pastors and churches. But perhaps these very sacrifices will be rendered a blessing, in bringing the churches to a more simple dependence upon divine aid and in wakening and putting forth their slumbering energies in the cause of Christ.

"In relation to the needful qualifications of our Pastor for the particular station which the Board designed to assign him, there can be no diversity of opinion among us who have long enjoyed his faithful and able ministrations.

"We have thus hastily glanced at one view of the subject, and though we have used great freedom of thought relative to the claims of this side of the question, we are still deeply impressed, and doubt not the church will be equally impressed, with several considerations, among many others, which seem to render it desirable that our Pastor should not abandon his present post of ministerial labor.

"We notice, First,—The scope of his present ministerial influence is wide and important. This consideration must bear with great weight upon our minds, if for a moment we take into view the claims of our own growing community, the extreme destitution of the surrounding country, the scarcity of educated and efficient men in the bounds of our Association, and the loud demand for enlightenment in every part of our Southern country. If we are not entirely mistaken in our views, no part of our whole country is so poorly prepared to spare an efficient pastor as our own. 'The harvest truly is great, but the laborers are few.'

"Secondly,—The wants and expenses of our church require the continued labors of our present Pastor. His immediate removal must to all human appearances be attended by many checks and drawbacks upon its prosperity. If the standard-bearer suddenly falls when the hosts are rallying, confusion must ensue; or if a master builder leaves his work unfinished, his plans may be speedily abandoned. And, although we would not forget that God is able to protect his own cause, we also remember that he does this by the use of suitable instrumentalities. We consider that much depends upon the influence and exertions of our present Pastor. Should he now leave us, who can tell the consequences? Who can tell what will become of our present congregation? of the many lambs of the flock? of many plans of benevolent effort, which are yet in their incipient operation? nay, of many impenitent ones who steadily hear from his lips the proclamation of mercy?

"Thirdly,—We cannot overlook the fact that a pastor's usefulness greatly depends upon the measure of confidence and respect in which he is held by the community, especially among the congregation where he labors. In this particular, we believe we have a strong reason why our Pastor should not abandon his present important station. As a man and a Christian he is held in the highest estimation in our community, and as the Pastor of this church and people he occupies a large place in their respect and affections.

"Fourthly,—We are strongly impressed with the consideration that his labor in his present field may be greatly promotive of the cause of Domestic and Foreign Missions.

"Fifthly,—We think it worthy of consideration also, that in this climate both our Pastor and his family have enjoyed a large share of health. In this respect great uncertainty must attend the contemplated change.

"These are some of the thoughts which this deeply interesting matter has suggested to our minds. In view of them we cannot but hope that our beloved Pastor may be led by the unerring hand of God to the same conclusion to which our own minds have arrived, viz., that nothing short of a most imperious sense of duty can reconcile us to the sundering of the ties by which we are now harmoniously and happily united as pastor and church. Finally, we commend both Pastor and church to that gracious God who is ever ready to give us wisdom to discern and strength to perform whatever he would have us to do or suffer for his glory.

(Signed by)   Standing Committee,
H. O. WYER, Chairman,
(THOS. CLARK and twelve other
names follow).'"

On motion, this report was unanimously adopted. It was also voted that the clerk furnish our Pastor with a copy thereof, and that the Committee continue to act in the case.

May 1.—At a monthly meeting of the Committee our Pastor presented in writing his decision upon this subject; he also orally presented the reasons on which that decision was based. It was then voted to desire those reasons in writing, and that this document from our Pastor be communicated to the church at its next monthly meeting.

May 4.—At the monthly church meeting the following document was presented by the Committee:

LETTER OF MR. BINNEY TO THE CHURCH COMMITTEE.

SAVANNAH, May 1, 1843.

"DEAR BRETHREN:—The deeply important question of duty submitted to my consideration by our Foreign Missionary Board, has been the subject of most anxious thought and earnest prayer for the last four months. Under other circumstances, it would have been decided with much less solicitude in that number of weeks. But situated as I am, in so extensive a field of usefulness, with so strong an attachment to the people of my present charge—and in view of other important considerations of your communication—it became very difficult to settle. To those at all acquainted with the infirmities of our nature, it is unnecessary to say that this difficulty was increased by the matter of fact view which years of pastoral labor had prepared me to take of the subject; the exceeding sacrifice requisite on the part of myself and family; together with the fact that with very rare exceptions I have received no encouragement to make that sacrifice; while from numerous sources, by letter and in person, I have been urged to the contrary. The claims of the Mission have been sustained entirely by information, already in my possession, of the wants of the heathen, and a consciousness of my solemn responsibility to him, under whose commission I act as a gospel minister, and to whom I must so soon render my account.

"During this inquiry I have been encouraged by the assurance, that if a man lack wisdom, he may ask of God; and that if in all our ways we acknowledge him, he will direct our steps. Certainly, my dear brethren, you have joined me in fasting and prayer, that God's will might be known in this important matter. That God

10*

could and would answer those prayers and afford us light, I had no doubt.

"The time has come when my duty alike to you and the Board requires a decision. This is the more evident to me from the fact that for the past three months no new suggestion has been made from the many who have kindly endeavored to throw light upon my path. So familiar have I been with the main merits of the question,—with the condition of my own church and vicinity, and the wants of the heathen—that little was left me, but personally to apply decisions long since made of the subject generally.

"I am aware of the extreme uncertainty respecting the future, of the possibility that my conclusions may eventually appear wrong. But I am necessitated to judge by the light I have, and to walk by faith where more light might seem desirable. For the result, I depend upon his gracious aid, whose direction and support I have earnestly sought, and who has hitherto been my sufficiency.

"It might be added that, however much trepidation is felt, it arises alone from possibilities and not probability. I have as much assurance and comfort from the conclusion as could reasonably be expected by any other man under similar circumstances. It is really no easy matter to walk by faith.

"In view of all this, I could not retain a good and peaceful conscience, were I to remain in America. I have, therefore, been constrained to conclude that it is my duty to sever the very tender ties that bind me to you; to leave this land of so many delightful associations for the desolations of that far-off country.

"It is already intimated above, but it might be proper here more formally to assure you, that this decision has in no way been affected by any dissatisfaction with my present condition. I could not ask a greater sphere of usefulness. From no church has the minister of the gospel probably received a more uniformly respectful and affectionate treatment, or a more hearty cooperation in his labors for his own church and the cause abroad. This is also true respecting our pew-holders: to whom I feel deeply indebted for the kindness with which they have regarded my labors, and for the cheerful and liberal pecuniary provision they have made for my support. I have never wished more. It is pleasing to reflect that all this meeting my highest desires has been of a character that might be trusted for the future. Indeed, so peculiarly have I been impressed with these considerations, that I could hardly fail to regard myself your pastor until death. It was my earnest desire and full expectation to spend my life in your midst; to be, by the grace of God, your spiritual adviser, in prosperity and affliction, even to the dark valley of the shadow of death; and to aid you in rearing your sons and daughters finally to occupy your places in the Church of Christ. I had not for a moment thought otherwise until this question of duty was officially submitted to my consideration by the Board. I know of no situation in this country that could induce me to leave you; but to the cry of the spiritually desolate, having no God and without hope, personally presented to me, I cannot, I dare not, turn a deaf ear. To do so would blind my mind, sear my conscience, harden my heart, and greatly darken my own prospects for eternity. After that, of what value could I be to you. The wail of lost souls from heathen lands would ever be present to me, and what but the indignant frown of him whom we most love, could I expect? The love of Christ and the wants of men ready to perish, alone constrain me to leave a most affectionate and faithful people, whom I most tenderly love.

"In presenting more definitely the reasons which have led to this decision, let me refer you first to the wants of the world. I shall by no means argue the Christian character of missions, nor fill a sheet with missionary details. With you, this is certainly not necessary. To say nothing of your many previous opportunities, if after nearly six years instruction in private, in social meetings, and in monthly concerts, in frequent allusion, and especial missionary discourses in the pulpit, any of you are still ignorant or faithless upon this point, I have no hope that you can appreciate my present intention.

"In the spirit of our Saviour, then, contemplate six hundred millions of persons ultimately susceptible of all the improvement and temporal happiness of this land, but now groveling in heathenism; and twenty millions of immortal souls with light sufficient to leave them without excuse for their sins (Rom. 1. 18-32), living without God, and dying without hope, annually driven away in their sins to the bar of God, and thence to everlasting death. The influence of the gospel, the love of Christ applied to their hearts, would make them happy in time and save them eternally. Here remember that solemn inquiry—'What is a man profited if he shall gain the whole world, and lose his own soul; or what shall a man give in exchange for his soul?' Can any sacrifice on our part be compared with an annual loss of at least twenty millions such souls?

"If you refer to the particular field assigned to me, the necessity of more laborers appears under peculiar circumstances. The Karens are a numerous people, and waiting for gospel light. The small amount of labor thus far bestowed has met an unusual divine blessing. Already about five thousand have come to Christ, and the number is rapidly increasing. But where are the needed laborers? Who will preach Christ to them? And who will go forth to shepherd and feed the lambs and sheep of this distant fold? Our only reasonable hope can be in native preachers and teachers. If left to themselves, they must ere long have a corrupt Christianity, worse, it may be, than even their former state.

"One who loves Christ must tell it to others; but he can tell no more and no otherwise than he knows. Without a miracle then in his behalf, the darkness of his mind must mingle with and corrupt his notions of religion; and those confused corrupt teachings are to mould Karen Christianity. Now who will engage to discipline their minds, and richly furnish them out of the abundance of God's glorious gospel? If our hope for the people is in native teachers, our hope for the teachers is in their previous instruction; and to whom shall they look for that instruction if not to us? It is to this work I am invited.

"Whether, therefore, we view the field in general, or the particular station to which I am called, the claim is immediate and unspeakably great.

"You will find a second reason in the exceeding difficulty of supplying these wants. This appears, not only from the fact that so large a portion of the heathen world has yet received no attention, but equally from a full view of those to whom the gospel has been sent. Our effort hitherto can be regarded only as an experiment upon a small scale, and under very unfavorable circumstances. To this day, no one of our stations has received adequate attention. In most, we have but here and there a solitary man, rapidly descending to the grave, not so much from the effect of climate as from excessive labor. In some of our most important posts, the fall of even one man would suspend our operations for months or even years.

"There is, probably, in the hands of those to whom God has given this gospel in trust for the world, money and men sufficient for the whole field. So long, however, as the Church retains its present low standard of action, the meagreness of funds and the paucity of laborers is as real, and the inability of the Board to obtain them as great, as though God's trustees were actually destitute of means. Hence, those who appreciate the claim and have the ability must decide duty and perform labor as if really alone in the Church. In this respect, I have felt a deeply solemn responsibility resting upon me.

"A view of the particular field of my future labor will present additional difficulties. The man needed for this must enter upon a new climate, habits, studies, etc.; and must, therefore, be so young as to afford a reasonable expectation of so long a period of labor as to reach results that will require years of patient effort; still he is to enter upon duties of such responsibility as demands the discipline and experience of some age. He must love the heathen and be willing to make some sacrifice. His constitution must be adapted to a warm climate, and the habits of his mind fitted to work in prospect, without immediately seeing any prominent fruit of his labors. He ought to have no pecuniary embarrassments. Such a man would probably be a married man. If so, his wife should be qualified to be a helper in the work, and willing to forsake all for that purpose. And then, how important that they be not encumbered with a family of children!

"Many men may be found possessing any one of these in a far greater degree than myself. But how seldom are these ten or a dozen particulars blended in one! However deficient I may feel myself in any particular qualification, it would be presumptuous in me to reject the unanimous opinion of those by whom I am known, so far as that opinion has been expressed to me. Though so often advised not to leave my present field, yet in every case, by yourselves and others, this point has been, not only fully admitted, but immediately and unequivocally expressed. Now, if such are the difficulties of finding the man, shall he, when found and addressed by name, blench? Shall he decline the work? Can he do so and remain innocent?

"I have referred only to the obtaining of men, but there is equal, if not greater difficulty in our funds; and it is an additional consideration, if this man is so situated, as at the same time to effect this point. There is no want of money in the Church, only in the disposition of our brethren to bestow it. How is that disposition to be reached? Undoubtedly every man who makes new and great sacrifices for the cause affects it by his example. In this respect God has greatly blessed me. By giving me years of very favorable settlement, I have much to surrender. It directly touches this question of funds, that among other things I must give up an annual income of at least twenty-one hundred dollars. My own heart and conscience have often been quickened to duty by the great sacrifices of our missionary brethren, and will not the same effect follow in this case? Surely, if special reasons exist, why I should go to the Karens, the great reason remains why all should supply the requisite means to evangelize the world.

"I hope, my brethren, that this disposition to give will be effected another way. We take your hearts into heathen lands. Parents know that where the heart is the money will go. And may I not hope that, when far away, you will remember me, pray for and support me? Will you not thence be led to a greater interest in, and effort for, the cause generally? And will not this be equally true of many others? There is yet another way by which this disposition may be uniformly moved—that is by inspiring confidence in such decisions. The Missionary cause is often regarded as mere matter of declamation. I fear this is too frequently the case, and in such men as would cause great surprise, were it all told. Even the sacrifices of some are in the same spirit attributed to a warm imagination, or a hasty decision. I have been so long known by my brethren to be practically the reverse of all this, that I can but hope my influence may in this respect be peculiarly happy. You know I can not well endure a man who attempts, by imagination, to befool my judgment or to carry my passions by storm. Then not only have I calmly weighed this call for four months, but I am not aware of greater feeling respecting it at this time, than I have generally had for the past thirteen years. What has come to your observation is equally well known to the companions and advisers of my earliest Christian walk. By many of them I am remembered mainly as one consecrated to the cause of Missions.

"I cannot avoid the impression, that contemplating all this, so desirable in the man here needed, renders it a very fearful matter for me to decline this service. If I cannot go, to whom may the Board look, who is more favorably situated? If it is not my duty, on whom is the duty more plainly devolved? It is certainly no easy task to select such a one.

"You are prepared now to hear, as my third reason, that I was early impressed with this duty; indeed, solemnly consecrated to this work. After many weeks' agonizing conviction of my condition as a sinner, there was a night when I dared not sleep, nor even retire, without an interest in the Saviour's love. As I sat alone at midnight searching God's word, every fear fled, every sorrow was banished, my heart was relieved; indeed, it was filled with peace. But it did not occur to me that I was forgiven or that I was regenerated: I had forgotten my own condition, but oh, the preciousness of that glorious gospel! I thought, if I had a thousand worlds, I would cheerfully give them all, could the heathen have that Bible. Their condition alone seemed to occupy my mind. To bear to them a knowledge of the great salvation, first awakened in me a desire for the ministry. For that I commenced my preparatory study, and when, in consequence of ill health, that delightful prospect was darkened, I seriously thought of giving up all attempts to preach the gospel. I should have done so but for the advice of wiser men. When I last saw Missionaries sail from Boston, so painful was the thought that I could not follow them, that I solemnly resolved to see no more leave our shores until I could accompany them—these feelings have never left me. When I first met you in the Monthly Concert, you may remember I stated these facts, and that though providentially forbidden to stand on heathen ground, I was still a Foreign Missionary. You all know with what interest I have from month to month, and every year, presented this subject before you; and that however much I have felt and done for my own charge, I have manifested no less interest for this best of causes. I have given but one reason at any time for remaining in this country, that I was not fit for a foreign field. Now that God has kindly removed that objection has he not a right to hold me to my early consecration? True, circumstances have changed. I am now surrounded by an affectionate people and many comforts, and am blessed with the confidence of my brethren. For all this I have felt, and do still feel, truly grateful, and it is no easy matter to sever these ties. But did he hand them to me that they shall become my idols? Solemn vows are upon me. Shall I not take them up, now that I may?

"My fourth reason is found in a review of divine providence in this matter. I have often asked in much surprise, why, while the harvest was great and the laborers were few, God should reject one who so ardently desired this work? But if it is his will that I should enter the sphere now opened, this difficulty is solved. At no previous time, until perhaps the last two or three years, would I have dared to enter upon this work. Even now my health would not admit the many exposures and irregularities which necessarily attend the usual Missionary service.

"God has, for some years, under favorable circumstances, detained me in this land, until I am measurably prepared to commence this work; and, at the same time, he has presented such associations and responsibilities as would have forbidden my engaging in it, however well qualified. During this time, he has been gradually preparing just such a field as I could enter. At no previous time, perhaps, would it have been best to commence; but now the call is immediate and imperative. God has led the blind by a way that was not understood, and has brought together the man and the work at apparently the proper juncture. A little while more, and I should be too old; a little while more, and the field would be overrun with weeds of rank luxuriance. Then, again, who informed the Board of this man? How came they, after the decision by our brethren that it was proper to call a pastor, to select him, so little known in our public bodies, from among the large number of ministers in the United States, so many of whom were likely immediately to be suggested to their minds? Why send to the low country of Georgia, to take one out of so few, instead of selecting from the large number of well qualified men in the New England States? Why not apply to some one of the many that in Worcester, by their votes, approved, and solemnly pledged themselves to this work? I have asked them no questions upon this point, and know not who or what has thus influenced them. Until the morning that I received their letter, I had not even dreamed that it might be my duty now to go. But for the want of a better solution, I say it looks like the providence of God, after having prepared the field, and given the man a heart to the work, directing the Board to that very man though surrounded by so many more likely to go.

"If, then, God in his providence has thus made the man and the field to meet; if, at the same time, he has prepared me to take your hearts, and those of many brethren in other parts of our land with me, thus to secure your sympathies, prayers, and co-operation in the work of saving souls,—may I not suppose that all these combined indicate somewhat very different from blind chance? Is it not clearly the voice of God's providence? And should we not reverently receive such instruction? Truly, it is thus that he aids us in seeking our duty in his word and at the throne of grace.

"A fifth consideration is derived from the present state of the Missionary cause. To me, this has, for some time, appeared to

11

rest, if not to retrograde.   The most solemn appeals fail to
secure either men or money.   I refer, not to the fact that some
few may decline this service when addressed, or that our funds
have this year fallen short of a former year by upwards of $3,000.
There may be more men and money in the service than ten
years since.   But I allude more particularly to the solemn
consideration that present wants are 'not as cheerfully and
amply met, as were the wants of former days.   We have prayed,
'Thy kingdom come,' and God has mercifully answered the
prayer in part; but it has imposed upon us responsibilities, it
has made upon us demands, that we are slow to meet.   The
population of the heathen world has increased; each station has
progressed; new fields of labor have providentially opened;
and the labors of wicked men against Christ and his cause have
augmented far beyond the increase of our efforts to convert the
world to the cross of our Lord and Saviour.   And this has
occurred amid the unparalleled prosperity of our churches at
home.   We have money, until it is like a gangrene to the piety
of our members.   We have numbers, until a large portion of
the church have become the veriest idlers in the Lord's vineyard,
or are engaged mainly in carping at and retarding the effective
labor of others.   It is not my purpose here to account for this state
of things; but if my life would help to remove it, I ought cheerfully
to surrender it.   Rather than in any way to increase it, let a mill-
stone be hanged to my neck and me be cast into the depths of the
sea.   I believe every one does increase it who turns his back
upon the claims of the world, whatever sacrifice it may demand.

"In my last year's missionary discourse, I suggested the probability that the time was not distant, when the claims of this
cause would become the touchstone to the sincerity of our professions of Christianity.   The time has come when those who
know the facts in the case must respond, in men and money, to
the beseeching cries of the heathen, or forfeit a good conscience
and the approbation of God; and, may I not add, greatly endan-
ger souls for eternity.   This is a time when deep anxiety per-
vades the friends of Christ and the heathen.   Shall I add
to that anxiety?   Shall I increase the lethargy that possesses

so large a portion of the Church, by flinching from difficulties, and then presenting excuses which others will not approve, and which I myself cannot peacefully trust? It cannot be; the present state of this cause demands unreserved consecration, and the most prompt and hearty action in the service.

" The last consideration I will mention, is the effect of my decision on others. All Christians are closely observed, particularly in this line of gospel ministry. Their conduct is rigidly compared with their professions. To this we certainly should not object. Should we unwisely do so, it can neither do away the effects of our conduct, nor relieve us from the solemn responsibility thereof. We should, therefore, let our light so shine, that others seeing our good works may be led to glorify God. This is true in proportion as we have publicly espoused Christ and his cause. It is well known that I have always spoken freely upon the claims of Missions. I have pleaded for both men and money; and have often professed my readiness personally to enter the foreign field, if others, qualified to decide, thought me fit. Not only then may I be judged as a Christian and a Christian Minister, but as an avowed friend to the cause. And what but incredulity in our professions could be expected to follow my conduct, should I now practically deny the whole of my former instructions. Not only would the worldly-minded distrust me, and thence the cause, but would not Christians, and even my ministering brethren feel their confidence weakened in the Ministry? Would they not be liable to infer that, however good this subject may be for declamation, it is deemed too cross-bearing for practice? When next we approach them with the claims of God and the heathen, may they not say to us, 'They bind heavy burdens and grievous to be borne and lay them on young men's shoulders; but they themselves would not move them with one of their fingers?' Indeed, in so saying would they not utter a truth capable of ever after keeping us silent? May not one difficulty, now found in obtaining the right men and sufficient funds be that this has been expressed or even suspected? How fearful, too, would this influence be upon the people of my own charge! You know with what

plainness I have ever preached to you the gospel. I have kept
back nothing which I deemed for your good, the Bible being
my guide. I have not sought your praise or pleasure; but
your welfare, your piety, your usefulness. I have often and
earnestly presented you the requisition of God for self-denial,
and the right use of your property, and I must do you the
justice to say, that in no instance has any complaint reached
me on account of this plain dealing. But I am too well aware
of the fact that you have not always believed me. Certainly, if
you had, men of property especially would either have given
more freely to supply the wants of a perishing world, or have forsaken a ministry from which they heard so frequent reproaches.
So also in our Church and Congregational concerns, I have
often asked you to make sacrifices for their welfare. And
though I have never said go, but come; yet I am not ignorant
that, in some, there have been moments of suspicion that my
object might be personal interest. Of this I do not complain;
it was natural. I have far more reason for gratitude that you
have so cheerfully endeavored to execute my plans. But
should I now cleave to the many comforts around me, would
not the mind very naturally misinterpret the act? Would not
some eventually conclude it far easier to preach than to practice,
and even justly say, 'It always appears his duty to take good
care of himself?' Could I, after that, preach as I have hitherto
done?

"And if such be the influence upon your minds, what must it
be upon that portion of my charge who have no personal interest in the Saviour. They are honorable men, and have a right
to expect consistency in their preacher. However much they may
be pleased with a declamation, will they not scorn the instructions and warnings of a man whose sacrifices consist only in
words, who demands from others what he is unwilling to attempt
himself? Will they not transfer their emotions to their intellects,
from this to other subjects, until from despisers of me and thence
of my office, they become skeptics of the worst cast, and ultimately lose their souls? Not only do I see the possibility of this,
but I see not how it could be otherwise. To prevent this would

require better reasons than it is in my power to give. I would not dare they should weigh me in my own balance.

"But to all this, my dear brethren, why should I subject myself, the ministry, the Church, the cause, and the souls of my people—souls committed to my charge, which before God I have solemnly promised, if possible, to lead to Christ and heaven? Sincerely I have preached what and no more than I thought the Bible contained. Honestly have I asked, without fear or favor, that my Master's claims should not be rejected. I have not presented principles which I could not myself believe, nor duties which I would not at least try to practice. Thus far, with the allowance due to the infirmities of our nature, I feel assured you can bear me witness, that my life has not falsified my verbal instructions. Surely I ought not now to hazard that point by cleaving to the comforts and kind friends, so mercifully loaned me for a time by our Heavenly Father.

"May I not hope the reverse of this will attend my cheerful compliance with duty? If, holding as I do, so much worldly good in my hand, I voluntarily resign it; if I now sacrifice my all, the result of a kind Providence over me for years, solely to obey Christ and benefit souls,—will it not be a voice, to my friends at least, that must be heard, an appeal that will be felt? Thus acting honestly and cheerfully, as I have desired others to do, and as I have professed my own readiness to do, will it not place beyond every reasonable doubt the sincerity of my past instructions? Will not my ministering brethren be strengthened thereby, especially when I can sincerely assert my firm conviction, that every honest minister of Christ would do the same or its equivalent, should duty be made plain? Can it fail to induce them and private Christians, by prayer and effort, to join us in this holy work? Will it not happily influence the minds of our brethren, hitherto opposed to Missions? Often have they suspected our motives when pleading this cause; they have feared that for our selfish interests we were imposing upon our brethren, whom we sent abroad, and upon those from whom we solicit funds at home. But after having so long been engaged in this work here, they cannot deem me ignorant of what has been supposed to be

11*

behind the curtain, and assuredly they will not charge me with folly sufficient to cast away so many earthly blessings, in order to become the mere tool of designing men to accomplish wicked purposes. If for a moment they have ever deemed it possible that even our Missionaries are seeking to advance their temporal interests, they cannot fail in this case to see their mistake. What earthly recompense can that heathen land make me? Will they continue to say that none go who have any thing to lose? and will not correct views in this case lead to suitable impressions respecting the cause generally?

"I cannot but think, where circumstances require such a sacrifice, and the demand is cheerfully met, it is adapted to strengthen men's faith in the ministry and its teachings, in the Church and its professions. To avoid dangerous and to secure healthful influences is with the gospel ministry of the first importance. I deem it well purchased at almost any amount of sacrifice.

"I have endeavored to present, briefly as possible, some of the reasons which have induced my decision. I have not decided from contemplating any *one* of these; but each in its place and all combined leave a conviction on my mind that cannot be resisted. Should you, under such circumstances, retain me, I am confident that you would have only a Jonah, whom you would soon seek to cast into the sea. I trust I am not understood to imply that any obligation rests upon me to the general cause, which does not equally belong to every member of Christ's body. For this particular field, special considerations must be weighed by me. It may not be the duty of all to go to Burmah, or to any other foreign land; but surely we are all Christ's, and ought as a church to obey his last command, to send the gospel into all the world, until it be preached to every creature. Nor can any one of us be absolved from our part of that momentous trust.

"I hope, also, that, when I allude to sacrifices, I am understood to speak only after the manner of men.

"I confidently believe you will not only cheerfully resign me to this cause, but that you will with me give liberally, uniformly, and to the end, of your substance to accomplish this glorious work. That the Great Head of the Church, who purchased it with his own blood, and who loves it far better than we can do, will provide for its wants, I cannot doubt. In him alone is my trust for you and myself. To him, my dear brethren, I commend you.

'I remain very truly your affectionate pastor,

J. G. BINNEY.'"

After the reading of this paper, it was voted to receive the same, and refer it to a Special Committee, consisting of Brethren A. Harmon, T. Clark, W. W. Wash, and the Church Clerk, with power to act or report at pleasure.

It was also voted that a copy thereof be presented to the pew-holders at the earliest opportunity.

June 1st. At the regular monthly Church Meeting, the above-named Committee reported as follows.

"We recommend to the Church the adoption of the following:

"*Resolved I*, That this Church gratefully acknowledges the divine goodness to us, in the delightful relation which has existed between us and our beloved Pastor for nearly six years, and in the many blessings bestowed upon us during that time.

"*Resolved II*, That we deeply feel the loss we sustain in his removal, but in view of the document he has presented us, we cannot but approve his decision, and regard it as a dispensation of God in which, however afflictive, we ought cheerfully to acquiesce.

"*Resolved III*, That when our Pastor leaves us, he takes with him our highest confidence and affection; that his fidelity to this Church, and the sacrifice which we know he makes, are sufficient promise of his fidelity in a foreign land.

"*Resolved IV*, That by our Pastor's consent, the Committee appointed at the last meeting be authorized to print in pamphlet form, our proceedings upon this subject."

The resolutions were unanimously adopted.

When the question of going to Burmah was settled, he and Mrs. Binney went at once to Augusta, Georgia, to visit the Baptist Church and people, by request of their young pastor, Rev. Wm. T. Brantly. Then commenced the acquaintance between these two, which ripened into a warm and lasting friendship. Though on leaving his native land for Burmah, he received several gold pens as mementos of friendship, the one on which was inscribed "W. T. Brantly to J. G. Binney," was ever kept on his table, in the bracket of a bronze inkstand, the gift of another dear friend, and mostly used by him. It is the pen now used to couple their names on this page.

This visit to Augusta was remembered with great satisfaction, and made frequent subject of conversation in after years in the wilds of Karen jungles. The people everywhere received them with open hearts, and listened to his addresses on missions with eagerness. Everywhere, however, the effort was made to dissuade him from leaving Georgia. The great destitution, and the need of such men, were strongly pleaded as a reason for his remaining in the State. Especially was the ignorance and apathy on Foreign Missions presented as a reason why one so well informed and so earnest should remain to intercede in its behalf. The perils and discomforts of a sea voyage of four or five months, loomed up before them, and well they might. That would have been a vivid imagination that could have exceeded the reality.

An event occurred here which seemed well adapted to impress upon all minds the truth, that perils are not confined to times or places, but that our " times are in his hands."

While in Augusta, Mr. and Mrs. Binney received the hospitalities of William Turpin, M.D., the honored father-in-law of Mr. Brantly, who with his wife was also staying at his house, a mile or two from town. After an early evening meeting, held in behalf of Foreign Missions in the town, Mr. and Mrs. Binney entered the carriage of Dr. Turpin, which had been sent in to convey them home. The clouds were threatening rain, and it was very dark; but as the road was good, and one with which both coachman and horses were very familiar, no danger was apprehended. When but a short distance out, however, a vivid flash of lightning, followed instantly by a terrific crash, caused the horses to spring to one side, and precipitate themselves and the carriage down an embankment. As the carriage was thrown upon one side, Mr. Binney was able to open the door of the opposite side, and thus escaping, aided by the flashes of lightning, they reached the road. Though unharmed, their condition was not an enviable one. The rain was pouring down in torrents; the coachman and horses in the ditch, and though the former declared himself "all right," the latter made no sign. It was fully half a mile to the nearest shelter, which by the advice of the coachman they attempted to find. In this they were successful; but the owner was alone, with the exception of an old negro woman, and so much under the influence of Georgia whiskey, that he was neither able to go to the scene of disaster with Mr. Binney, nor fit to be left with a lady. After much persuasion, however, with the help of the old woman, he started out to aid in extricating the horses and carriage, but the drenching rain brought him, partially at least, to his senses, and he rushed back, declaring to Mrs. Binney, that he would have nothing to do in helping a runaway match out of their difficulties. "Nothing but an attempt to escape over the border to get married would ever have taken a young couple out on such a night."

Mr. Binney secured the lantern, however, and the horses and carriage were brought on at length, neither seriously injured; but it was thought best to walk home and not risk them again. A warm reception, a warm room, a warm bath, and a good night's rest, brought all right so far as Mr. and Mrs. Binney were concerned; and, as it was rather a serio-comic affair, had it ended then, it would have afforded equal occasion for gratitude and mirth. But it did not end there. Mrs. Brantly was in very delicate health, and the fright she experienced from the perilous adventure of her friends brought on convulsions; and the next day the doctor had little hope of her recovery. For several days the life of this almost idolized wife and daughter hung in the greatest suspense. It pleased God, however, to spare her life and restore her to health again.

Soon after this Mr. and Mrs. Binney attended the Georgia Baptist State Convention held in Madison. Here many new and pleasant acquaintances were formed with the brethren of Upper Georgia. The subject of Missions was discussed, and their claims enforced, both socially and publicly, and much interest was awakened. The friends there had positive proof that one man at least believed in the duty and practicability of obedience to the Saviour's last command, to "preach the gospel to every creature."

There, also, the old argument was brought up, that Georgia was emphatically mission ground; and was met, also, with the answer, that for the ignorance that prevails, either among the poor whites or the colored people of Georgia, the Master will hold its Christian citizens responsible. The force of the answer was felt, and many and hearty were the confessions of neglect in this respect. It was very evident that Domestic as well as Foreign Missions received a new impulse.

At the close of the session, the spacious house being crowded, all passed before the desk and shook hands in turn with their missionary friends, and with many tears and benedictions said their last farewells. Even little children wept as they looked upon the faces and took the hands of those whom they deemed martyrs for Jesus' sake.

Dr. Binney returned directly to Savannah; closing up his affairs, both public and private, with all possible despatch, he preached his last sermon to his church and congregation, and embarked with Mrs. Binney for Boston on the first of July. The last Lord's Day was a memorable day to the church; the place was literally a "Bochim," a place of tears. The next day citizens of Savannah of every rank and condition followed them to the ship, one of the regular line of sailing packets plying between New York and Savannah; for this was before the days of railroads and of the swift steamers which now bring the cities so near to each other. With the usual passionate impulsiveness of the colored people, they literally wailed and screamed, as their friends stepped on board the vessel that was to carry them forever from their sight. All their friends were extremely kind; and their esteem and good wishes were shown, not only in words, but also in numerous presents, precious mementos of their Savannah friends when they should be far away.

Their passage to New York was a little foretaste of what was to follow. They had head winds with high seas, and were fourteen days in the crowded vessel, in the hottest part of the year. To add to the discomfort, sugar, ice, and all kinds of vegetables gave out several days before they reached New York, and even bread was becoming scarce.

CHAPTER IX.

PREPARATIONS FOR DEPARTURE.

July to November, 1843.

FROM the middle of July till the time of their embarking for Burmah, the following November, 1843, Mr. and Mrs. Binney made their home at the house of R. E. Pattison, D.D., Roxbury, Massachusetts. He was then the Home Secretary of the American Baptist Missionary Board, having its headquarters at Boston. From this home Mr. Binney went abroad, visiting Associations and other meetings, not only in Massachusetts, but in other States, doing what he could for the Mission cause. Everywhere he produced the impression that he thoroughly believed in the claims of this cause to which he had consecrated himself. He preached one sermon many times that summer and autumn. As it was not written, it was probably somewhat varied to suit occasions, but the outline was the same; the text was, "Lord, what wilt thou have me to do"? He repeated this sermon, generally, by special request. He would leave home having prepared a different subject, not even taking the analysis of this with him, but would be urged to repeat the sermon preached on such an occasion, and he would yield to the request. He never wrote it out in full, and when requested to do so, would say,

"I don't think I could. Perhaps a reporter could do

so; but I am too much in earnest; I lose the inspiration as soon as I try to write it."

Each repetition cost him a great expenditure of labor, and brought on nervous exhaustion, like making the sermon anew; or even greater than new sermons generally did.

Among other cities, he visited Buffalo, by request of Rev. E. Tucker, pastor of one of the churches. His heart was thoroughly enlisted in the Foreign Mission cause, and he gave Mr. Binney an opportunity, not only of preaching to men of means and influence in the city, but also of becoming personally acquainted with them. Before leaving Buffalo, Mr. Tucker planned to spend a day with his friends at Niagara Falls. He took them in his private carriage, as the day was fine, and it would afford them an opportunity of viewing the Falls from the most favorable points without great fatigue. After spending an exceedingly pleasant day in this way, Mr. Tucker discovered that he could obtain a remarkably fine view by walking out to the very verge of the stream upon an immense tree which had fallen above the cataract. Its topmost branches were actually laved by the current, and many of them had been broken off by its force. He was quite transported by the view, and walked back and forth several times to persuade Mr. Binney to enjoy it also; but while expatiating on the ease with which it could be done, his foot touched the water and was tripped from under him in an instant. He threw himself prostrate upon the tree, and clung to a branch, but was unable to bring up the unfortunate foot. Mr Binney took in the position at a glance, and walked out boldly, caught him by the collar, and with almost superhuman effort brought him to the tree in safety. Mrs. Binney, seeing her husband's purpose, shut her eyes and did not move till she heard Mr. Tucker exclaim, "All right," and Mr. Binney respond with authority, "Now, Brother Tucker, behave yourself!" Mr. Tucker brought himself upright, and with a look of distress, clapped his hands to his head, exclaiming, "But, Brother Binney, you have lost my hat; I paid ten dollars for that beaver last week." Mr. Binney, who had a keen sense of the ludicrous, shouted with laughter, in which Mr. Tucker heartily joined. When they had composed themselves, Mrs. Binney suggested that they had seen enough for one day, and it would be well to call the carriage. This was promptly done, and Mr. Tucker went back to Buffalo with a wet foot and bare head; but all were thankful that so pleasant a day had a comical rather than a tragical ending.

The preparation for a sea voyage of four or five months' duration and for living in a country almost unknown, and where many necessaries were not to be obtained, was a very different thing from preparing for Burmah now. The crossing of the Atlantic in a fine steamer is an every-day occurrence, and requires little addition to one's usual wardrobe; then, a few days in Scotland or England enables one to start again refreshed, on another fine steamer for thirty-five or forty days more; and for this it is easy to calculate and prepare. Then again, little is needed for Burmah; all the real necessaries of life can now be procured in Rangoon as readily as in New York City.

Then, ignorance of what was really desirable made the preparation more difficult than it otherwise would have been; but the work was done mostly by Mrs. Binney, assisted by the deft fingers—not machines—of a few kind friends in Roxbury. Many last visits were paid; and when all was completed it only remained to have a farewell meeting; this was held in Bowdoin Square Church, Boston, November 5th, 1843.

Mr. Binney's address on that occasion is given entire, that the views with which he entered on the work and the spirit which actuated him may appear in his own language.

ADDRESS OF MR. BINNEY.

"The present occasion is one of deep interest. Not only is it so to the Church generally, which is moved by whatever affects any portion of Christ's cause; and to our own immediate relatives and friends, who regard it as one of the last stages of a process which is soon to separate us from them; but particularly is it so to the parties immediately concerned. The Board are about to increase their already numerous responsibilities, and cannot but be anxious respecting the result of our appointment. The missionaries to-night occupy a position whence we can readily observe what has been and is about to be relinquished, and with some certainty, anticipate the, to us, untried circumstances and labors to which we are designated. Our age and past circumstances prepare us to feel the solemnity of now confirming our former resolutions.

We are not surprised, therefore, that many inquire, why, at our period in life, we are induced to enter upon the uncertain vicissitudes of a foreign field. In the few remarks that I may make this evening, let me first glance at what has induced this determination.

It is not, dear friends, that this step involves no sacrifice on our part. We do not, indeed, anticipate many of the trials to which the pioneers of this cause were exposed. Some of these arose from a combination of circumstances such as seldom occurs. Others were peculiar to new and untried fields. Such is the condition of our places of destination, that we do not apprehend a violent death nor imprisonment; though we are too well acquainted with the instability and caprice of arbitrary governments, not to know that possibly we may be subjected even to these. Such also are the facilities of intercourse between these stations and the churches at home, that it cannot be necessary to expose us to great deprivations of any of the comforts of life. To anticipate them, therefore, would be an uncharitable suspicion of our brethren and friends, which we have not for a moment indulged.

But if extraordinary trials may not await us, we cannot forget that the happiness or the suffering of life depend mostly on its more ordinary events. Its every-day bestowments are the most essential to our welfare; and these, to no small extent, must be relinquished by every one who becomes a Foreign Missionary. We know the privileges of this free country, and we have enjoyed its literary, social, and religious associations; our homes were stored with comforts as yours are to-night. We loved our people, and they loved us; our numerous relatives and our other personal friends are unspeakably dear to us; our very language is replete with the most tender associations; hitherto in our anxieties and labors, we have had the sympathy and co-operation of many friends, and in perplexing circumstances we have been associated with those ready to counsel us, and to share with us our responsibilities. I speak the sentiment of you all, when I say, that suddenly to part with any such tributaries to your happiness would deeply afflict you. You know what sorrow is experienced when Divine Providence lessens your comforts, or removes even a single loved one from your family circles. What, then, must be our feelings, when called to relinquish nearly all, of every class, at about one and the same time? Believe us, no one who has the sympathies of a man and the tender attachments that a Christian should possess, can become a foreign missionary without great sacrifices.

Of this we are well assured. Our age and habits forbid the indulgence of mere romance. Missionary labor is now too well known, as an every-day business, fitted to test our patience and exhaust our powers. We have seen too much of men and things, to be deceived respecting the position we are really to occupy. Besides, we are too well acquainted with the true state of missionary feeling and action at home, to indulge in mere imagining. It is a painful fact, taught us by years of pastoral labor and observation, that the missionary is not remembered as he should be by the great body of church members. True, there are exceptions to this; and to us it is a consolation which no language can express, that there are a few who will daily remember us and our labors, in earnest prayer to God, and from whom we may expect prompt and persevering co-operation. May our Heavenly Father long spare their lives and their means of usefulness, and may he greatly increase their number. But how very few there are, who are conscious that the wants, and especially the usefulness, of the missionary are the subjects of their daily secret pleading with God! And even to the "Monthly Concert" prayer-meeting, how very small a part of the church come up to pray the Lord of the harvest, either to send forth more laborers, or to bless those already in the field! How few pastors succeed in obtaining a general attendance of their people upon this meeting! Alas, how few pastors so much as expect all their people to be interested in this work of praying for the missionary cause! Even in our cities, it is often thought necessary to invite the meetings of different churches, in order to secure an ordinary assembly. And then, how small is the number of those who cheerfully make sacrifices, that they may be able to give liberally to this cause! And how much smaller is the number of those who faithfully labor to induce others to give! And when once they sincerely engage in this work, how easily do other subjects divide their ranks and divert their efforts! Upon their constancy in prayer, and in effort for this cause, our success largely depends. With so intimate an acquaintance, then, with this whole subject, it would indeed be strange, if we were not soberly to contemplate the work upon which we are about to enter.

No, brethren, we are not influenced to this step by the sup-
position that sacrifices are here no longer required ; nor because
we have failed to see that necessity. Not only is the sphere one
of necessary self-denial, but we entered upon it with our eyes
open.

Nor is it because we depreciate the wants of our churches at
home, that we are induced to embark in this cause. With these
we have long been familiar, and they have enlisted our sympathies and secured our efforts. But we are painfully impressed
with the disinclination of our brethren to enter the foreign field.
Notwithstanding the destitute condition of much of our own
land, yet in our older country communities, churches and
preachers are multiplied until they are brought almost to every
door; and in our cities and larger towns, evangelical ministers
are crowded together, and many are running to and fro ; so that
not a few find it difficult to obtain a settlement, and the efficiency
of others is often sadly diminished. We are confident, therefore, that others will soon fill the desirable stations we vacate ;
but where are the men, ready and waiting to enter the wide
doors of usefulness which are constantly opening abroad?
Again and again has the cry of the missionary, fainting amid his
toils, come up into our churches in vain for help. Even the
awakened heathen have joined in that request, until their thrilling appeals have forced tears from our laymen and flaming
speeches from our ministers. Some have been led to say, "Go,
go to their rescue ;" but alas ! how few respond to the appeal
with,—"Here am I, Lord, send me." It is this that moves us,
that so few devote themselves to this work.

Nor is it that we are led by any new and special impulses peculiar to ourselves. We have no desire to rid us of the enjoyments of home; our circumstances and employments here are
by far the most congenial to our natural tastes; and we confess
that at times our hearts even recoil from the peculiar condition
of the heathen land. We can see no obligation resting upon us,
that does not rest upon Christ's disciples as such; and we know
of no divine wrath that awaits us if we go not, more than also
awaits our ministering brethren who remain at home. We seri-

ously doubt whether many of the members of our churches, who live so much for worldly good,—and many of our pastors who still cleave to their native land, have not, at some period of their Christian course, had impressions like our own. Indeed, we solemnly believe that they have often heard the cry of the heathen, and the command of Christ, and have been troubled thereby; and that had it not been for the difficulties of the foreign field, the influence of near friends, and the allurements of this happy country, they would have known their duty. We say not this for the sake of complaint, but that our own feelings may not be mistaken upon this subject. After an intimate acquaintance at home with young converts, with members of our churches, and with our ministering brethren, as learned from their own declarations, we can find in our own experience no impressions which most of them have not more than once felt.

But if neither of these considerations has induced our decision, so neither one nor all of them can be permitted to keep us from the path of duty. Our views of the cause outweigh any number of difficulties, and constrain us to go on, not knowing what may befall us.

In reflecting upon the state of the heathen, and in comparing their temporal condition with that of our own happy country, we have ever supposed that this wide difference arose from the fact that upon us were showered the benign influences of Christianity, while upon them came only blighting and mildew;—their false gods and their necessarily false principles have, like bands of locusts, overspread the nations and desolated all that was lovely and conducive to true happiness. We confess, our sympathies have often been moved by this reflection, and we have wondered why the gospel might not be made to impart these blessings to the whole family of man; though we are not certain that this view alone would secure our determination.

But when we remember their eternal prospects, there can be no longer any question, how much expense may be justified, to make them acquainted with the great salvation. We do honestly believe the Bible to be God's own word, that all its assertions are true, and that all its promises and threatenings will be fulfilled. We cannot, therefore, expel the thought that "The wicked shall be turned into hell, and all the nations that forget God;" that "There is no other name under heaven given among men, whereby we must be saved," than that which the gospel presents; and that the heathen, though very ignorant, have some knowledge which they do not improve, "so that they are without excuse." On the other hand, "The Scripture saith, Whosoever believeth on him shall not be ashamed. For there is no difference between the Jew and the Greek; for the same Lord over all is rich unto all that call upon him. For whosoever shall call upon the name of the Lord shall be saved. How then shall they call on him in whom they have not believed? And how shall they believe in him of whom they have not heard? And how shall they hear without a preacher? And how shall they preach except they be sent?" With us, therefore, there is no question, that about six hundred millions of souls, precious as are our own, are exposed to the wrath of God, and to endless misery in hell; that millions of souls are every year hastening into wretchedness infinitely more dreadful than the worst of their temporal state, which so easily excites our compassion; and that nothing known to us can save them from this unspeakably awful prospect, but the minister of the gospel, proclaiming "the Lamb of God who taketh away the sin of the world."

Now what, dear brethren, are our earthly interests compared with the welfare of millions of souls, each of which, our Saviour has taught us, is of more value than the "whole world?" Is it possible for us to retain our confidence in God's word, and yet to evade the awful pressure of this thought? For years it has been before us, and we must turn infidel in intellect or in heart before we can banish it. As truly as the Bible is the inspired word of God, so truly can nothing but the preaching of the gospel rescue these millions from the woes of hell: nothing else can light up in their hearts the anticipation of that rest in heaven which so much cheers and comforts us to-night.

Immediately connected with this reason is another. Our Divine Master has commanded his church and ministers to give this gospel to the world. We say our Divine Master has so commanded. He is assuredly that much to us, or he is nothing. Whatever he bids, we must do; or cease to be his servants. Upon that condition alone did we become his; and that condition, that we take up our cross daily, that if necessary to obey him, we hate father and mother, and brother and sister, and houses and lands, yea, and our own lives also,—was by us distinctly understood.

Now Christ has commanded us to go into all the world and preach the gospel to every creature. Should a doubt still linger whether on account of the greatness of this sacrifice, it might not be declined; let his sayings still linger in our ears, while he adds —"If any man will save his life, he shall lose it."—"It is enough for the disciple to be as his Master, and the servant as his Lord."—"No man, having put his hand to the plough, and looking back, is fit for the kingdom of God." Now, our brethren through the length and breadth of the land have heard this command, but from various considerations they decline the service. It is not for us to inquire, how far they may be safe in so doing; it is enough that Christ commands the work to be done, and that by his church. If others will not go forth, as they certainly do not, then that duty must be ours. Should he come to remove the candlesticks from unfaithful churches, and to turn dishonest stewards from their office, we would count any sacrifice as trifling to be allowed our place in his service.

One other consideration has greatly conduced to this decision. Our Missionary Board have requested us to go. We have always regarded that body as the agent of the churches. They are elected from the denomination at large, by delegates assembled from every part of our country, solely for the consideration of this subject. To them it is committed, in a special manner, to watch over the interests of Christ's kingdom in foreign lands, and, in behalf of the churches, to do all in their power that the last command of Christ may be fully obeyed. According to the best of their judgment, they are to select fields of labor, to commit these to the care and efforts of faithful men, and to inform the churches, not only of their proceedings, but of the means necessary most effectually to do the work assigned them. And every reasonable request for aid should be promptly and cheerfully afforded by those for whom they act. When we committed to them the care of this department, we certainly did not expect them to conduct its operations at their own expense; we virtually pledged to them all necessary means. Besides, the churches having thrown upon them the responsibility of this department, we, to no small extent, regard them as acting by the authority of our Saviour, as well as by the appointment of their brethren; and their request for any amount of aid, in men or money, necessary to give the gospel to the perishing, is urged upon us to the extent of our ability, by the command of Christ himself. Nor does this at all infringe our right of private judgment; for we ourselves are to judge of that necessity, as we hope at the last day, in peace to meet the brethren at the bar of God. To this thought we should add, that under present circumstances, we must act by some delegation of trust, or not obey the commission of Christ. We can do but little, if anything, effectually in this field, merely as individuals.

Such have been our views of our relations to the Board, and of our obligations to co-operate with them. We believe they have been as economical in their department as could reasonably be expected; that the fields they have occupied were judiciously selected; and that they have scarcely begun, yet, to meet the pressing wants of the world. As they can proceed only by the assistance of the churches, so their requests for that assistance have never yet exceeded the actual necessities of the work assigned them. Hitherto they have asked our prayers and our money; and without waiting for personal application, we have endeavored to afford our aid. When they have issued special appeals, we have made special efforts to meet the crisis. They now tell us that they need, not only money, but men; and that, should it upon prayerful reflection appear our duty, they wish our personal service in the foreign field. What could we say to this? We had committed to them the responsibility of directing this business of winning souls from among the nations; but they have returned upon us the solemn responsibility of co-operating with them; at the same time they inform us how we may best aid in their object. Shall we reply that they have progressed sufficiently far in converting the world unto God? Never, never! so long as millions of immortal souls are yet ignorant of the great salvation. Shall we say, that the Lord's treasury is exhausted,—that no talent of his yet remains buried in our napkin,—that we have done all in our power? Before God we dare not assert this. True, that which is here required has become so much a part of ourselves, that it can now be taken, only as by the drawing of blood. Still, it is not our own; it belongs to the Lord; and by his grace we can render unto God that which is his. What we can do, we ought to do, in this case certainly; and hence our decision.

Yet think not that, having learned our duty, we are otherwise than most cheerful in its performance. Never were we happier than at the present time.

Having stated briefly as possible a few thoughts respecting ourselves, allow me to consider a moment, the question,—What is the duty of the churches in this matter? What, dear brethren, is your duty? That you will constantly remember us in your prayers, and so far as circumstances allow, afford us comfortable support, we cannot doubt. This is understood. The field is divided. We take one department, and you retain the other. We "go down into the well," and you "hold the rope." But there is one feature of this obligation which may not be so generally apprehended, and which may be illustrated by the expression just quoted. If any one descends into a well to perform a labor common to himself and to him who remains above, the latter is obligated, not merely to hold the rope for the safety of the former, but to afford him such facilities that he may most successfully accomplish their common object. It is surely wrong to require him in the well, because he has already the most difficult department, also to work to disadvantage; unnecessarily to expend his strength and to impair his constitution. Yet such has been the condition of missionaries: their own maintenance has been sufficient; but they have been compelled to work to disadvantage. Often have they frittered away their strength, and impaired their constitution, for want of facilities, and especially for want of fellow-laborers, to accomplish that for which they went forth. How often have you heard the agonizing cry of your brethren, assuring you that they were almost exhausted from over-exertion, and that the work all about them remained unaccomplished for the want of necessary assistance; and imploring you, by all that was momentous for time and eternity, to send them help? This is what at times oppresses us: the thought that you may not perceive, or that you may not fully appreciate, this part of the home obligation; that we may be left at the bottom of the well, without the facilities for working to advantage, and that, consequently, all our trials may prove comparatively in vain,—this is painful beyond expression. A comfortable support is not the object of our solicitude; *that* we could more readily obtain at home. It is, that we may be enabled to *accomplish the work* for which we relinquish those many blessings which you retain. We have been reminded this evening of our solemn obligations to Christ and his church *for the results* of our labor. To the sentiments advanced we add our most hearty *Amen.* We reflected upon them before our decision, and they have appeared to us far more appalling than all personal deprivations. Were it not written, " Lo, I am with you alway, even to the end of the world," and, " My grace is sufficient for thee," those sentiments, so true and solemn, would dispel our every thought of entering the field of foreign missions. But judge, dear brethren, the extent of our sorrow, if to this and to all our other sources of solicitude, there be joined the painful consciousness that we are expected to make bricks without straw; if we are held accountable for results which are utterly beyond our control, from the want of your full co-operation. We know that God will not be deceived. Yet we may be exceedingly unhappy even respecting this part of our responsibility. A tender conscience may so severely judge us, that eternity alone may render clear to us the true cause of our failure. I know, dear brethren, that you now understand us. I think I hear you say, "That were indeed unjust; that ought never to be; the

13

Board should afford you every facility." But, alas, what can the Board do? Nothing but direct the means supplied by the churches. It is by the churches, through them, that these facilities must be afforded; and each one in this assembly should feel his personal responsibility to the missionary.

But your greatest obligations are to Christ, our common Lord, and to his cause in the world. Christians generally have not clearly apprehended these; at least, they have not done so in comparison with what they deem obligatory upon those who enter the foreign department. Christ gave his command to his disciples *as such.* He taught them all, that they were not their own; that they were to enter any department of his vineyard, where, according to their talents, they might most effectually serve him. However varied, then, may be the particular duties of Christians, the principle of consecration is one. In whatever department they may be, to the performance of its duties they are to devote every ability of soul and body, of time and property. Every other one is as truly bound to live wholly for Christ and his cause, as is the foreign missionary,—to do as much, and to suffer as much, up to the wants of the cause and to his capacity. And this consideration is paramount to every other. The responsibilities of no particular department can require more; nor can the favorable circumstances of any sphere require less, *so long as millions of souls are in a perishing condition.*

It is in accordance with this view, that, under God, we become ministers or missionaries. Nor has any disciple of Christ a right to devote his talents to the calling of a lawyer, physician, merchant, mechanic, or farmer upon any other principle. Nor, according to this, has any minister of the gospel a right to yield to the inducements of a home settlement, if his aid is more needed abroad; provided he is qualified for that sphere, or provided that by *severe discipline* he may obtain that qualification. It is not enough that he does good. He is obligated as the disciple of Christ to do the *most good* in his power; and that often depends as much upon the necessities of the field as upon the amount of labor performed. If any seriously doubt this, it is surely time for such carefully to review the first principles of discipleship; and in earnest to implore the instruction and direction of God. In eternity they may learn that this is the very foundation of true submission to God.

If such is the principle of consecration, what then is the responsibility resting upon Christ's disciples in this assembly? Is it not the duty of some to enter personally into the foreign service? I see before me many young men, who are ministers of Christ, many who are candidates for that sacred office. To you, dear brethren, do we most solemnly direct our appeal this evening. It is to be the business of your lives to unfold to others this principle of consecration, to urge them to unlimited fidelity to the Master. Can you consistently or successfully do this unless conscious that you are disposed to practice accordingly? You are not ignorant of what Christ requires, nor of the perishing condition of millions of your fellow men. Nor are you unaware of the fact already stated, that in New England and in many of the older States, ministers of the gospel are multiplied, until their usefulness is often seriously impaired. Why then spend your life in doing a work which would be equally well, and perhaps better, performed without you? Why, especially, do this, when millions of men are left annually to perish in their sins, without the knowledge of that salvation which it is your business to preach? Are you sure that it is alone to glorify God, and that you are where you can do the most good? Have you a comfortable evidence that the Saviour has made this your duty? Will that evidence bear agitation? Has he never seriously impressed you with the contrary? and what have you done with those impressions? Do you here urge your love of the refined and literary, your worldly relations and prospects, the great sacrifices required, and particularly your want of qualifications? What missionary, whom you would recommend to this work, must not experience the same or similar difficulties? Tell us, dear brethren, can it be possible, that he who upon earth had not where to lay his head, and who in the Garden and on Calvary drank to the very dregs that most bitter cup, in order to provide salvation for sinners, really approves your unanimous resolution to remain at home, while a world is perishing in your hearing? Has he. appointed only here and there a solitary one to preach his salvation to perishing millions; and has he made it the duty of the mass of his ministers to remain with the few, where they are more comfortable but less needed? Did he die for America only, or was it for the world? O ye disciples of this *crucified One*, to whose gospel you are indebted for all that you are, and for all that you anticipate, arise, and look out upon this wide scene of desolation. With your own views of Scripture truth, enter with these millions of heathen the eternal world; stand with them before the judgment seat; and hear and see for yourselves the result of this neglect; then say, can you turn your backs upon such fields, and with a quiet conscience remain at home, where you are of comparatively little service? We solemnly urge upon your consideration the fact that such multitudes are so entering eternity every year; and that it is in your power to guide many of them to the cross and to eternal life.

But the great body of the members of the churches may not go to the heathen; nor is it needed, if they will sacredly observe their obligations at home. To this class belongs the largest part of this assembly. In connection with your labors for America, you are to co-operate with the Board to the extent of your ability, until Christ's command is fully obeyed. Your bodies and minds, your time and attainments, all belong to Christ; by them you obtain money, which is equally his. You are his stewards, trading upon his capital, for the promotion of his interests. Your powers and time must be diligently employed, or you will bury his talents in a napkin; you must live frugally, or he will charge you with having perverted his funds for your own indulgence; the remainder you must consecrate to his cause so long as it is needed, or he will eventually condemn you for having lived unto yourselves, and not unto him.

Is it inquired, how far you should practically apply this principle? We think, dear brethren, *you* are best able to give the answer. How far do *you expect the missionary* practically to apply it? There may be at times peculiar circumstances to modify the form of his sacrifices, and so far they must differ from your own. But generally, you and he are alike the servants of Christ, and subject to the same rules. You can have no more right to live to yourselves and to your families, than he has to live to himself and to his family; that is, neither has any such right. Why should not the American pastor, the lawyer, and the physician; why should not the merchant, the mechanic, and the farmer, live as entirely for Christ, and as sacredly obey his commands, as the missionary? Why should not the sisters of the church here be as self-denying and as faithful to this cause, as their sisters in foreign lands? Did they not alike come to the cross for salvation? Were they not all pardoned upon the same consideration? Is it not one vineyard, into which they were all received as laborers? And are they not all to act upon one principle? Of whom is it said, "Ye are not your own, ye are bought with a price"?—of the missionary, or of all Christians? Is it not emphatically said, "*No man liveth unto himself*"? Weigh, my dear brethren and sisters, the reasons why it is *our* duty to enter upon this work. Do not the same reasons press your entire consecration to this cause? Is there no language to *you*, in the dreadful condition of so many perishing ones? Are you not a part of those disciples to whom the Saviour commands, "Go ye into all the world, and preach the gospel to every creature"? Again prayerfully ponder the instruction of the Holy Spirit in Romans x. 11–15; and remember, that upon the amount of your co-operation will depend, under God, the number of those who personally enter this field of labor, and the efficiency of their efforts. The fact that the missionary is thus dependent upon your aid removes every doubt respecting the extent of your obligation compared with his. Again, the Board has informed us how we might best aid this work; and have not you, too, heard its appeal? Again and again they have told us of the unoccupied fields, upon some of which the first kindly influence is to be exerted; while upon others the gospel has operated until they are ripe for the harvest. If these considerations might justly move our decision, when surrounded with the rich enjoyments of this Christian land, ought they not also deeply to affect you? The position, dear

13*

brethren, which you occupy is most fearfully solemn. The world is perishing in your hearing, and Christ requires you to spare no labor or expense for its rescue. You stand in the very passage-way to the heathen, through which the missionary can pass only by your aid. If you prove false to your trust, you will block up that way, unless God in mercy to a fallen world removes you; very few will pass it; the heathen will continue to perish in their sins; and you,—who can portray your feelings, when with them you stand at Christ's judgment-seat to answer for the buried or the wasted talents of your Lord?

We know of but one way to evade these considerations. Young ministers do so respecting their personal service; because there is no more money to support additional fields and laborers. Others do so respecting funds, because men are *not waiting to be sent forth*, who are kept back only by an exhausted treasury. But neither of these pretend that Christ's command is obeyed or that the work is done. They plead the unfaithfulness of each other, in order to excuse their own continued neglect of duty. However much this course may now evade the appeals of their brethren and silence their own consciences, it will not obey Christ nor save the world. It will not suppress the wailing of damned spirits for eternity; nor cause the arches of heaven to reverberate with the songs of millions saved through *their* instrumentality. Brethren, believe us, or rather believe the whole tenor of God's word,—this may answer for a time; but it will not suffice when he who died for sinners, and who gave his commission to the Church, "maketh inquisition for blood." It will be no trifling matter then to find the blood of souls upon their garments; to hear the unutterable, eternal anguish of the heathen charged to their neglect.

Allow us to suggest a remedy for even this evasion. Let the Board select any and every man whom they think best fitted for this work; and let them solemnly appeal to him, if he is willing to go on two conditions; first, that those who are best qualified to judge, shall deem him fitted for the sphere; and second, that the Board are able to send him forth, with a reasonable prospect, under the influence of Christian faith, afterwards to support him.

Let them thus leave this responsibility at the door of each man's heart, to decide the matter for himself, as he hopes in peace to meet his Master at the last day. Let them then record every man's name who consents to go, and make this record known to the churches, that their members may understand, not only the wants of the world, but that men are waiting to enter upon the service, who are prevented by want of means only. In like manner let them appeal to the churches for funds. Every one knows, that in that treasury of God's there is enough and to spare, if its resources were drawn and applied to the right purpose. Long, long before the disciples become as their Lord, and have not where to lay their heads, will this, his treasury, afford ample means. I know not how we might dare to ask him for more, until at least the capital now lying dead in the hands of his stewards is applied to the work. Let, then, the Board, without reference to the number of men at present waiting for this service, apply in person to the rich for their abundance, and to know how far they may be relied upon, if foreign laborers can be found; let them also encourage the poor to forward their several mites, so that the means of greatly enlarged operations may be supplied; and let the state of the treasury be made known to our young men. Let the men and means no longer wait for one another, and mutually encourage neglect of duty.

Thus let the ministry say, — "We wish to remove this reproach, that man cannot be found to do Christ's work, even among those purchased by his blood. *We are* waiting to be sent." On the other hand let the body of the Church say to their young ministers, and to their young members yet engaged in worldly avocations:—"In the opinion of our brethren, we are necessarily prevented from going to a foreign land, but we are Christ's; and if you will go, we here will live as sacredly for him as you do there; and will give you the means to work to the best advantage, *if it takes all* we have, *and all we can honorably obtain.*"

We believe this would remove that last common evasion. For as "face answers to face in water, so the heart of man to man." Besides, great confidence may be reposed in the spirit of Christ in his disciples, when it is fairly tested.   We cannot believe, if there were sufficient funds, that there would be any want of men ; or if men enough stood ready for the work, that there would long remain any want of funds.   Yet, we are now as truly responsible for this neglect, as we should then be; and the consequences to millions of souls are as deplorable for time and for eternity.

Pardon us, dear brethren, the freedom of these remarks. I speak for myself; and in most respects, I think I may safely say, I speak for my brethren also.   If we had not most deeply felt the sentiments here presented, you had not seen us here to-night, about to go forth as your messengers to the heathen.   We have, probably, passed our last Lord's Day in the land of our fathers, and in this city of most tender recollections.   A day or two more, and we shall see your faces no more upon earth.   We go down into an exceedingly deep well,—and very solemn thoughts possess us, as we wait a moment at its mouth.   Dear brethren, will you hold the rope? *Will you give us while there the facilities to work to advantage?* We can not doubt it,—and the God of all blessings will bless you in so doing.

But we shall meet again.   Until then, let us labor faithfully, knowing that there remaineth for us a rest in heaven.

CHAPTER X.

VOYAGE TO MAULMAIN.

1843—1844.

THE ship was expected to sail immediately after these services, but was detained till November 17th. In consequence of this delay, Dr. Pattison, the Home Secretary, was obliged, in order to meet an engagement in Philadelphia, to leave before they sailed. This was a sore trial to the parties concerned. Dr. Pattison had not only ever been a very dear brother to Mrs. Binney, but had also sustained an almost paternal and even maternal relation to her. When first coming up into womanhood, and in such delicate health that physicians and friends thought her an invalid for her probably brief life, she left the paternal roof, for the first time, to live with this brother, who had just been settled as pastor over the First Baptist Church in Providence, Rhode Island. A change from the region of the lakes to the vicinity of the sea, it was hoped would be beneficial to her health. And so it proved to be; but it brought, also, home-sickness, yearning for the precious mother's tender care, and for the dear father, the only sister and other brothers as well; and this brother was her guide and support, striving to take the place of all she had left. More than all these, his preaching met her pecu-

151

liar need, and he became her spiritual father, and she the first-fruit of his ministry. He had buried her in baptism, given her the hand of fellowship, welcoming her to the duties as well as to the privileges of the church of Christ. He had assisted her in her efforts for mental, as well as spiritual improvement; he had married her and taken her husband into his loving heart, so that they were to each other all that an elder and younger brother and sister could be; and now they were apparently to be separated forever, so far as this life was concerned.

There was not then the most distant thought of a missionary's return to his native land. Two or three had done so, but the circumstances were very peculiar, and the thing was not approved of in "high places." Could there have been a ray of hope of their ever meeting again, how different the parting. As it was, it appeared to be simply a living burial. But the carriage which was to convey him to the railway station was at the door, and the farewells must not linger. Dr. Pattison bore them bravely, but his sister's heart was almost broken. For a moment she thought, if he loved her as she loved him, he could not have left her thus. Mr. Binney withdrew at once to his chamber, but she did not follow. No one should witness her agony. In a moment the parlor door was opened, and the loved brother, with tears streaming down his face, entered to hide himself from observation. Instantly they were clasped in each other's arms, and tears and sobs were mingled. There was no need of explanations; none were made. She was the first to speak. " Go, now, my precious brother; we shall meet again, where there will be no more scenes like this." The bitterness of this living death was passed. Nothing more trying could follow. Her sainted mother's happiness could not be lessened. The dear father—the tender-loving father— had so long " walked with God," that a translation to the bright world above any day would not have been matter of surprise. He rejoiced that God had counted him worthy to give a daughter so dear and a son whom he had taken to his heart of hearts, to the mission cause. The pastoral work was a great, a solemn work, which angels might tremble to assume, were they commissioned to do so ; but somehow *this* work seemed more like the Master's, who gave himself for sinners. It brought us very near to Jesus. It was thus he discoursed ; and his prayers brought Jesus very near to all who were with him in those days.

Then there was Mr. Binney's own dear father, who had been brought into the kingdom late in life and who " could not see the necessity of seeking a more extended field of usefulness, or of going further from home than Georgia." He had been called to pass through sore trials ; again had met with pecuniary losses, and his son was his stay, his support. How could he spare him ? Surely not till ample provision had been made for his future comfort. All of his son's careful savings were invested for his use and that of a widowed sister, who was to live with him and care for his comfort. Mr. Binney did not deem that, though called to leave all the endeared relations of this life, his filial obligations were cancelled. If filial love had not been so great, the example of the dying Lord would have forbidden it.

But soon the farewells—final farewells to many and supposed to be such to all—were said, and they set sail.

Fortunately, Mr. Binney's journal of the voyage has escaped the fate which most of his journals have met. Extracts from this will be given, sufficient to show the character of this five months voyage, in an ordinary sailing vessel, designed for merchandise and not for passengers; and also to show his character, brought out by trying circumstances.

CHARLESTOWN, November 17th, 1843.

To-day public service was held on board ship; prayer by Rev. William Hague, of Boston, after which came the long-dreaded event, bidding the last adieu to those we love. Truly, none but those who have experienced it can tell its bitterness. May God, for his Son's sake, permit us all to meet in joy at his right hand. After fruitless efforts to shove off into the stream, the ship was secured for the night, but one wharf from that from which we started; and Mrs. Binney and self gladly accepted the kind invitation of Dr. White to leave our cold, damp cabin and spend the night with his family in this town.

18th—This morning a fair wind, though very rainy. About half-past nine o'clock we left the wharf for the stream, where we anchored until eleven o'clock, waiting for our supercargo. On his coming on board, the ship got under way, with a fine wind. The last friend I saw was my dear brother Joshua, who came off to us in a boat just as we set sail. Very dear brother, farewell! May every temporal blessing be yours, and above all a saving interest in the Lord Jesus Christ.

Our company consists of Rev. Edwin B. Bullard, wife and child, Mr. and Mrs. Thomas S. Ranney, and Miss Julia A. Lathrop, with Mrs. Binney and self, of the Baptist Denomination; Rev .Mr. Dow and wife, of the Free Will Baptist Denomination; and Rev. Mr. Gunn and wife, of the Lutheran Church; supercargo, two clerks, Captain Henderson, mate, second mate, steward, colored boy and cook, eight seamen, and four boys before the mast; in all thirty-three souls on board. A precious cargo, indeed! God of the winds and waves, wilt thou take charge of our ship, and bid us safely, speedily, and happily to our desired port. To thee we commit ourselves and our all; in thee alone we confide.

19th—All the passengers but myself sick; still a fine wind and all goes well, except the ship is too much "by the head." Commenced to-day to read the Old Testament in course in English, also the New Testament in course in Greek. Precious Lord's Day!

It may be as well here to say, that the manner of spending his time at sea was fully reported in a letter to Dr. Peck—near the close of this passage—which is given entire; his health was good; his freedom for five months from all responsibility was delightful; and he revelled in hard study, not from compulsion or a mere sense of duty—but from choice. His unvarying cheerfulness and satisfaction were a subject of frequent remark.

22d and 23d — The ship encountered very severe storms, nearly every passenger sick. Thanks to my Heavenly Father, I suffer nothing in that respect, and my dear wife suffers less than I expected... Never before have I witnessed such tokens of God's power. A few weeks ago I looked on the Falls of Niagara and called the scene sublime; but to-day, in comparison, I call them beautiful, and this mighty tossing and heaving of waters I call sublime. * * * To the extent of our sight the waters are lashed into fury, and their spray driven away like the light snow before the driving wind. Our frail bark, as though proud of the opportunity to display her sea-worthy qualities, scuds before the wind in safety, now plunging into the waters, then mounting the waves in triumph. Surely he that hath said to this mighty sea, "Hitherto shalt thou come and no further, and here shall thy

14

proud waves be stayed," can put his hand beneath us all the voyage through, and make the winds and waves bear us safely to our destined port.　God of wonders, I thank thee that I have seen this display of thy majesty and power.　Sanctify it to my growth in grace, and to my usefulness.　In the evening, the tumult so far subsided as to make it possible for several to be on deck.　It was truly delightful to see so many of our company, and to hear so many voices join to "Praise God from whom all blessings flow."

25th—Awoke to find a calm, the ship making about two miles an hour.　About ten o'clock, A. M., the whole ship's company were put into the greatest consternation by the cry, "A rope! a rope! somebody overboard!"　All ran—I looked about and inquired "Who?" but, receiving no answer and not seeing my wife, rushed to the side of the ship, and what a sight!　A boy had fallen overboard, and two noble fellows had jumped to the rescue; they had caught the rope thrown to them, but with the boy found it impossible to get on board.　The mate, fine fellow, dropped himself down to their help.　At the time I first saw them, all four were in the water, dipping down several feet every time the ship rocked; the boy seemed almost exhausted, and his hand kept slipping from the rope.　We feared all four might be lost, but after hard work they lifted the boy on deck, and then the rest.　After all were safe, I wiped away a few tears that I found stealing down my cheek, and thanked my Heavenly Father that he had not so soon broken our little number by death; that he had spared the boy's parents the dreadful event; and prayed for the choicest blessings upon the noble fellows who had rushed to the rescue at the risk of their own lives.

To me the shock was dreadful; all the day my nerves remind me of this morning's event; and from what I see about me I judge I am not alone.　Sick and well—all are on deck.

26th—"This is the day the Lord hath made," and a delightful day it has been to my soul.　According to arrangement, Divine Service was held in the cabin, being too squally to have it on deck.　For the same reason, but few of the sailors were present, their services being required about the ship.　The captain, mate,

three boys, and ten passengers were present. I preached from
" Be ye also ready," and tried to improve the event of yesterday
morning, both for the good of those who are not Christians, and
those of us who are Christ's. May God make it a blessing. Have
had much comfort to-day in contemplating Ps. 68: 20, and Ps.
63: 70. Towards night, as I looked upon the heavens above me,
and the waters around me, I was carried back to the dear ones
left behind; father, sisters, brothers. The tears would come,
though I felt quite happy. It was an exceedingly tender reflection—" I shall see their faces no more on earth." Thanks to our
precious Saviour, I have a well-grounded hope that I shall meet
them all in heaven.

This evening I calculated my time and tried to worship with
my dear Savannah church. Precious privilege to meet in spirit
at the throne of grace! Retired at about ten o'clock, grateful
to God for the comforts of this delightful Lord's Day and
for the great happiness I feel and have felt so far during this
passage.

Every day's latitude and longitude, with remarks
about the weather, are given in this journal, with
sketches or drawings of all the different birds and
fishes, and every little island, so that the diary is quite
a "picture-book." Rather copious extracts are given
at first, as they show how the missionaries, collectively
as well as individually, spent their time on board ship,
for five months shut up together.

27th—The evening quite dark and wet; from nine to ten
squally, when the rain began to pour in torrents; and it was so
dark that nothing could be seen a foot from us, except by the
flashes of lightning. I resolved to witness all, and with water-
proof cap and overcoat on, remained on deck until the storm
had abated. I was rewarded by the sight of what seamen call
the "corposant," a brilliant light like the brightest star of the
first magnitude. I saw one at the mizzen-mast-head, and another

on the foremast yard arm. Verily, "They that go down to the sea in ships, that do business in great waters, see the works of the Lord, and his wonders in the deep."

28th—This evening at tea all but one of the company, Mrs. Gunn, were able to be at the table, after which the brethren and sisters met and adopted the following plan of duty on board, viz., Sunday morning, the ministers to preach once each Sunday in alphabetical order; Sunday, P. M., a Bible class, to study the book of Romans, of which I am asked to take the lead. On Tuesday at 3½, P. M., a social conference and prayer-meeting, to be led by each in alphabetical order. The Monthly Concert, to be held the first Monday evening of each month, and family worship each night in the cabin directly after tea; these are to be led as the prayer-meeting. The hours from ten to twelve, A. M., may be devoted to study, during which time there is to be no interruption by talking, singing, etc.

So the daily journal goes on; every day something of interest recorded, besides the " daily observations,"— the head-winds and the calms and all the varied incidents, hardly noticed anywhere but at sea in a sailing vessel, whose progress is so sensitive to any change. One day is Thanksgiving Day at home. "Home! that precious word! What a thrill has the writing of it caused! That home never to be revisited. But, we, too, have abundant cause for thankfulness for God's great goodness to us thus far. We should be very thankful." Another day: "Finished the reading of the 'Days of Queen Mary.' I pray, if consistent with the divine will, to be spared the tests of Queen Mary's day; but should I ever be so tried, and I may, may divine grace be sufficient for me. . . . O thou Lamb of God, be thou my sacrifice, and as my day is, so may my strength be. Make me an every-day Christian, that I by thy grace may be prepared for every extra demand upon my fidelity to thee."

Every Lord's Day with its appointments is noticed; the preacher and the sermon named, but never with criticism, only with desires for their usefulness to their hearers.

December 1st, 1844—This is my birthday, thirty-six years of age. A large part of my life is actually gone; soon it will all have passed. May my remaining days be more sacredly devoted to the glory of God and the salvation of men! I think I can honestly say, nothing seems to me so desirable as to live for Christ, and at death to enjoy his presence in heaven.

6th—This evening finished reading the Life of Rev. Mr. Thomason, Missionary to India, pp. 356. A truly Christian man, faithful in his work. May the reading of this book be sanctified to my increased piety. Oh that I had more of this love, humility, and self-consecration to the work! More of those characteristics necessary to the happiness and usefulness of a missionary! My most holy acts are so deeply sinful, that I sometimes fear that God may not at all accept the service I offer. But the comfort is in the thought that all our works are viewed through the merits of his dear Son. The blood of Jesus,—precious, precious blood,—is all my hope; and I would rather be received for his sake than my own. May I but have his smiles here, and his presence in joy hereafter. I am satisfied to be anything, and to do anything, which he directs. Dear Saviour, so fill me with thy love, that I may be enabled to honor thee, with my body and spirit, which are thine!"

It is exceedingly difficult to make extracts from the Journal. Every page is full of interest, and every faculty of his mind in full exercise; at one time the imagination vivid and fresh as a school-boy's.

All is new and fascinates. Over the bow the scene was truly magnificent. The ship seemed to be sailing through liquid sil-

14*

ver, whose waves, foaming and dashing against her, were thrown
to the lee-ward with such reflection of light that we could see to
read fair-sized capital letters.

Looking upon the scene, the wide waters appeared to be
studded with little islands of polished mirrors, dancing upon the
top of the deep blue ocean, and now reflecting upon us the
rays of the sun.

In looking over the stern of the ship this evening, the wake
and as far as the eye could reach, seemed such a boiling and
tumbling of liquid metals as reminds one of the lake of fire
mentioned in Scripture; but I have no language in which to de-
pict the scene, much less the effect upon my own mind. Now
beautiful beyond description, now sublime in the extreme.

Then follow theories as to the causes of all these
varied appearances, with the authorities, etc. He never
failed to " study up " everything that came before him.
His cabin was quite a curiosity, the sides being lined
with books and maps for reference, and as easy of access
as if in his own library. He was always a genuine lover
of the sea; and, though a cautious man on shore, was
considered rather reckless here; and some amusing incidents of having been "met more than half-way by
seas," and faring badly in consequence, are related.
Christmas is remembered, and the contrast drawn between it and former days, especially the last,

When I met so many hearty good wishes from the inmates of
my own happy home and from the dear people of my charge,
and when presents and good wishes came from many men, even
of other denominations, so that I felt myself to be both blessed
and a blessing. I seldom draw these contrasts, but when I do,
they are not wholly painful. I have never failed to draw comfort from the contemplation. Thus far, I have no doubt of the
propriety of the step I have taken, nor the first wish to have it

otherwise. Yet I did love my people most tenderly, and truly did I enjoy the many comforts arising from my relation to them. But I hope ere this some dear brother is filling my place in such a manner that I alone shall be the sufferer.

Then again comes the New Year in which he finds himself wishing the friends everywhere, North and South, a Happy New Year, "and desiring to renew the covenant I have made with thee and thy dear Son— the solemn consecration I have made of all to thy service and thy will." In reviewing the past, and looking forward to the future, he says, " I often think I am the happiest man living, for all my days are crowned with his loving-kindness."

March 4th—This morning's air is indeed refreshing, after spending the night in such confined, impure air. Our room is about thirty feet square, and seven and a half feet high, with the thermometer at 80°, in the purest and best state of the atmosphere during the day. There are eleven grown persons, beside the colored man, who is also steward, a colored boy, and the baby, to breathe the air all night. Then we have the steward's pantry, dining table, rusty chains, tarred ropes, old sails, etc., to make it more impure, with but little circulation of air, even with the hatches open. It is not quite so bad as the Black Hole of Calcutta, but sleep under such circumstances is anything but refreshing. And then, we have rats and mice, and cockroaches without number. Some nights since, the steward had not only his toe-nails, but his toes gnawed so badly, that we had to bind them up. Last night the rats gnawed the heel of the colored boy, who slept near the steward. This morning I gave public notice that "all them ar' passengers what has any heels or toes to be rat-gnawed, please bring 'em to the steward's office." However, there is not much fun in having one's toes or fingers gnawed by rats.

March 8th—This forenoon I read an article on " Discriminating Sermons," in the *Christian Review* for September, 1843. I have ever held the views there expressed, and tried to be governed by them in my ministry; but to-day in reviewing it all, and in contemplating the consequences of the opposite course, I was completely overwhelmed. While reading the first two paragraphs, on the necessity of such sermons, I could not refrain from bitter weeping. I pray God to spare my dear people from the consequences of any want of faith or of skill on my part. I did endeavor to do my duty in such preaching. I sometimes feared that I carried my views to an extreme, but the more I reflect upon it, the more I am convinced that it was not so. Were I to return to-morrow, I do not see how I would change the general character of my preaching for the better; but the bare possibility that my dear people may have suffered from the defects of my labors among them is truly agonizing. It is indeed a deeply solemn thing to be a preacher of the gospel and a pastor of a Christian church.

12th March—My heart is still greatly oppressed on account of my preaching in Savannah. I have not wept so much for many months. Oh, what a thought! to be an unfaithful or an unskillful minister! And what pangs proceed from the reflection that my people may suffer, not only temporarily, but eternally, through my defects. It seems as though my memory recalls the names of all the church; that if any one *has* suffered by my ministry, I may entreat God to grant that one a double blessing in my successor. Whoever may be their pastor, may he have very much of God's blessing for himself and the church.

I have heard much of these beautiful skies, but scarcely twelve hours pass without my exclaiming, at least mentally, "the half was not told me."

The ballast was largely ice, which although never opened for the use of the passengers, was daily becoming less. In consequence of this, the vessel rolled badly. This wrings from him the complaint in his journal, though it was never heard from his lips:

How delightful it would be to find some little spot where I could lie just for a few hours without rolling about, or sit without a great effort to retain the place! My back aches without intermission, for the want of support. It is just roll, roll, pitch, pitch, no matter where one is or what the position. Who ever thinks, on land, of thanking God for the favor which we so longingly desire here—perfect rest.

March 27th.—Our ice, almost our only ballast, fast melting away; consequently vessel rolling badly, our bread, rice, peas, etc., full of weevils, and other insects, our water pretty good, better than a few weeks back, when it was ropy.

30th.—The heat oppressive as ever, but to-day the captain took a studding sail and formed it into an awning over the quarter deck, after my planning. No one can tell what a difference it made in our comfort. It hardly seemed as though we could be in the same climate. Were I coming this voyage again, I would stipulate for a free circulation of air and an awning; the latter I would pay for myself rather than not have it. With all our discomforts we enjoy our religious privileges, and great harmony and pleasure in each other.

It certainly was wonderful that so many passengers, under such circumstances, enjoyed so great a degree of health. Yet some of them arrived in Maulmain a good deal enfeebled. Mr. Binney kept very well most of the time.

April 5th.—About 4 P. M., anchored in Amherst Roads, about five miles from the town; giving us a fine view of it and the lofty hills in the back ground; two pagodas in full view, and what I suppose is the tree under which our beloved Mrs. Judson lies buried. Strange emotions arose on first beholding this land of heathenism; but I cannot say that I felt any more than when in our native land; though I did feel that my *personal responsibility now lies to this deluded people.*

"April 6th.—This morning Brother S. M. Osgood from Maulmain came on board, and it was soon decided to take the ship there. At 5 o'clock, P. M., we anchored in the river opposite Maulmain, where we land. Let God have the thanksgiving of our hearts for, on the whole, so pleasant a voyage, and for our safe arrival. Soon we left the boat and went on shore where our missionary brethren awaited our arrival. I knew Brother Judson at sight. We were cordially received by all as brethren and fellow laborers. We are to make our home with Brother Hosea Howard till we can make arrangements for a home of our own. One thing strikes me with great force on entering this heathen land, viz.: the well regulated families of our missionary brethren. The children conduct themselves with the greatest propriety and refinement. Many of our ministers at home might, with profit to their families, take a lesson here. But the natives— alas! Every thing tells me where I am! The adults are generally more than half naked, and many of the children are quite so.

7th.—This is our first Lord's Day in this land of moral and spiritual darkness. In the morning we attended Divine service at the Burmese chapel. Brother Judson conducted the services in Burmese. His style of preaching, though simple, is very forcible. Though I could not understand a word spoken, yet I entered heartily into its spirit. He was evidently contrasting the future condition of the righteous and the wicked, and I thought he must be discoursing upon the parable of the rich man and Lazarus; and so he was, as he afterward told me. It was an affecting sight, to see so many of that people eagerly listening to the words of eternal life. About eighty persons present."

After speaking of the kindness of Brethren Simons, Judson and others in offering to share their homes with Mr. and Mrs. Binney during the rains, he says:

Though this was exceedingly kind I felt that I had long since settled the point, never to prefer a place of comfort to one of usefulness. I was compelled to decline all these offers, as all took me away from the Karens, whose language I must learn as rapidly as possible, in order to be useful among them. Resolved to await Brother Vinton's return from the jungle, when we may take some part of his small house or put up a light bamboo house near his place, as the brethren think best.

12th.—To-day we have been on board the "Charles" to bid good bye to our dear brethren and sisters Gunn and Dow. May God send them, the pleasant companions of our long voyage, speedily to their spheres of labor; and the ship, with our captain, and all on board, safely to our native land, and be very gracious to them all, being their Saviour and their God."

14th.—Another precious, precious Lord's Day, though our hearts are pained to see the heathen profane it. But they do so "ignorantly." This evening had a delightful communion season with the English Church. Seldom have I conducted the service with more delight to my own soul. The communicants sat so as to form an oblong; about forty of them belonged to the British regiment stationed here, all dressed in spotless white, with their two officers in military dress. It was very pleasant to speak to them, but I long so to have my tongue untied, that I may address these poor heathen around us respecting this great salvation."

CHAPTER XI.

COMMENCEMENT OF MISSION WORK.

1844.

AS has been seen from Mr. Binney's journal, the good ship "Charles" arrived at Maulmain, on the 6th of April, 1844, after a passage of 140 days from Boston. The want of proper ventilation, the crowded state of the ship, no awnings, and light ballast, all conspired to make the passage anything but a pleasure trip; but as no pleasure trip had been anticipated, it was borne with fortitude and usually with cheerfulness. Certainly, Mr. Binney's uniform patience and good spirits seemed to render others, whose opportunities of learning what they ought to expect had not been so great as his, more forbearing, but all were most thankful to be once more on land, where there was no stint of air, water, or space.

Just two weeks were passed in getting a house, and in becoming sufficiently settled to commence the study of the language. In order to be near the Vintons, with their large Karen school, it was decided to rent a house at fifty rupees per month. This was then a very high rent; but every other proposal took Mr. Binney away from the Karens, and thus from the best opportunity for

166

acquiring the language, and he thought nothing economical that would do that. A bright, intelligent young
man was employed as teacher, or "moonshee," as they
are called in India. He was about as well educated as
any Karen then in Burmah. He could read and write
his mother tongue; and knew a little of the first principles of geography and astronomy; that is to say, he
understood that the earth was round and not flat, and
that a new moon did not literally come into existence
every month, but that its changes were produced by
its various revolutions, and that the sun did not go
round the earth every day. Also he knew that America
was on the opposite side of the globe, and that it took
several months to come to Burmah by water. But he
knew a great deal about the plan of salvation. He
believed on the Lord Jesus Christ, and could repeat the
book of Matthew "by heart," and from the heart, and
he was a thorough believer in God's providential deal-
ings with men, and with himself in particular. A more
happy, cheerful Christian is not often seen; and his sayings were frequently quoted by Mr. Binney, even down
to the last days of life. He did not know one word
of English, nor did his pupil know one word of Karen.
The Karen and English manuscript dictionary consisted
of about three hundred words. There was no little
phrase-book, or other helps, but two or three children's
books, such as a Catechism, Todd's Lectures, and Dra-
per's Bible Stories, and parts of the New Testament.
Thus equipped, the language was commenced. A few
days spent in calling over the characters, served to give
the sound and inflections, and enabled one to read with-

15

out knowing the meanings; a few days more sufficed to fix them sufficiently to begin to translate.

The portion of the Bible already published was the best dictionary at command, and it was in constant use for the purpose of learning the meaning of words. Six and often seven hours of close application were given to this study. The "jungle bird," as our teacher called himself, began to droop and chafe under the confinement. Another man was called to his aid; so that one or the other was always at hand. Whether actually studying with books, or walking or working, or whatever he was doing, Karen was the accompaniment. Mr. Binney's devotion to the language led some of the missionary brethren to be anxious, and protest against it. Dear, kind Brother Osgood was greatly disturbed, and finally told Mr. Binney that no man could work with impunity in that way in the climate of Burmah. Yet if he insisted upon killing himself, he supposed he must be left to do it, but that he really should not be allowed to kill Mrs. Binney too. Mr. Binney urged, in self vindication, that he had pressed upon her the necessity of taking it more leisurely; that he knew she had not half his strength, and there was no doubt but she would acquire the language in due time; that he would really be obliged to any brother who would aid him in convincing her that it was better to leave him to go on by himself. Mr. Osgood left her with the earnest entreaty that she would take care of her health, first of all, and not be influenced by her husband's unwise course. Dr. Judson had been in the habit of calling frequently in the evening or morning for a few moments, and Mr.

Binney often walked with him, but nothing had been said of the manner of study. The next mid-day, however, while the usual lessons were going on, Dr. Judson most unexpectedly dropped in, and as he did so, exclaimed cheerfully—

" Well, well, this *is* pleasant; it reminds me of the days, when Ann and I sat together day after day with our moonshee, with no more facilities for acquiring the Burmese than you have for acquiring the Karen. Ann was able to talk with the people sooner than I, and I dare say Mrs. Binney will be talking Karen much sooner than you. Those were happy days when we were so learning the language together."

Mrs. Binney caught at the encouragement, and said:

" Yes, Dr. Judson, we think so too, but it seems to be decided that these happy days are to come to an end at once. My husband feels that he dare not permit them to go on longer. Friends are all protesting, and think I should follow on slowly, as I am able."

" Yes, I understand it; if you had a very steep hill to climb, which Brother Binney did not find difficult, but which you did, he must not think of giving you his arm to help you up, but should say, ' My dear, this is a very steep hill, I fear you will not be able to reach the top in a long time, if ever; good bye, my dear!'"

All joined in a hearty laugh, and nothing more was ever said on the subject by anxious friends, nor was Mrs. Binney left to clamber up the rugged hill alone.

After seven months spent in reading, translating, and speaking Karen as best they could, Mr. and Mrs. Binney left Maulmain early in December and went to a pretty

Christian village, named after the leading man who established it, Ko-chet-thing's-ville. On leaving Maulmain they were resolved at any cost to accomplish the chief object for which they were going in to the Karen jungle, viz.: to acquire a free use of the Karen language. That they might be sure of doing so they "burned their boats," and allowed no one to accompany them who could speak a word of English. After they left Maulmain, it was no longer optional with them whether they would speak Karen or English, but whether they would speak Karen or remain silent. They took no servant with them, relying simply on such assistance as untrained Karens could give. Not only their cook, but even the boatmen were Karens, and this brought them much into all kinds of small talk.

Though Mr. Binney kept a full journal of the first year of this work, yet he destroyed it all. With the aid of Mrs. Binney's journal and his letters this narrative will be continued. Under date of December 8th, her journal says:

We left Maulmain on the 3d inst., and this is our first Lord's Day in the Karen jungle. As we embarked on board the little boat for the new scenes of labor before us, I thought of many loved ones in my dear native land, and wished it were in my power to give them a picture of our circumstances and appearance. Our boat, such as is generally used on these rivers, was large enough for our mattresses to be spread out under the thatched roof; in front were three seats running across the boat and occupied by four boatmen and a little boy, whom we had brought up to learn to read. At the stern was our Karen teacher, who steered the boat and acted also as captain, and my Karen girl, who had been with me in Maulmain; last and least our little dog and cat, that felt privileged to snuggle down together at the foot of our bed. Both being, like ourselves, strangers to this mode of travelling, were afraid of every thing and every body, except of us and each other. As another family had taken possession of our house, we resolved that the pets should share the comforts and discomforts of our jungle home with us. Our furniture, which the poor Karens thought really luxurious, consisted of a trunk, a box or two, a light covered basket, a small box filled up after the manner of soldiers' marching boxes, with two cups and saucers, a couple of knives and forks and spoons, and a few plates, with some little necessaries for the table, all so packed as to bear rough handling; a small rocking-chair and table were tied on top of the boat.

We left at dark, very tired with a hard day's work, and were not sorry to sleep till ten o'clock, lulled by the motion of the boat and the singing of the boatmen. At this time, the tide having turned against us, we tied up until it should again be in our favor. At the first dawn of day the Karens were up, and we were on our way till about 8 A. M., when we stopped to cook on shore. By means of flints, similar to the tinder-boxes used when I was a child, the Karens soon kindled a fire and cooked both for us and themselves. They are so used to this way of cooking out of doors, wheresoever they can find dry fuel, that they do it very quickly. We had a nice cup of coffee, which I prepared myself; a cold roast duck and hot rice, and relished our breakfast very much. I should have added, we spread a table-cloth on the dry ground and, seated on low stones, were very comfortable. After breakfast we proceeded without further interruption till 3 P. M., when we again stopped to cook. Our Karens were very happy, especially the girl and teacher, who had been with us in Maulmain. Having been thus separated from their homes and friends for seven months, they were now returning to them. Having slept one more night on the boat, we reached early in the day this village which the Karens call Ko-do-ko but the English call Chet-thing's-ville. It is beautifully situated on the east shore of the Salwen. The opposite side of the river is sheltered by high hills or ledges of slate, so that it presents a

15*

very picturesque appearance; and the reflection that this is a
Christian village, that these rocks and hills have echoed the
name and praises of Jesus, that here the Redeemer has seen the
reward of his sufferings in the redemption of many souls, makes
it very interesting to all who love him.   It cannot but be an
attractive spot to us, the scene of our first real beginning of mission work among this rude and ignorant people.   Here we hope
to spend four or five months, our chief business being the acqui-
sition of the language, but meaning at the same time to use it as
fast as we can in instructing and warning those about us.

When we reached the village the Karens greeted us
in large numbers; but seeing our inability to say much
to them, did not hesitate to express their great disappointment that Teacher Vinton had not come instead.
The teacher could not preach and the Mamma could not
teach the women and children.   This was rather a
damper on our spirits, but we told them we had come
among them chiefly to learn their language, and looked
to all to help us; that we had only been in the country
seven months and could read and write very well, but
now were hoping to speak very soon.   They seemed
comforted and expressed great surprise at the acquire-
ments which we had already made.   Mrs. Binney got a
little school started and, with the help of the children
and domestics, was soon speaking quite fluently.   Mr.
Binney who had less necessity for speaking often looked
on and listened in amazement, and was obliged to admit
that Dr. Judson had prophesied truly.   It was his turn
now to need help, and he was often obliged to call on
his wife to act as interpreter.   Feeling that he could not
speak so readily, he seemed unwilling to try even as
much as before leaving Maulmain.

This disinclination or inability to converse with them seemed to trouble the Karens. Some of the leading men took the "Mamma" one side and asked:

"Why does not the Teacher talk as well as the Mamma? Is he not going to preach to us and the heathen around us?"

The moonshee gāve a little comfort, assuring them the Teacher did talk to him when alone.

They replied, "Yes, but the Mamma speaks with every one."

Evidently, they were anxious. Every evening the whole village came together for worship. Mr. Binney soon began to take a seat with the pastor, read a chapter, give out the hymns, and lead them in singing; then the pastor would pray, make some remarks on the chapter, read, and close the service. He would sometimes say, 'will not the Teacher pray?" but he always declined.

One day he seemed very quiet and thoughtful, but continued reading, translating, and discussing matters with his moonshee as usual. Mrs. Binney was busy with her school and talking with the people; but she was not quite light-hearted. She was beginning to sympathize with the Karens in their anxiety that the teacher should at least make a beginning in talking with the people; but she did not express this solicitude. She had assured the Karens, that he had always done what he undertook to do, and that she was not troubled; but in the course of the day she had felt obliged to go over the whole thing, again and again, in her own mind. "He certainly was very desirous to acquire the language, and was working very hard, but he was not making use of what he learned. Dr. Judson had told him that he would not be able to preach much before he had been in the country about two years. Was he making that his aim, and, therefore, not attempting now? This was only the eighth month, it was true. It was not yet time to speak fluently, but he could ask for a drink of water, or inquire of a mother after the improvement of her sick child." These thoughts annoyed her. Still she trusted him. She was sure he would come out all right in some way; but her trust was something like that which many Christians exercise: they trust the Lord, yet carry the burden still.

Evening came; Prahai, the pastor, and the Teacher went into the desk together. Mr. Binney gave out a hymn, joined earnestly in the singing to the close, and said "let us pray." And he did pray, and that with a freedom and earnestness which carried every one with him. When he asked the Lord to help him to speak to this people of the wonderful love of Jesus to sinful men, there seemed to be an implication that he meant to try to tell them of it; but as that would be quite impossible, it appeared probable that he had not used the language quite correctly, and was only praying for the pastor. However, after the prayer, he read a part of a chapter from one of the Gospels and, as he read, explained in a simple and earnest way the word of Jesus. Mrs. Binney became alarmed. She was sure he could not proceed far without breaking down. He never could commit a sermon in his *own tongue* to memory; he certainly could not go far in Karen. He must be reciting, and would have to stop soon. As her seat was in the doorway, she slipped out of the chapel, but she could hear in her own room all the same. She rushed out to the cook-house to get away from the sound of the impending crash. Several Karen women came running after her, asking eagerly, "Is the Mamma ill? Does she want hot water? What can we do for her?" She was brought to her senses; she informed them she would wait for the water till after sermon, when the cook would attend to it. All went back quietly, the preacher was not disturbed, but still went on talking and seemed likely to continue to do so for a long time. However, just as he closed the clock struck, and revealed the fact that the entire service had occupied about forty minutes.

The Karens gathered about him. They were so glad; they understood all that he had said. He could preach, and now they would bring in the heathen around to hear him. There was a good deal of excitement. The Mamma busied herself in making tea, and found other topics of conversation; and he had preached several times before he knew of the comic, well-nigh tragic, effect of his first sermon upon her.

There was no farther difficulty. The ice was now fairly broken; and, if practice would make perfect, he was on the high way to perfection. The Christians began to bring their heathen friends and neighbors to him, and he went out into the near villages, laboring with the help of his teacher and others, for the conversion of souls.

An extract from a letter from Mr. Binney to the Foreign Secretary, Solomon Peck, D. D., will show his first impressions of the people in their jungle homes and his efforts for them during that season.

You will, perhaps, ask, "What were your first impressions on seeing the Karens in their own homes?" I was painfully impressed with the great work yet to be done for them. I thought, "If this is their condition after all the effort that has been made in their behalf in this Christian village, what must they have been in their heathen state?" I could hardly think it a fair specimen, and considered that they must have retrograded since the missionary had been here. But soon strangers came in from other places, persons who were not disciples, and who had not been influenced by the missionary labors, and I then saw how much had been done for the Karens by the gospel. The contrast was very great—so great that I could immediately distinguish a disciple from one who was not. On seeing what has been done, we feel encouraged to hope that the work, though difficult, will continue to make progress. I do not think the Karens so docile as many at home believe. I should regret to find them, as I had feared, ready to be shifted about in any direction, by the nod of a superior. They are, it is true, generally influenced by a good reason, but they must first see that reason. It is best that they *should* seek a good reason, and that we should be prepared to give it, before we expect them to act.

Mrs. Binney finds her little school of twenty or more Karen children very interesting, and not difficult to govern. She has a woman to assist her, so that she is not confined to the school-room altogether. Our religious services are, on the Lord's Day morning, a meeting of the children, a kind of inquiry meeting, to ascertain their character and conduct during the week from their own testimony, and to give them such instruction as circumstances require. This Mrs. Binney is able to conduct, with the assistance of a very intelligent and pious young woman. At 9 A. M., we have preaching; at 12 M., Sunday-school; at 2 P. M., a general prayer-meeting; at sun-down, the people meet again, when they sing, pray, read a portion of the Scripture, accompanied with some few comments or a short discourse. This last meeting they have every evening at early candle light. Brother Vinton commenced this course, and it seems adapted to their present state. My class of men, old and young, in the Sunday-school, I find deeply interesting. I enjoy it.

The preaching I do not enjoy as yet, as my attention is greatly engrossed by the use of a new language, and the fear that I may not be rightly understood. I hesitated much to commence preaching so soon, knowing that what I had learned of the language, especially before coming here, had been chiefly obtained from books, and I had only been about eight months in the country. But there were subjects which I wished brought before the people, and I feared the assistants would either say too much or not enough, so I broke through the difficulties and talked to them about twenty-five minutes. The people understood me better than I feared, so that I have been encouraged to go on preaching and talking. We already feel that we are doing the people a little good.

Last Lord's Day evening I talked to them from John 5 : 39, and after pointing out the reference of the text to the Old Testament, and its application to men of those times, I urged upon them the peculiar reason why they should read diligently the New Testament,—the Old Testament not yet being translated. I told them that their not being able to read was no excuse ; that, though already old, if they loved God and wished to know his will, they would learn to read. Yesterday morning, early, the Chief of the village came to Mrs. Binney, and told her he wished for a spelling-book, for he must learn to read the Bible. Until within a few years he had lived among the Pwo Karens; since he had been with the Sgaus he had made one effort to learn to read, but it took so much time from business, he thought he could not afford it; but now he was resolved to read God's word for himself. He is now hard at work with the children in the school."

Another very interesting case of an old man from a neighboring village, who never heard the gospel before, is mentioned.

I cannot tell you the feelings with which I labored to point this anxious inquirer to the way of life. It is the first time that such a responsibility has rested upon me, where there was such a

state of mind, in this new language. Most sincerely do I pray that he may not cast from him these serious impressions; but he goes back to his heathen home, to be surrounded by sin and darkness. God can do his own work, even without instruments. I mention these cases, not because they are singular in general, either here or at home, but because they are peculiarly interesting to us, under our peculiar circumstances.

We shall return to Maulmain at the close of the dry season, and I have no doubt I shall have as many students as I shall be able to teach for the first year. Should you send a man to help Brother Vinton, as is really needed, allow me to suggest that he be a man to preach, not to make books.

Before deciding on a permanent location for the Theological Seminary, Mr. Binney wrote to Brethren Mason and Abbott very freely, asking their opinions of the desirableness of locating the Institution at either Tavoy or Sandoway, or at any place nearer their fields of labor. All the correspondence, which is very interesting, is at hand, but an extract from the same letter, quoted above, will give the gist of it.

In my last letter, I mentioned that I had received no answer from Brother Abbott respecting our location. Since that time I have received a letter from him, dated October 1st, 1844, in which he expressed a very hearty interest in the establishment of such an institution, and pledges his full coöperation. Respecting the location, referring to my questions, he says, "You ask, 'Do you think Sandoway should be the place?' No, I do not. 'What are the considerations?' Climate and locality." Again he says, "My opinion is that the Institution should be located at Maulmain, and it seems to me there can be but one opinion in the Karen Mission. I should decidedly oppose its being further from Sandoway. It would be very agreeable to me to have another mission family here, and I could call lots of students, and things would go on swimmingly for awhile; but that would only be the beginning of the end. No. Although Tavoy would be a good place, yet the interests of the Karen Mission require that it be located at Maulmain, and the interests of the Karen Mission are ours."

The whole letter of Mr. Abbott is worthy of a missionary; manifesting the kindest feeling, and affording valuable suggestions.

Mr. Mason says, as I mentioned in a former letter, that "if a general Institution be established, Maulmain is the place." I hope to see Brother Mason in a few weeks, when we can converse more freely on the subject. My own feelings are now, as when I saw you last. I have come here to work for the cause. If my brethren prefer another place, I have no objection. I will go cheerfully to any place they may decide on as best adapted to secure the object. Respecting the question of a general or a local Institution, the more I know of the state of the Mission, the more fully I am persuaded that circumstances require the best possible division of labor; that there is too much work to be done, and, after our best efforts, too much work will be left undone, to allow any two men to do what one man can do as well alone. Still, you will not infer that I would wish the Board to decide upon a general Institution against the wishes of the brethren at Tavoy. Far from it. A general Institution could not succeed under such circumstances. For it to succeed well, it must have the confidence, the prayers, and the cheerful coöperation of all who are expected to send pupils.

When Mr. and Mrs. Binney arrived in Maulmain, the headquarters of the Maulmain-Karen Mission were in close proximity to the Burmese Department, both being in the city. Mr. Vinton, then the only missionary in the Karen field, was very desirous to establish a Karen village in the suburbs of the town, thus affording an opportunity for Karens to carry on agricultural and other pursuits near by. He hoped thus gradually to

16

bring them under the influence of civilization, and also to make a kind of home for the schools. Another extract from the same letter will throw further light upon this plan. It will be remembered this letter was written while still at Chetthings-ville.

In my last letter to you, I mentioned that the question of a new location for the Karen department was not yet settled. Since that time it has been decided, and two houses will be ready at the commencement of the rains. I was in favor of the measure, so far as mentioned in my last. Since that time, I have felt more and more the importance of some such course. Every week strengthens my opinion that unless the Karens make further progress in the habits of civilization, nothing which is done for their intellectual or spiritual welfare can be permanent; that is, self-perpetuating and independent of foreign aid. They will always need the oversight of a missionary. This reconciles me to almost any effort that promises success in that direction. If it fails, we must,—what? Give it up? I think not. To do so would be to relinquish all hopes of permanent results by our labors. We must try again. Of one thing I am certain; the step has not been taken without long and prayerful consideration, and the most fraternal regard to my wishes by Brother Vinton. I only regret that my inexperience in the country and with the people has made me unable to advise or act largely in the matter. We feel that very much is at stake, both for ourselves and the Karens, yet we leave the result cheerfully in the hands of our Heavenly Father, and hope for the best.

An extract from Mrs. Binney's journal will complete the history of the first season in the Karen jungle.

February 2d, 1845. Mr. Binney has now been preaching for several weeks, both on the Lord's Day, and at other times, and I find myself slowly improving in the ability to teach and talk with the people. I am encouraged to think that time and hard work will finally make us at home in this language ; but nothing else will do it. It will not come to one by ever so patient calling and waiting. To-day Mr. Binney has had several applications for baptism. The inquirers seem to be sincere, thoroughly in earnest, and appear every way well; but he has put them off a little, in order that he may have opportunity to consult with Mr. Vinton, who will be up soon, and who knows many of them personally. They are very reluctant to be put off a day, but after being told that the *Teacher* wished to defer their baptism a little, and that the responsibility would be his and not theirs, they were better satisfied. I am sure our Pedobaptist friends would not, if they were here, accuse us of laying too great stress on baptism. These people were told over and over again, the nature of the new birth ; and its necessity, in order to qualify them for this ordinance ; but the Karens, like the primitive disciples, seem to place baptism in very close juxtaposition to repentance and faith. One of them said to-day, " How am I to know, and how are others to know, that I have renounced the service of Satan, and become a disciple of Jesus Christ, unless I do what he commands me to do ? No, no, I have done with the service of the devil, and I want to show that I have." This man has recently come from the Shan Country, has had very little religious instruction ; but this season he learned to read, and now reads the Gospels hours every day. He is the same man Mr. Binney speaks of in his letter to Dr. Peck, and for whose return to his heathen home, he felt so much anxiety, lest his serious impressions should be lost.

February 12th.—Alone to-day in the Karen jungle, my husband having gone to Maulmain for a few days on important business. I have been thinking, in my loneliness, much of my former views of missionary life, particularly of my views at the time when I professed conversion. I thought deeply of the duty of Christians toward the heathen; and, although at that time I enjoyed very precious privileges, I thought I would gladly give them all up for the privilege I now enjoy of laboring among these benighted ones. But I had very vague and incorrect views of the work required. It seemed to me, as I believe it seems to many Christians, like doing for the advancement of the Redeemer's kingdom on a large scale, as we say, "a wholesale business;" instead of looking upon the missionary, more truly than any others perhaps, as patiently and laboriously instructing the ignorant; reproving sin; and, though on heathen ground, meeting the same devices of Satan as at home, and in the same manner; finding every means ineffectual without the Spirit's aid; and withal, having to contend with the same temptations in his own heart, which paralyze the energies of the Church at home; the same love of ease, aversion to patient, self-denying labor in a quiet way; the same love of human applause, which would lead to doing "some great thing," instead of following the indications of God's providence, which would perhaps lead to laying foundations, on which other hands alone will build.

My views of the duty of the Church or of my own personal obligations have not lessened, but vastly increased; neither would I be anywhere else than where duty has so plainly called us; but I feel more and more the need of special grace for a work like this. I never saw my dear husband more uniformly cheerful than he is here, alone and with hardly the bare necessaries of life; and though we speak often of the contrasts of the past and present, and the dear ones are remembered in our daily prayers, yet I never witness the least regret.

Thus rapidly did the four months of jungle life pass away.

Just before returning to Maulmain an incident occurred, which perhaps would not be thought of sufficient importance to be noticed here but for its results. Mr. and Mrs. Binney, accompanied by their moonshee and a group of children, and often by others, were in the habit of taking a walk of an evening by the river Salwen. The western bank was a high ledge of rock, and hid the sun from the level eastern shore, on which the village stood, long before it set to the country around. This enabled them to go out earlier than otherwise they could have done.

On an evening of a sultry day, the Karens being still at their evening meal, Mr. Binney suggested to his wife that it would be pleasant to slip off alone, and have a walk and a chat without interruption. They had thus walked perhaps a half hour leisurely on the shore, when, at a considerable distance, they perceived the huge horns, and soon the entire head, of a domestic buffalo emerging from the water. The creature seemed to have scented them from afar. Its glaring eye-balls, distended nostrils, and fiercely defiant attitude were fearful, especially when it was recollected that these animals were the mortal enemies of the European race, and, in the jungles, as much to be feared by them as the tigers. They dared not turn to retrace their steps; but Mr. Binney called at the top of his voice for help. Slowly, however, they walked backward, facing the animal as best they could; but their path lay parallel with the stream; and the fierce creature, though confining himself as yet to the water, was perceptibly gaining upon them. Mr. Binney would occasionally brandish his walking stick and "look daggers" at their pursuer, when he would seem for an instant to be afraid, but as soon as they resumed their retreat, would recover his defiant attitude. All hopes of avoiding a conflict were failing, and Mr. Binney told his wife to run for her own life, while he would assume the offensive as the last resort, but she was urging a further persistence in the same course, when a child's voice was heard—"Stand still, Teacher! Stand still, Mamma!" In another instant a little figure darted past

16*

them, caught the buffalo by the string in the nose, and turning its head about, shouted out—" Now, now run fast." No second order was needed. In a short time after starting for the perilous walk, half the men of the village had turned out in pursuit of the " Teacher and Mamma," knowing that it was not safe for them to be out alone; but they would have been too late. The little boy had saved them. From that time Gnah-poo was almost as their own child, and will be heard from again.

CHAPTER XII.

EDUCATIONAL WORK IN MAULMAIN.

1845–1850.

THE last of April, 1845, Mr. and Mrs. Binney took possession of their new house on the new Mission premises, called Newton, a little way out of the town. The following is an extract from Mrs. Binney's journal:

There have been many obstacles to prevent our taking possession of this place. First, many of the brethren had doubts as to the healthfulness of the location. Although abundant testimony was procured that there was not more sickness there than in other parts of Maulmain, yet appearances were unfavorable. In the rains it is surrounded by water, and portions of it affected by the tide in the dry season. This difficulty was overcome by the facility with which the ground could be drained, but a more serious obstacle has arisen from Government having failed to meet expectations. When the purchase was made, a large part of the land was unoccupied, beside the Mission compound. Mr. Vinton and Mr. Binney's plan was to obtain a grant of this for a Karen village, and thus an important step would be taken in bringing this wild people in contact with European civilization, and make a home for Christians coming to town, either for business or instruction. Since the great fire, the Government has forbidden Burmans to put up their frail houses in the city, and they have sought land here until every nook and corner is occupied, so that the Karens will be in a state very similar to that in which they were before they left the city. Still, there were other considerations which induced the purchase, and we have taken possession alone; the Vintons were to follow in four weeks with their schools. While we do not seem to have an inch of room to spare in our new house, yet we have all we really need, and are content. As to physical comforts, we feel that God has been better to us than our fears, and he has thus far prospered us wonderfully in our efforts to acquire the language. I trust our faith for the future may be greatly strengthened by his past goodness. As to my husband, he is as happy as any man can expect to be in this world; he is so cheerful, almost jubilant, that I have a kind of fear, perhaps presentiment, that some great trial awaits us.

April 26th—I took a sad, probably a final leave of Mrs. Judson this morning. She has gone on board ship expecting to sail early to-morrow for America, but we doubt whether she lives to reach England. It is the last resort. Poor Dr. Judson! He did not wish to return to America, but God in his providence has compelled him to do so.

June 15th—Mr. Binney preached his first sermon before his associates, the Vintons, to-day. Not having preached before any but the natives till this morning, he seemed a little nervous, but God has certainly been better to us than our fears. When we took our first Karen lesson, but little more than one year ago, we should have been very happy could we have been assured of doing so well. Not that we "have attained," but the prospect is encouraging. Brother Vinton is more than satisfied with Mr. Binney's success, and all praise the sermon. If hard work and earnest prayer will prevail, the result is certain. Mr. Binney has his school well under way; he gives himself mostly to Biblical Instruction, while I help him in teaching arithmetic, a little geography, etc.

More than half of these sixteen pupils are from the Rangoon District, having made their way overland through forests and dense jungles, often sleeping by day and traveling by night for fear of their Burman rulers; thus risking even their lives for the knowledge of God's word. Several of the pupils have brought their wives and little children with them, so that we have quite a charge for the beginning. They are in many respects an interesting class, but are so uncultivated that their uncouth ways and dirty habits annoy me. I find it very hard to bear patiently with them, and gently teach them another way. I look upon this as one of my greatest trials, but one in which I dare say I should meet with but little sympathy. When I see how little this disturbs Mr. Binney, and especially when I see the familiarity of the Vintons with them, I keep very silent on the subject. Indeed, I am ashamed and humbled, but still suffer just the same. Jesus ate with Publicans and sinners.

The Mission Premises, when purchased, had no buildings and the grounds were entirely uncultivated, so the place could be laid out from the beginning according to the taste of the missionaries themselves; that is, they had the opportunity of using the small means at their disposal as they chose. Mr. Vinton was overwhelmed with work and care, and was glad to leave this department to Mr. Binney. He not only built his own dwelling-house, school-house, and dormitories as he chose, but arranged their relation to other buildings and to the whole plan; the laying out of the roads, gardens, walks, and the buildings for the schools under his care were all planned by Mr. Binney.

He and Mr. Vinton would go out with the Karens of both schools an hour or more in the early morning and evening, and work on the drains and roads, going themselves into the work as if they loved it. Not only that, but in order to keep the houses and compounds clean, they often took the lead in the use of rakes and shovels. This kind of work told rapidly upon the place, converting it from a most unsightly

marsh and jungle into an oasis.   English friends, seeing
what was being done, sent carts and coolies, now and
then, to assist in enclosing the grounds by a fence and
hedge.   Others sent money for the erection of necessary buildings.   One lady met the expense of a pretty
school-house for the Theological Seminary.   A pious
officer gave the means for laying the brick walks from
the dwelling-house to the chapel, and from thence to
the Karen dormitories, and covering them with a
thatched roof, so that in the rains by day or night they
could be reached without exposure.

But this work, in addition to teaching several hours
daily, was telling upon Mr. Binney's health.   Mr. Vinton and the Karens protested, and he felt obliged to desist.   But he could do so without detriment now.   The
prejudice against the kind of work had been overcome;
they had learned now to keep their places tidy, and
learned, too, that it must be done; that if they did not
do it the Teacher and Mamma would do it themselves.
They looked upon it as a part of their education, and he
never was obliged again to work with his pupils in
order to get work done.   He often did so to show them
how and to encourage them, but there was no longer
any objection from his pupils to work for the sake of
exercise and to save expenditure of mission funds.
Still, the extremely filthy habits of this people, grown
up to manhood, were very difficult to deal with.

Mrs. Binney had kept the little boy, the hero of the
buffalo adventure, with her, and had spent a few minutes
at a time, as a little leisure presented, in teaching him
English.   He was like her shadow, following and assist-

ing her on all occasions; a mutual and strong attachment, continually increasing, existed between them, and she found him a most efficient helper in making suggestions to the people as to their habits, which she scarcely had courage to do in person. This led to the idea of establishing a school for children.

At first a little girl was taken into the family, almost as bright and promising as Gnah-poo. She was also very useful, and kept about the place like a daughter. The little boy, with some help, taught her to read English, and they both learned to speak it with wonderful facility; they were mere children, and it became to them like their native tongue. Then seven or eight were brought in, and soon the school numbered thirty, to which number it was limited. A gentleman gave them a school building the second year. The parents were required to give their children entirely to the school, and there was never a case of violated faith. Mr. Binney took a general oversight of the school, especially of its financial interests, but gave no lessons. In it, Mrs. Binney spent four or five hours daily, and taught the school largely " to run itself." Every pupil was made to teach what he or she knew, to those who knew less, and so almost all became teachers. No pupil was allowed to speak Karen in the school-room; of course, the moment they left the school they were surrounded only by their own people and used their own language. The Old Testament had not yet been translated, and these children would give to the pupils of the Seminary all they learned from the English Bible. There was no difficulty in keeping a small number clean and tidy, and as they were in the house and took turns in doing the work of the house, their influence was like a charm over the Theological and other Schools in the Mission Compound.

Mr. Binney was looking forward, with great pleasure, to the day when some of these lads would be able to use his library freely.   Both schools were continued as long in the dry season as possible, having only a short vacation.   Mr. Vinton, however, was obliged to return home, and Mr. Binney, in his absence, spent more or less time in visiting the churches and doing such work in the jungle as he was able.

But while there was great progress and much cause for gratitude, Mr. Binney found these years of mercy mingled with many trials.   From the first, there did not seem to him to be, on the field, the same appreciation of the importance of the work to which he had been designated, as he had expected to find.   The Karens were a wild, jungle-loving people, and, until very recently, the subject race.   It was perhaps natural that those who had worked for and with the Burmans should look upon the Karens as hardly needing such an Institution as he was contemplating.

Dr. Judson, after a few weeks acquaintance with Mr. Binney, wrote him an earnest letter stating his opinion that he should abandon his plan of a Theological School for Karens and enter the Burman Department as a preacher.   He gave very fully and freely his reasons for this opinion.   They were very complimentary to Mr. Binney, could not well have been more so, and were especially enforced by the consideration that there was no man then in all Maulmain who was giving himself wholly or indeed very much to preaching to the Burmans. It is to be regretted, that neither Dr. Judson's letter nor the reply is preserved; both were worthy of the men. Mr. Binney, in common with the friends of missions everywhere, looked upon Dr. Judson as the embodiment of wisdom, self-denial, and all Christian graces, and it was a sore trial of his faith in his work to be met at the onset by such an opinion from such a source. He hesitated and faltered, but, after a careful and prayerful survey of the whole field he felt compelled to differ from him and to pursue his original purpose.

He had but just decided this question when Dr. Mason and Mr. Vinton presented to him a plan, carefully drawn up, for them all to work together in the Educational Department, having equal powers and equal responsibilities, and in the dry season all would give themselves equally to jungle work. This was pressed with great earnestness by Mr. Mason, and when Mr. Binney felt compelled to decline the proposal, Mr. Mason avowed himself so opposed to the plan of one General Institution, to be conducted by one man, that he declared his intention to labor for a similar school to be established at Tavoy; and before Mr. Binney had been a year in the country Rev. E. B. Cross, just from the Theological Institution at Hamilton, was sent to Tavoy, believing himself in every way empowered to do the same work for Tavoy as Mr. Binney was doing for Maulmain. The next year Rev. J. S. Beecher, also a young man just from the same Theological Institution, was sent out to establish a similar school at Bassein. Local influences

17

seemed likely to counteract what he deemed the great motive for his coming to Burmah, and all these things led to much correspondence and an immense expenditure of strength and time.   He must, under the circumstances, have had stronger faith than is usually found, not to have been sorely tried, even depressed.

Under date of April, 1848, Mr. Binney sent to the Board a carefully prepared "Plan of Education for Karen Native Preachers," embracing to some extent the whole plan of Education for Karens.   A part of this was published, but the original plan as written by himself is inserted here.   It is long, and probably will not interest all readers, but those who have borne a share of the burden of Educational Work in Burmah cannot fail to perceive by the light of experience, how clear and far-seeing were his views, and also how perfectly devoid of all self-seeking was his aim in carrying them out.   If the work could be' done without him, much as his heart was in it, he was as ready to lay it down as he had been to take it up.

MR. BINNEY'S LETTER TO THE FOREIGN SECRETARY.

In a letter received about a month since from Mr. Cross, he says, "Mr. Peck wrote me some months ago inquiring our opinion about the propriety of having three theological schools instead of one."   I hence infer that the Executive Committee have the subject under consideration, and I trust intend ere long to decide this important question.   From the first, I have had but one opinion respecting it.   There should be but one Theological School, designed to be permanent, and to be continued during the dry season.   I have previously offered a few thoughts respecting it; but as every month and an increased knowledge of the state and wants of the Karens have the more ·confirmed my early impressions, I beg through you to present to the Executive Committee my present views of the whole subject. I trust the importance of the issue will be a sufficient apology for the length of this communication and secure for it a consideration.

There is, perhaps, a liability to blend points in themselves distinct, and which require a distinct provision. In this confusion of the subject, three schools may appear desirable. The necessities of the older class of assistants are thus made to control the provision to be made for a younger and entirely different class, respecting which there is no such necessity.

I. The class of older assistants have families, and some of them large families, which renders it expensive and for them very difficult to attend school at a distance. They are the best qualified of any we have to preach, and are therefore needed during the dry season to operate in the jungle; so their journey to school must be annual. Again, they may at times be needed even during the rainy season, to look after the churches; of which the missionary in charge must be the judge. He must be permitted to send and to recall this class of assistants according to the exigencies of the field in which he labors. If they attend school at a distance from him, he can have no opportunity to consult with their teacher before taking them from their studies. Under such circumstances there could be no mutual understanding, and consequently a school could not long prosper, even if it continued to exist. For the instruction of this class, it is necessary to make provision at each station; where the missionary in charge and the teacher of the assistants can have frequent consultations. I can but think that the instructor of this class would be far more successful were he in charge of churches, as others are. He would, during the dry season, become intimately acquainted with the work and all its circumstances; and following with his own eye his pupils as they go forth preaching, he would learn their practical defects, and be better able to adapt his instruction and discipline to the very work *now* needed among the Karens. Besides, being in charge, like his brethren, he would better appreciate the present necessities of the churches, and would more cheerfully yield to the wants of his brethren, though it might produce some irregularity in his classes. Because this class of older assistants ought not to attend school at a distance, some have inferred a necessity for three Theological Schools; but no such inference legitimately follows. It only shows that instruction during the rainy season is needed at each station. For the instruction thus needed, as well as for that of school teachers at each station, provision is made so soon as the station is provided with men sufficient to do the jungle work of the dry season. Supposing the station to have only two men in charge of the churches, one may teach this class of assistants, and the other may instruct in other branches. Two such men are certainly needed for the jungle labor of each station. The criterion by which we are to decide how many men are required for the Karen Mission is, how many are requisite to preach, and to look after the assistants and churches. Wherever you make suitable provision for this, there will be men enough in town during "the rains," to give all the instruction needed for the station, and to prepare such books as are requisite for the time being. This does not include the men engaged in translating the Bible and making dictionaries; because these men have not time for jungle work, unless it be an occasional tour for their own recreation. This will appear if it be remembered how long the Karen Mission has been established, and that, to this day, the translation of the Old Testament is yet scarcely begun. Genesis and a part of the Psalms are alone even in manuscript. The New Testament only is printed. The first edition is exhausted, and the correction for another edition is but just begun. The Dictionary is, I think, no farther advanced. The first letter only of the Alphabet is printed, and even the vocabulary, brief as it is, is but about half done. Yet, both Mr. Wade and Mr. Mason have done much more than half their work upon missionary ground. Hence, I suppose, provision must be made for the churches independent of the translator and dictionary maker, and that provision will be ample for all the educational necessities of each station. The great proportion of education in reading, writing, geography, and arithmetic should be given in the jungle by native teachers who may themselves be instructed during the rains as suggested above. This would greatly reduce the number whom you now feed and clothe in town. The necessities of the Educational Department and those of the churches, at each station, will go hand in hand, and will gradually cease to need the labor of the American Missionary. If we do our duty, with the blessing of God, ten years, more or less, should see the Karens at the heads of their own churches and schools, (so far as peculiar to each station,) and supporting them too. Supporting them because both willing and able to support them, and I may add, because thus conducted by themselves. If at that time they determine to have all their teaching done at their own door, and to pay for it, I should cease to feel a part of the objections which now arise in my own mind—the part connected with our present mode of supporting Foreign Missions.

II. It will be seen that, though the above does much by way of a gradual improvement of the people, and for the preparation of teachers and preachers, it does not do all that may by a judicious system, be done at a small additional expense,—small, considering it is for a nation,—a nation so generally ready to receive the gospel as are the Karens. It does not provide for a class of men more thoroughly disciplined and educated, who, before ten years shall have passed, will be needed to fill important posts in the churches, and for the people, and to wield a controlling influence in their councils. It does not provide for a class, now too young to preach, but who after a few years study the year round, might constitute a suitable connecting link between the older assistants and a more thoroughly trained ministry. It makes no provision for a class of children and youth, already in the churches and rapidly increasing, who are too young for teachers or preachers, and who, if not taken by us, will be wandering about the jungle, and who ought to be immediately placed under a rigid course of instruction. This class, from the object in view, must be small. None should be received but the most promising, and those who may be retained for a number of years, free from parental interference.

17*

It is for the two latter classes that I suppose a General Institution needed, to be continued the whole year, with suitable vacations. Even in the vacations they should be under the direction of their teacher. This would evidently require two departments, one for Theology and one for other studies. The former must of necessity be under the charge of a competent missionary, the latter for some years certainly, may be taught by a competent young lady, and its general supervision taken by the man having charge of the Theological Institution.

English should be the classical language. Should the classical department or Normal school, as it might be called, ultimately outgrow the care of a lady,—which will not soon be,—it would be necessary to have two men, one at the head of each department. The instruction of the Classical School could not be given by the teacher in Theology. Not because of the number of the pupils, but from the diversity of studies and the number of classes. Here, then, one man is required the year round for a Theological Institution, and to take the general oversight of the Classical Department. Small as the class may be, judiciously selected, we must take care of it, or the Roman Catholics will ere long do it for us.

For the general supervision of this Institution, you may have to provide, long after the Karens may themselves be competent for every other department. It should be for all, at every station, for whose instruction you make provision the whole year. It should include both Sgau and Pwo Karens. Mr. Bullard, previously to his death, had decided to place even his older assistants in my school. It will be seen that none of the objections to attending school at a distance, raised for the class of older assistants, can apply to the younger classes ; and that the necessity for instruction the year round exists only with reference to this select portion, which must from the nature of the case long remain comparatively small. It differs, also, from the fact that the other, being attached to a particular station, should be under the advisory direction of the station itself, while this, belonging to all the stations, should be under the advisory direction of all the stations—an ultimate appeal being in all cases to the Executive Committee. To meet the above, the Institution might be visited annually, biennially, or triennially—more or less frequently by a delegation from each of the stations. This, while it would afford your Missionaries opportunities for consultation respecting the general interests of the Mission, would also be calculated to secure to the Institution the sympathy and aid of all the stations, to prove a wholesome, and perhaps necessary check upon any liability to loose theory or practice in the Institution, and to afford to its head essential aid in adapting his labors to the prospective wants of the Karens.

The expenses of the Institution, whether for traveling or ordinary support, should be charged by itself, and not to any one station, and its location should be central. To this, might also be sent all the classes of older assistants connected with the station in which it is located ; they to be subject to the direction of their own station, in the same manner as the older assistants are to each other's station ; provided, that while they were at their studies they should be subject to the rules of the school.

Respecting the location of the Institution, I have ever said that I was willing to be at any place which the brethren might prefer for the object. At first, I had no opinion about it, but now I think it should be in the vicinity of Maulmain. The reason will be seen by a reference to the map. It is to provide for Tavoy and South Maulmain and east ; and northeast, over the mountains, for Arracan, Bassein ; and around, for Rangoon and beyond. This location was, I think, approved for a General Institution four years ago, by all. Mr. Abbott was of opinion that it should be at Maulmain, and Mr. Mason said, If there is to be a General Institution, it should be in the vicinity of Maulmain. Some, however, thought it should be at Amherst. To this there could not be much to object. It would have its advantages ; especially, during the dry season, it would be favored with the salt water air and bath. The present Karen houses could be removed at small loss above the expense of taking down and putting up again, perhaps also a trifle for transportation. Still, if the brethren all thought best, I should prefer Maulmain, as it has good medical attendance, and chiefly, perhaps, because I am already here.*

1. More than one institution unnecessarily expends men and money. That it is not necessary appears from the above. I fear many do not calculate correctly when they estimate the expenses of these schools. A Christian minister's life and influence are worth something, and ought not uselessly to be expended. In estimating the pecuniary expense, we are liable to include only the bills returned as direct charges for this object. We are liable to overlook the yet greater items for the missionary's outfit, passage, dwelling, salary, &c., and the whole list of contingencies for sickness, traveling, for health, and the children's support, till the age of sixteen years. This is no trifling bill to be assessed on the few pupils to be found at each station the year round. But to multiply this by the number of stations as a provision for theological education in the very infancy of the churches, and that from funds, much of which is collected from the poor on the express plea of urgent necessities, appears to me in a much stronger light than I have wished to state.

2. The question of one or three is not really the question at issue. If there be more than one, for the same reasons there should be as many as there are stations a little removed from each other. We now speak of three, because our field, for the time being, is so divided. Let Bassein be opened to our missionaries, and some new provision must be made for them. Rangoon, so soon as men can remain there, will need the same; and when churches begin to multiply over the mountains, you must establish yet another; and thus to what extent no man can tell. They will certainly be needed for Rangoon and for the mountain Karens, far more than they are at both Maulmain and Tavoy. These two stations may better be associated than any other two stations ever likely to come under the mission. I have pupils now in my school from many days' travel beyond Rangoon, and who were more distant from Sandoway than they were

---

* It will be remembered that Rangoon was still under Burmese rule, and that Maulmain was the capital of British Burmah.

from Maulmain. If, then, the necessity for three schools be now admitted, they must be indefinitely increased hereafter, and we should count the cost before we launch upon such a system.

3. Such a multiplication of Theological Schools is out of all proportion to what is doing, or can be done, in other departments of missionary labor. If only the amount of labor said by missionaries to be now needed at each station, be regarded, to say nothing of the wide fields opening on every side, (I have now in my mind three different fields, which I have within six months been invited to visit, where they have never seen a teacher among them. Their chiefs told me, if a teacher would visit them, their people would listen:) it would appear how utterly impossible it is for the Executive Committee to provide other laborers in proportion to this large number of schools.

4. One Institution would enable the Executive Committee to do what they do more effectually even in the cause of education for Karens, than they can do with three schools. Not to insist upon what has already been written to us respecting retrenchment, (my own school the past year was saved only by the generosity of my associates; and, as it was, the reduction of the amount allowed to the Theological School compelled me to refrain from doing what my pupils expected and what I thought to be necessary for the improvement of my pupils;) there can be no doubt that there is a limit to the ability of the Executive Committee. I cannot believe that the American churches will ever give adequate support to so many Theological Schools for the same people. I repeat, that the necessity for an additional man in a General Institution, should it occur, will arise, not from the number of the pupils, but from the number of classes and diversity of studies. It requires as much time properly to prepare for, and rightly to conduct, a small class as it does a large one. I have thus far found my largest classes make better improvement than the smaller classes. There is no magic in the successful teaching and training of a well-qualified ministry; it is not to be done in the lump. Every mind must be individually reached by instruction specifically and often repeated, and this demands the most thorough preparation before recitations; and no teacher

can neglect this, even among Karens, but at the expense of his pupils' improvement. Can our Mission supply such instruction to each station the year round? I think not. Whatever the Committee may wish and resolve to do, the churches will not afford the means.

What, then, shall be done? The having a large number of schools, half supported, and of necessity half taught, can give only a popular education. It cannot give what the Committee wish, and what the welfare of the churches demands—a good foundation upon which to build a well-educated ministry. Is it not better to make a suitable provision at some one point than thus to scatter our resources? But this is only one branch of expense. To those acquainted with educational efforts, I need not enlarge.

5. Above, I have said, that the churches will not afford the means. It should also be stated, that even if they were willing to do so, the men and money are more needed at home, both for the preaching of the gospel and purposes of education, than three Theological Schools are needed for the Karens. I speak from a personal knowledge of what is needed at home. Without going into our western and south-western States, I have myself seen the destitution and the array of error even in some of our old States, without the means to remove the one or combat the other.

Our State Conventions and Home Missionary Societies witness the same. I have, also, been four years in daily intercourse with the Karens and with Karen missionaries; I have heard the wants and circumstances of each station read, explained, and discussed. It is after all this, I must honestly say, that were I to be at home again with my present knowledge, I could not give either my own money, or ask for that of others, for such a multiplication of schools for Karens, until those destitute places of our own land had been first supplied.

6. Pupils educated together will be more likely to understand each other, and to co-operate together in all their future labors for the Churches and Nation. It is not merely that they are subject to the same and mutual intellectual influences, but their moral and

social habits will be formed together, and they will become accustomed to each other's views, feelings, expressions, and actions,
under the most favorable circumstances. The advantage of this
in the infancy of the churches is incalculable.

7. Three Theological Schools will prove a strong temptation
to require the older assistants to study during the dry season,
when they ought to be in the jungle preaching and assisting the
churches. No man qualified to take charge of these schools
will sit down five months in the year to teach five or six pupils,
without casting a longing look into the jungle after the preachers.
Soon the period for teaching will be shortened, or the number of
preachers in the jungle will be diminished; nor will the good
judgment of the station always be a sufficient antidote to this.

8. For the same reasons, three schools will prove a strong
temptation to encourage unsuitable persons to study for the ministry. The number at each station who ought to study the year
round must for a long time be small. If we duly consider the
character and ability of the men, and the weighty reponsibilities
hereafter to devolve upon this class, we cannot avoid this conclusion. I refrain from stating here my own experience respecting this and the previous reasons; but this perhaps I ought to
say, that I have good reason for distrusting my own ability to
resist these temptations. It is not a very difficult matter, while
spending the money of others, to have a large number ot
persons whom we may call students! The difficulty is to sift out
the chaff; and there is a temptation to be remiss when we know
that a due strictness would leave but little wheat.

9. The plan of three schools must entail upon Karens a system
of education which for ages they cannot themselves support. In
other words, it confirms them in a state of dependence on others.
No one acquainted with the condition and prospects of the
Karens, and with what is needed to support a system of education, can for a moment suppose that the Karens will for ages be
able to support such a burden. Is it right, then, for us to place
a nation in such circumstances? Not to urge the bad economy
of the act, have we any warrant that our means at home, or the
condition of this country in years to come, will allow us to con-

tinue our aid to the extent supplied? It is exceedingly doubtful whether, for half a century or more, Karens will be able wholly to relinquish the aid of others. But with their Translation and Dictionary made, and with one or two efficient men at the helm of their Educational Department, they ought to be able to sustain their own operations in a much shorter period. And they could support one such Institution by their united efforts, when they would yield to despair at the thought of supporting an Institution at each station.

10. This system of three schools is calculated to foster in the Karen churches the idea, that they are not required to deny themselves for the general good. It lays the axe to the root of the tree. It begins its work with the very men whose business it is to press home upon the conscience of the churches the self-denying requisitions of the gospel. It practically, if not theoretically, teaches him, at the very commencement of his ministry, that his local preference and his convenience are first of all to be consulted; and all this is while he is in every respect dependent on others. If they do these things in the green tree, what will they do in the dry? Of what possible benefit can such a class of men be in the ministry of Jesus Christ—an office which no man can hold with success and with a good conscience, without self-denial? With such a ministry, what must be the state of the churches? Besides, where are we to look for the men who will "leave father, mother, brother, and sister, and houses and lands," as they may possess them; who will peril even their own lives, —to preach the gospel on the mountains to the "Red Karens," and to obey our Saviour's last command? I cannot think that a missionary body should foster in the churches and in the ministry the quintessence of anti-missionaryism.

DIFFICULTIES IN THE WAY.

I ought not perhaps to close, without alluding to some of the difficulties in the way of adopting but one Institution.

1. It has been said, pupils will not come to a distance to attend school. I give my own schools as a practical refutation of this. I have had, and now have, pupils from the most distant Karen

churches under your patronage; and their journey hither has been, on almost every account, the most difficult. Some have come alone; some have brought their families; and some have sent their children, boys and girls, to remain with us so long as we may think best. Such is their confidence in their teachers that they feel satisfied if they can have their children with us; and respecting this matter they will do as their teachers desire them to do. What is yet more satisfactory to my own mind is, that those from a distance are decidedly among the most diligent and successful in their studies, and the most patient and happy during the dry season.

II. The expense of getting these pupils to us, has been objected. This estimate of expenses overlooks, as noted above, the heavy bills for the missionary, his family, etc.

III. It may be said, It is unnecessary for us at present to decide definitely. Let the schools go on, and a system will adjust itself to circumstances. It is doubtless true, if you begin with one, it will be easy to enlarge the number. Almost any station would be glad to have a school at its own door. But I submit to those acquainted with educational efforts, with all the piety of the church and ministry, Whether, if we begin with a school at each station, it will be easy and natural for these stations to relinquish them, and to unite in one Institution; whether years of indulgence in this matter will make men more self-denying. This objection only asks time, and it will give to each station all its desires, so far as to expend for local ends what little we can have. Circumstances will, doubtless, secure dry season instruction somewhere. The question is, Shall we have one, or many schools, the year round? From the first, I have thought that the only way not to have three, or more, is to have one and to sustain it.

IV. It may be urged that the men are here; that their jungle work is done in some two months, or so; and that they may then as well teach a school as do nothing. But why (if it be so) are your missionaries in the jungle so short a time? Most certainly not because of anything in the climate which prevents, for men of business, of ordinary constitution, go with perfect

18

security during the dry season—they do sometimes go even in the rainy season. Your missionaries can, doubtless, go during the dry season, if they have physical ability. If they have not, they ought not to come as missionaries to this country. Indeed, unless it be some special exception where long experience is needed in the language, as for a translator or maker of the Dictionary, if they become unfitted for the work, they should return home. If it is necessary for the Mission to support them, let it be done among the churches who give the money. Missionary ground is no place for a hospital, any more than the battle ground is for the invalid soldier. But why in the jungle for so short a time? Assuredly, not because missionaries are not needed in the jungle, for you are constantly urged to send more men for this very work. Is it true that the Mission must support four or five men at a station, to be with the churches only two months in the year, when two men could do the whole work in four months? Nor is this relieved by saying that missionaries need only to remain in town, and to give direction to native labor through the jungle; for the number of men so urgently requested cannot be needed to sit down in town, to take the oversight of these few churches and this handful of assistants. The fact is, the men are not needed for any such purpose; but they are greatly needed themselves to travel in the jungle, to examine with eagle eye the state of the churches, and to know by personal observation what the assistants are about; whether they faithfully labor as assistants; and, if faithful, whether their efforts are rightly directed. Without all this, whatever men may say, the missionary presides over the churches and their assistants in the dark. The whole dry season should be honestly and faithfully devoted to the interest of the cause in the jungle; and it was while the Wades, Masons, Abbotts, and Vintons were thus laboring that God so much blessed the Karen Mission. I know this is hard, self-denying work, and most sincerely do I honor the men who faithfully do it. But hard as it is, it was for this they came here; and if they repent their decision, they ought honestly to say so, and return home.

V. Possibly the Executive Committee may feel, if the missionaries were agreed, we could act; but this is a thing which cannot be forced. I once thought unanimity essential to a decision; but I then supposed the difficulty grew out of something peculiar to missionary work. That, I cannot now believe. In the Karen Mission there is now as much unanimity as could be expected. But it should not be overlooked that this point is not to be settled merely for the few men now here. They are present .it may be to object to-day, but before the year closes they may be taken away. Their objections, therefore, should not be allowed to rule the decision.

VI. I am aware there is practically another difficulty, and I am not certain but the Executive Committee may feel it to be even greater than any yet named. Three men are upon the ground; two of whom are commissioned to take charge of Theological Schools, and the third is at least in part to be engaged in similar employments. If, then, these men do not consent to do other work, are not the Committee, it may be said, obliged to sustain them in the work to which they were sent? The difficulty is real and great, yet what shall we do? Must the Mission support us here, as supernumeraries, merely because we were sent here? I think not. Whoever may be to blame in the matter, a due regard to the welfare of the cause ought to provide some remedy. If a man has health for the work, and is unwilling to deny himself to meet the exigency, he certainly is not the right sort of man to·be the teacher and pattern of the rising ministry in these Karen churches. Most cheerfully, under the circumstances, would I resign my charge to another and become a jungle-missionary. It is the post of honor in the Karen Mission. But my brethren know 1 am physically unfit for the work. It is not that I should not long live; I could not do what is absolutely necessary to be done. This was well-known before I came here, and my constitutional vigor has not gained since my arrival. When Mr. Vinton returned to America, the field was left destitute, and I thought it my duty to do what I could, however much it might fall short of what was needed. I accordingly dismissed my pupils until the next rains. So soon as Dr. Kane, Surgeon to one of the regiments here, learned my intention, he sent me the following :

"My dear Mr. Binney, understanding that you contemplate a sojourn in the jungle during the present dry season, I feel I am only performing my duty in telling you that I consider both you and Mrs. Binney to be most unsuited for any such mode of life, from your state of health. I have now had nearly a year's medical experience of you both, during which I formed the opinion, that from the general delicacy of your constitution considerable care and attention are requisite to enable you to preserve your health in this country. As these conditions cannot be complied with in a jungle residence, I have considered it my duty to warn you in time and thereby relieve myself of responsibility, though not of anxiety, on your behalf ; and hope the circumstances will excuse my obtruding my unasked opinion."

Mr. Mason, proposing most kindly to take my place in the jungle, writes : "My dear Brother Binney, I have grave doubts of its being the duty of yourself and Mrs. Binney to go into the jungle this season, and that simply on the ground of your health. The season seems particularly sickly, and you have much less vigor of constitution to meet it than you had when you last visited the jungle. Should you go, the probabilities are quite as strong to my mind that we shall not have your labors next rains, as that we shall ; or that, having them, your system will be so shattered that it will not be long before you are compelled to leave the country." But my pupils had already been dismissed, and I thought it best to do what I could.

Such, therefore, being my own state, I cannot become a jungle missionary. Mr. Beecher has good health, and if I am not much mistaken in the spirit of the man, he will be willing to do anything to advance the interests of the churches. I do not believe he will allow himself for a moment to stand in the way of a General Institution ; how it may be with Mr. Cross, I am more doubtful, because I do know him or his circumstances. I know he considers himself sent to sustain a Theological School, in no wise differing from that at Maulmain. He has a young family about

him, and may feel he cannot become a jungle missionary. He
may also be very unwilling to return home. I believe the difficulty—should there be one—to be in the disposal of Mr. Cross
and myself, and however painful it may be, I have resolved to
remove it. I cannot do jungle work, but I can return home. I
love the work in which I am engaged, and should the Executive
Committee decide to have one Institution, and should they think
it best to commit that to my care, I am prepared to devote myself to it as heartily and cheerfully as when I at first came to
this country. But it was not to please myself nor to promote my
own interest that I came; nor can I remain from any such consideration. I came, not to embarrass, but to assist the cause.
Should, therefore, the Executive Committee wish for one Institution, and in deciding should they, to meet the difficulty here presented, be unable otherwise to remove it, I hereby authorize
them to recall me. I resign my place to my brother Cross. It
may be more difficult for him with his family, than it is for me.
Let him immediately enter upon the work; and let a good jungle missionary take his place at Tavoy. I say again, I would
prefer to remain here if needed, but would rather return home
than be one of three men to do one man's work. I would rather
return home, than to spend missionary money, and entail upon
the Karens such a system of education.

That the God of all wisdom may enable his servants rightly to
decide, and energetically to pursue, what is best is my earnest
prayer.

Very sincerely, your brother in gospel labor,

J. G. BINNEY.

An extract from a letter written by Mr. Binney to the
Board, February 22d, 1848, after his return from a tour
in the jungle, will give, perhaps, a more clear idea of the
kind of labor involved; and show how well grounded
were his convictions of his inability to do justice to it.
These convictions were held, while yet considering the

18*

question of entrance on the position to which he was first called by the Board in 1843.

I have not attempted what Mr. Vinton had been accustomed to do, knowing that it was out of the question. I have no constitution for such work. In this conviction I was quite confirmed by what I saw and heard during my recent tour. This traveling in the jungle is no boys' play ; it is no mere relaxation of study. I see not how any man who feels himself called of God to that work, and assumes the care of this people to himself, can retain a good conscience and not work, work hard and work incessantly while in the jungle. He must be exposed to the sun by day, and, at times, to the dews of the night; he must go sometimes in his boat, sometimes upon his elephant, and often on foot. Circumstances compel all this. He has no alternative but to do this, or else to leave the work undone. The work is about him, presses itself upon him, and if he cannot do it, he should at once resign his place to some one who can and will do it.

At the close of the first year of the " Karen Normal School," Mrs. Binney, to save Mr. Binney's time, wrote a report of it to the Foreign Secretary. Some extracts of the report will give more fully the reasons for its establishment.

It was deemed important to keep the Theological School in session during the dry as well as the rainy season. The Karens, though anxious and willing to come during the rains, have always manifested a great impatience of remaining a day after the Monsoons had broken up. They have well been called "the jungle-loving Karens." Some difficulty, therefore, was anticipated and felt in keeping the school together. Particularly were the young men's wives averse to remaining, and we felt it extremely important to secure their influence on the right side. It was thought, if a select school of children could be kept up during the year, the women would feel more at home, and, therefore, be willing to remain.

Again, the habits of these adults were fixed, and although we have never deemed it advisable to Europeanize these people, yet it was felt that Christianity should influence them to habits of industry and cleanliness. Few, however,—perhaps no one who has never made the attempt to improve a people similarly situated,— could imagine the difficulties we met in our first efforts. However much they might approve of any course, their national custom afforded an unanswerable argument against its acceptance. We found it hard to overcome their indolence, as they could not see the necessity of doing what Karens had never done. Many things which we deemed desirable and practicable they deemed impossible. We had no precedent among their own people to plead. Of course, compulsion does not comport with the office of a missionary, nor does it suit his policy, for we should probably have been left without pupils. It seemed, therefore, to Mr. Binney to be greatly to the interest of the Theological School, to establish such a school as this on the same compound. The children are easily influenced. To secure our approbation is usually a sufficient motive to influence them to almost anything we might wish. Of course, there are exceptions to this rule, but usually Karen children are extremely improvable. It was thought that the example of these children, in a course of training and improvement, would prove a more powerful stimulus, and accomplish more for the adults, than any direct effort we might make for them. In this we have not been disappointed. Seeing these children always dressed cleanly and tidily, with the knowledge that the labor was performed by themselves, made the women quite ashamed of their untidy appearance, and a change was soon visible, not only in their own persons, but in their little children, and even in their husbands. The influence was felt by the very men who, a few months before, had thought any attention to these matters quite unnecessary for Karens. During the last few months the improvement of the adults has been quite as great as the children's, and has followed closely in their wake. They have not only kept their persons and houses cleaner than formerly, but have been more cheerful in their hours of labor and study. The example of the children in abandoning the chewing of the betel nut is also beginning to be felt by them. This is a custom, not only of the Karens, but also of all the natives of this country. It is, however, a filthy habit, and universally admitted to be injurious to health, and actually often costs Karens more than the rice they eat. No pupil in the Normal School chews it, neither do any seem to desire it after a few days' abstinence.

Another reason, and perhaps the one why we deemed such a school desirable, was, that if we ever have any well educated Karens, we must begin with them young, and keep them with us till the object is in some good degree accomplished. The books in Karen are yet so few and so elementary, that for many years to come we cannot look for a thorough education, except through the medium of English. This is not a small work for the natives of this country, and not to be accomplished unless it be begun in childhood. We hope, however, there will be a few in this school who will not only master the English language, but be able to read the Bible in the original, and judge for themselves of the correctness of their translations. We hope, also, that some of the children will, at no distant day, be able to add to the literature of their nation. Others who may not desire to pursue so thorough a course, may be qualified to become successful and respectable mechanics and agriculturists, and thus lead the way in the civilization of this already Christian people.

It is not designed to educate persons who are thus to become only the more capable of defending infidelity, but Christian children, who are already hopefully converted, or concerning whom we have as much hope as concerning any equal number of children in America, perhaps more, as no Karen Christian has yet had children grown up without being converted. Karen Christians expect their children to be converted, and labor and pray for it, with an earnestness which might make Christians in more favored lands blush.

No further extracts will be made from this report, except to show the character of the lad Gnahpoo, who was the germ from which sprang the Karen Normal School of Maulmain, the beginning of "Higher Education" for the natives of Burmah. He was in every respect so promising that by his own earnest request he received an English name, and was called Everett Pattison. He dated his first serious convictions, and his fleeing to Christ as the true Ark of Refuge from impending doom, to the reading by the Mamma, in a very imperfect manner, when she first went to Chet-things-ville, one of Todd's "Lectures to Children," translated by Mrs. Vinton. On that very occasion, when trying to explain a little more fully than the lecture had done how Christ was to the sinner what Noah's ark was to those who fled to it from the coming flood, she had been quite discouraged, and felt it would be utterly impossible for her ever in that foreign tongue to do much good. Even then, as appeared in after years, the Spirit was blessing those imperfect efforts, not only to the saving of some souls, but the soul of one who was to be a rich blessing to his people.

Five of these children have been baptized; two since they came into the school. Of others we have strong hopes. One of the boys, Everett Pattison, has often been the subject of very serious impressions; twice he has been on the point of asking for baptism. Last year, about the time Mr. Binney's pupils were returning to Burmah Proper, he expressed a wish to be baptized. He was rejoicing in hope, but having listened to the instructions given by Mr. Binney to his class as to their duty, should they meet with persecution,—as there was every reason to suppose they would,—he seemed distrustful of his own heart and did not venture to go forward. He admitted that they were the instructions given to the early disciples, but feared, were he put to the test, he should love his own life better than his Saviour. How differently did these instructions appear to these young men and to this lad, who felt they might be practically applied at any time, to those receiving the same instructions in our own country! Mr. Binney dared not even now lower the conditions, and no one could judge of his own heart so well as himself. A few weeks afterwards he came into Mr. Binney's study on a Sunday morning and, with great solemnity of manner, said:

"Teacher, will you baptize me to day? I do believe I love Jesus so much that, if called upon to suffer for his name, I should not deny him. I am willing to take the solemn vows upon me, trusting alone in him for strength for every trial."

The great event of interest this year was the ordination of four of Mr. Binney's first pupils. The Ordaining Committee, or Council, was composed of all the missionaries, Burman and Karen, within a convenient distance, with the leading men, preachers, and deacons of the churches. The ordination services were not unlike those on such occasions at home, but it will be imagined that in solemnity and intensity of feeling it would seldom be equalled in our own native land. Under date of March, 1849, Mr. Binney reports:

The close of this term was a time of deep interest to all. The four pupils composing the first class were about to leave us, and go forth as ministers of Christ. They were among the first placed under my care, they were selected from the others and formed into a class by themselves, because they were among the few, who, it was supposed, might be safely trusted with power to administer the ordinances. Two were from this vicinity and two from Rangoon. They are all acceptable preachers.

Pra-hai has powers which would do honor to many of our pupils at home. He is perfectly self-possessed and graceful in his manner, has a good voice, clear in the conception of his thoughts and equally so in his mode of presenting them to others; his peculiarity is, he preaches with great point and power to the heart and conscience. He never beats the air, and seldom selects a subject too deep for his abilities and the object sought; he is also a strict disciplinarian, willing to place himself under necessary discipline or restraint, and ready to ·discipline others if necessary.

Ky-ah-pah has an active, discriminating mind, and is very ambitious; were he in college at home, he would be satisfied with nothing short of the valedictory; he is greedy of knowledge, and has a happy tact in communicating it to others. Though he knows more and has more mental power than any Karen I have seen, his active independent mind has given me some anxiety; but he has grown so much in the graces of the heart within two years; has manifested so deep an interest in the welfare of the churches; is withal so conscious of how little he really knows, that I cannot but think in his own improvement, and in many duties and responsibilities which he will meet in the vicinity of Rangoon, he will find ample scope for all his mental activity.

Au-paw is within a few days of Ky-ah-pah, and they are expected to work together. They love, and have great confidence in, each other; they are opposites in every respect. Au-paw is very deliberate in all his thoughts and actions, careful how he commits himself, yet independent when once his opinion is formed; he has been tried in the furnace of affliction and found to be pure gold.

Ta-hoo is to be numbered among the elders; he is one of the earliest disciples in this vicinity; has a good mind, though rather slow; and what he knows, he teaches with good effect. He has too much attachment to the simple gospel as he first learned it ever to go astray; his deportment is such that he cannot fail to commend the gospel to his fellow-men; he will, doubtless, do well in the discipline of the church." .

It is interesting, after a lapse of thirty-two years, to compare this account, once the predictions of their future course, with the actual course taken; to see how Mr. Binney's clear perception of character, which was rarely at fault, enabled him to state what, with a change of tenses, would now be their history. In transcribing Mr. Binney's account of Pra-hai, it occurs to the writer that the Karens called him " Teacher Binney the Second," and that Mr. Vinton once said to Mr. Binney, " I do not think Pra-hai an imitator, but, so far as the difference of circumstances will allow, he is your fac-simile." He has all these years quietly pursued the even tenor of his way, never swerving to the right or left, and will doubtless be loyal to the Master to the end.

Ky-ah-pah, concerning whom Mr. Binney expresses some anxiety, became impatient of restraint, would not listen to his meek and loving friend Au-paw, but though he thought he was strong, he fell, was deposed from the ministry, and brought great grief to those who loved him, especially to those who loved the Master. Thanks to preserving mercy, his was a solitary case.

Au-paw was called to suffer great persecution, and probably died a victim to its effects, but his faith never failed.

Ta-hoo still preaches. Old and quite blind, he quotes the Bible, chapter and verse, calls sinners to repentance, and doubtless will preach on, till the warning voice and tender accents of entreaty are exchanged for the victor's triumphal shout of praise.

Thus trials and mercies were mingled. Each year marked increased progress in his schools. He looked upon the Normal School as almost indispensable to the full development of the other. He went into the jungle, visited the churches, and did what he could for several years ; but each year the time was shortened, and finally he was obliged to give all his time to his work in town. On Mr. Vinton's return to America, he gave back the oversight of assistants, and everything else that he did not deem his legitimate work. The division between North and South in missionary organization had taken place, and this cut him off in a great degree from the sympathy and co-operation of his Savannah friends. They had promised, and he had expected, much of both. This, to a mind like his, was very depressing. Not that they loved their pastor less, but Burmah was the field which fell to the lot of the Missionary Union to cultivate, and the South needed their help. The Missionary Union also during those years was greatly embarrassed, and "demands for retrenchment" were "the order of the day." The Maulmain Missionary Society and personal friends, however, kept the work from being entirely abandoned. Again, some of the missionaries themselves had become very anxious for a division of the business and responsibilities of the two departments of the mission, which had hitherto been one; most of the Karen missionaries felt the time had come for a separation. The Burmese missionaries mostly thought it unnecessary, and opposed it. Mr. Binney approved of the division, and united with his brethren in requesting it. When the Board replied by asking the Karen missionaries to reconsider their request, he wrote an exhaustive letter, which, after being read to his brethren, was sent to the Board. The most important reason given was that "as there was considerable difference of opinion as to what was appropriate mission work, he thought it better, for both departments, that each be responsible for *its* own work."

19

Others, especially Mr. Ingalls, of the Burman, and Mr. Mason, of the Karen Mission, wrote about the same time, urging the importance of giving the preaching of the gospel to the people greater prominence, and asking for a man to be sent for the special work of preaching to .the Burmans, as those on the ground were not at leisure to give themselves wholly, or to any great extent, to this work. Mr. Binney took great pains to state that he found no fault with any man or class of men, but adds:

I do not think it necessary for me to explain to you my views of education. Surely I am not opposed to the most vigorous system of education for Christians and their families, but I cannot think such an amount of labor and funds should be expended with so small a number of converts, while there is so little preaching to sinners.*

Such a decision would be more likely to secure to both departments the benefit of mutual counsel and advice as Christian brethren and ministers. In the present state of things, if one be opposed to the wishes or measures of another, the other at once supposes it is an opposition which will be enforced by a vote, and there is an end to all influence of one upon the other. But let the fear of that vote, with its power over the wishes, be removed, and I cannot but think that Christian ministers bending under the weight of their own responsibility will gladly obtain light and counsel wherever they can find it.

---

* It is due alike to Dr. Binney and his brethren to state that his views of that part of the educational work done in Maulmain, concerning which there was the greatest diversity of opinion, known as Mr. Howard's School, were considerably modified in later years by its results; and though he continued to feel that preaching received a disproportionate share of labor and expense, he was free to acknowledge to those to whom it was still in his power to admit it, that he had placed too low an estimate upon the importance of this work.

The division was finally accomplished, but not without some friction and mutual misunderstandings among men with the same desires and singleness of purpose in bringing them to pass. As has been stated, the brethren were earnest in this matter. "More preaching," was the rallying cry, and the ball Mr. Binney first set in motion gathered size and momentum, till it well-nigh crushed his own work. His own views were clear, and clearly defined, but he was an educator. Therefore, in the minds of many, he must give education the first place in mission work; he must even deem it a means of evangelizing, while, in fact, he would not educate at all until evangelized. Even men who were regular attendants at the Board meetings placed him on the wrong side. This misunderstanding was hard to live down; he took no other measures, however, to set himself right; the work was done, and he was satisfied. In his own mind, the relation of preaching to education seemed so natural and simple, he could not think himself misunderstood where there was a real desire to understand him.

Soon after this division, the Karen missionaries at Maulmain put into Mr. Binney's hands a communication, which embodied their view of the measure for the relief of the pressing wants of the mission. The following extract will show their feelings towards him and indicate what they desired to have done in the hour of their pressing and painful need.

We have selected you, dear brother, to carry into execution our plans; not because we can spare you best—we could dispense with the labors and influence of any other man in the

Mission at a less sacrifice—but because you are the only man among us that we believe able to execute them. The greatest compliment, then, which we can offer you, is your election to this special mission, and we will offer you no inferior one.

We propose to you that with the least practicable delay you return to America to obtain all adequate supplies for the Karen Mission, at the following minimum estimate : For Tavoy, two mission families, one of whom shall be principally devoted to the Pwos. For Sandoway, two missionaries, one to be principally devoted to the Pwos. For Maulmain, three missionaries, two of whom shall be principally devoted to the Pwos, but all to pledge themselves to study both dialects.

Mr. Binney was expected by this plan to do every thing in his power to secure from this country the needed help. He did not, however, think it best to accept the mission proposed to him. At the same time he deeply sympathized with his brethren in their deep anxiety, as a letter written to Dr. Peck fully shows.

This letter was written soon after Mr. Bullard's death. Mr. Binney heard from a messenger, dispatched for the purpose, that he had an attack of Asiatic cholera, and hastened to his bedside. He was just in time to take his hand, already cold in death, but still able to return an affectionate pressure ; to pray with him a moment while still holding it ; and then Mr. Bullard's work on earth was done. They had come out together, understood each other, and were working together to bring the Pwo and Sgau Missions into closer relations, especially in their educational work. Mr. Binney had very earnestly desired to see this accomplished, and, besides his personal grief, he felt that the Mission had sustained an irreparable loss. He writes as follows :

My Dear Brother Peck:—I fully intended to write you by this mail something more definite respecting our educational matters; but alas! what are plans when there are no men to execute? Our dear brother Bullard is no more with us. No man but a Karen missionary in Maulmain can estimate the loss which the Karen Mission has sustained. My feelings when I closed his eyes in death cannot be described. It was one of the few instances since I became a disciple of Christ in which my heart plainly rebelled against God. I felt that it could not, must not be. But it was momentary—the thought that God reigns, somewhat relieved a burdened heart. But this, in connection with sick Karens to look after, together with three attacks myself of bowel complaint within a week, one of which had every symptom of cholera, was far from preparing me to receive the intelligence that we must also retrench for want of funds.

My own school is full of promise; and though I am feeling far from well, I long to plunge into the active duties of the next term, which commences in a few days, to drown the thoughts and feelings originated by the state of the Mission. I love my pupils and work, but *this load upon the heart who can bear!* Brethren Abbott, Brayton, and Mason are away. Brother Bullard has taken a final leave, and then, as though this were not enough, we have not means to keep up what little is left to work upon.

I hope our brethren at home will not talk of the mysteriousness of Providence. There is no mystery which men and means *rightly appropriated* would not remove.

As ever affectionately your brother,   J. G. Binney.

Newton, Maulmain, April 21, 1847.

Notwithstanding the order for further retrenchment, the missionaries acquiesced in Mr. Binney's proposal to go on with their work, conducting everything according to the most rigid economy, and assuming the responsibility themselves. Thus, for that year, no part of the work was abandoned. The next year Mr. Binney writes the Foreign Secretary again:

DEAR·BROTHER: The Karen missionaries of the Maulmain Station held a meeting last Friday afternoon, which will not soon pass from the memory of those upon whom devolved the responsibility of voting. The Secretary laid before the meeting a statement of the pecuniary embarrassments of the department. It appeared from your last letter to the Secretary of the Maulmain Mission, that we are to regulate our expenditures for the year 1848 according to the reduced rates allowed us last year.

Then followed a statement of the amount allowed for each department, and the lowest estimate of what was needed to carry on the work which must be done if the mission be sustained at all.

The question now arose, "What shall we do?" We cannot assume the responsibilities as we did last year, when there remained some little ground of hope that the few remaining supporters of missions in this country would help us; and by their kind aid, together with the providence of God, which reduced some of our liabilities, we were relieved. It would be rashness to rely upon that aid another year: those friends have left the place. Besides, it is impossible for three or four men to assume the responsibilities for any length of time, which the American Baptist Missionary Union declines. Under these embarrassing circumstances, there was much said with perfect unanimity of opinion and feeling; but no one was willing to make a motion. Mr. Binney then stated, that he considered himself here the servant of an Executive Committee; that his business was not to provide funds, but judiciously and faithfully to use such as were committed to him; that considering what he was about to do as the necessity of circumstances in which the Executive Committee placed him, he felt relieved of all accountableness in the case. After this statement, he moved, first, that the Sgau Karen boarding-school be dismissed, and the pupils assisted, as far as funds will allow, to return to Burmah Proper. A dead silence ensued, no one would second the motion, and it was lost. He then moved that one-third of the Karen assistants in Burmah Proper, and one-fourth of all the other Karen assistants of this station be dismissed. Again a dead silence followed; no one would second the motion, and it was lost. He then moved, thirdly, that the amount allowed to the Theological Seminary be reduced to five hundred rupees, and that the number of pupils and period of study be adjusted to that amount. This motion was also lost, like the previous ones. Respecting the Normal School, there was a full expression of confidence and deep interest, and the conviction that nowhere would retrenchment for the year be more seriously felt; no one would move to reduce the amount for its support. The question then returned, What is to be done? After much further deliberation, it was finally proposed; and, because we could do nothing else, it was resolved,—

1. That we will conduct our operations as economically as may consist with the existence of the various departments of the Karen Mission; that we will hold ourselves jointly responsible to pay any balance that may remain against the Karen Department at the close of the year; and that we earnestly request the Executive Committee to make an additional appropriation, sufficient to cover the expenses of the year.

2. That should the Executive Committee feel themselves compelled to withhold from us their support, we do respectfully request that they will at once call us home, as we are useless here if deprived of the means of working with and for the people.

Other remarks follow, and the letter closes by saying:

We have thus given you a simple record of the doings of the meeting as the best, and indeed the only, appeal we can make in the case. That we may not be misunderstood, however, we will state respecting the second of the above resolutions, that it is not a hasty act. By a reference to the letters long since sent to the Secretary it will be seen that we have fully represented that the operations of the Karen Mission had been so trammelled, that the work had ceased to progress. It is no longer a matter of opinion; many retrograde steps are already taken; your Mission as a whole is fast sinking; and the course now being pur-

sued must inevitably ruin it, unless God, in his sovereign pleasure, does for it what we have no right to anticipate.   We are
your missionaries; and we wish, in all fidelity, to perform our
duties to you; but we are first of all ministers of Christ, and we
must perform our duties to him; we are missionaries to the Karens, and owe somewhat to their souls; we do not mean to forsake them.   We are assured that if the Baptist Denomination
say, they cannot support this Mission, God will put it into the
hearts of others to do what the Baptists decline.   We are Baptists, and whole-hearted Baptists; but we are first, and above all
Christians, and if our own denomination will not reap this field
already white to harvest, we most earnestly desire to get out of
the way, in order that others may be permitted to do it.   With
the assurance that we are most anxious to co-operate with you
and to abide by your desires so far as we can do so with a good
conscience, we remain affectionately

Yours in the Gospel.

With all these discouragements, Mr. Binney had
abundant evidence that the Lord was blessing his work,
neither had he the most distant thought of ever leaving
it, till called to his final rest.   But God's ways were not
his ways.   Mrs. Binney's physician, most unexpectedly
to her and him, urged the necessity of his taking her
"home" without delay.   The brethren of the Mission,
at a meeting called for the purpose, united in the request; and Dr. Judson, then very ill, and about to embark for the Isle of Bourbon in pursuit of relief from
suffering which he had little prospect of obtaining, advised him not to wait till it was too late ; the rainy season was close at hand, and there was no time for delay.
Miss Wright had just come out from America to assist
in the Normal School, and Miss Vinton, already in
charge, would remain with her.   This relieved him of

anxiety as to the Normal School. He wrote to Mr. Beecher, then at Sandoway, to come to the Theological School; there was not time to wait for a reply, but Mr. Harris consented to take charge till Mr. Beecher should come; and so, with only a few days' preparation, they left their loved work and took passage on board an English sailing vessel for London, just six years from the time of their arrival in Burmah.

Eighteen months before, Mrs. Binney wrote to her brother:

As you see by the date of this letter I have entered on my fortieth year; and yesterday was the fifteenth anniversary of my marriage; can you think of your "little sister" as being so very old? Yesterday, Joseph and I were reviewing the past; we have little time for reviews now; the present so engrosses us that we almost fulfil the injunction to "forget the things that are behind;" up to the time of our coming to this country, you knew my past, a part of it at least, better than I do myself; and if you knew our experience here, you would say I am sure, as my dear husband did yesterday, "Goodness and mercy still follow us in a very remarkable degree." Everywhere, as you know, but here more than before we came, we have been and are all and in all to each other. I receive all the tender love as well as all the confidence and respect that my heart desires, and we are both happy. You hardly need to have me say this; but while I am so far from you, I know you will let me say it now and then, if I like to do so. Joseph, I can see, is a little anxious about my health. I am not. I did not expect to live many years when I came to this country, and I remember our precious mother, when I was trying to hide her grey hairs by brushing them under, used to tell me that I would never be troubled in that way. My husband said yesterday, that if on leaving his Church in Savannah, he could have known that he would only live long enough to accomplish what the Lord has permitted us to do here, he would not have hesitated a moment. Do not be alarmed, lest if I grow worse, I should go home. We have not the most distant idea of ever seeing your dear face again, though I would give anything short of sacrificing conscientious convictions to do so. May the Lord deal as tenderly by you and yours as he does by us."

But when physicians and friends advised Mrs. Binney's immediate return, she for once was not consulted, but loving hearts and skilful hands planned and prepared all that was necessary for her comfort.

CHAPTER XIII.

ON THE SHIPS SUTLEJ AND ARAB.

1850.

SO quietly and quickly had all necessary preparations been made, that Mrs. Binney, almost before she knew it, found herself on ship-board, and putting out to sea, bound for her native land *via* England. But an unexpected delay occurred. Under date of April 28th, 1850, she writes:

Having left our precious, consecrated home at Newton, on the 22d inst., about ten o'clock, A. M., we immediately came on board and put our cabins in order, ready for sailing; several of the dear Missionaries and others, as well as many of the Karens, including the pupils of both schools, accompanied us to the ship, to all of whom we were soon obliged to say, "farewell." It was very trying to us to leave our dear Everitt (Ghnapoo), he is such a noble, manly, Christian lad, and loves us as a son. The poor boy was almost heart-broken, and would gladly have left everything on earth to accompany us, but he is so favorably situated for acquiring some knowledge of medicine in the hospital at Maulmain, that we thought best to leave him there. The Steamer Proserpine towed us over the "flats," where we anchored just off Amherst, almost in sight of our precious home. There we were obliged to remain six days, whilst the captain returned to town to attend to some business which he could not complete before we left. As we were hourly expecting his return, we were obliged to remain on board. We found our patience sadly tried; the weather was

very hot, and the motion of the ship much worse than if we had
been under sail. I was so exceedingly weak when we came on
board that I could not sit up much, and the heat and sea-sickness made me too ill to write a line till to-day. Almost every
night we have had severe thunder and lightning, with high wind
and heavy showers. It made us very sad, too, to think that we
might not only have been spared so much discomfort, but that
the time might have been spent with the dear Karens, several
companies of whom came down to see us after we left, as our
letters informed us. Six precious days in which to have coun-
selled, instructed, and comforted them, to have united with them
in prayer for each other, have seemingly been lost; still we comforted ourselves with the thought that even this, as dear husband
said last night, was included in the "all things" which would
work together for their and our good. Our season of labor
among them for the present, at least, is past, and it is a very
solemn thought.

About daylight this morning. we weighed anchor, and with a
light breeze, are leaving sight of land, and, though I cannot yet
realize it, are actually on our way to the land of our birth, of beloved relatives and friends, of tenderest ties and associations, to
which nearly seven years ago we bade adieu, as we then thought,
for ever. I had not at that time the most distant idea of ever
returning, and should have thought it sinful to cherish such an
idea had it been suggested. But I believe we have committed
our way unto the Lord, and he has directed our steps: it may
indeed have been our last adieu. We may, one or both of us,
find our last resting place in this never resting ocean on which
we have embarked. God grant us preparation of heart for all
his will, whether it be for soon meeting him in sudden death, for
prostration by sickness, or a faithful discharge of the active
duties of life in the new scenes before us.

We have a fine ship of six hundred and fifty tons; in all
twenty souls on board, but only one passenger besides ourselves,
Mr. D., a young officer in the Honorable East India Company's
service. With the captain, first mate, and three passengers, we
are five at table.

As soon as the ship was fairly out to sea, and all
things comfortably arranged, Mr. Binney proposed a
blessing at the table and religious services on the Lord's
Day, to which the Captain most cheerfully assented.
As any one knowing Mr. Binney would expect, these
services were not a mere form; he felt that he had as
truly a mission to perform as when among the Karens.
He maintained the strictest regard to his relation to the
officers of the ship and his fellow-passengers, but he labored for, and expected, "souls for his hire."

There were one or two Christian men among the
sailors, who were roused to a sense of their duty, and
helped by their prayers and personal conversation. At
times the captain and officers seemed deeply impressed,
but Mr. D., was determined not to be influenced by a
missionary. He became really insulting. Mrs. Binney's
journal, from which the history of the voyage is con-
densed, records his walking overhead with heavy boots
during prayer, stamping on the deck when he knew
they were sleeping at midnight, laughing aloud in time
of prayer, sitting up to a late hour smoking just in front
of their cabin. One marvels at the forbearance which
rendered such conduct possible. The Captain at first
seemed greatly annoyed, but finally probably thought it
to be for his interest to take sides with Mr. D.

But at length other trials brought matters to a crisis.
The ship had been well furnished with provisions, but
there was no proper steward to look after them; every
thing had been used lavishly, and carelessly exposed to
the monkeys, kids, and goats on board. About the
time when the ship reached the Cape of Good Hope

20

there was no tea or sugar left, the flour had become mouldy, and the rice even worse. Everything that could be killed had been used to supply the call for fresh meat, and the case was becoming alarming. Salt junk and seamen's bread, that was not fit for them to eat, was all the food left. Head winds were encountered at the Cape, so that fifteen days were spent in the effort to round it.

During the first ten days of this time, the ship was a pandemonium. All on board apparently began drinking to excess; the Captain's stores of liquor had become low, but Mr. D., had a good supply left. Finally, one evening, while Mr. D., was using very obscene language, Mr. Binney reminded him that there was a lady within hearing. This very proper remark highly incensed Mr. D. He immediately went to his cabin, and in a moment came out with a drawn sword, rushed upon deck like a mad-man, threatening Mr. Binney's life and pursuing him in every direction. Mr. Binney called upon the Captain for protection; the men sprang forward ready to disarm him at the Captain's word; but he refused, saying, " My business is to sail the ship; settle your own quarrels."

With difficulty Mr. Binney escaped, took refuge with Mrs. Binney in their own cabin, and secured the door. Mr. D., however, inserted his sword through the venetian blinds, and remained for some time watching for an opportunity to make good his threats; but finally retired to his berth, where he slept off his insanity by the side of his unsheathed sword. In the morning, finding himself in this perilous condition, he reproached the

Captain for allowing him the use of the sword while in such a state.

On leaving the cabin, Mr. Binney told his wife, that he thought she might banish fear, as he felt pretty sure that whoever was the nominal Captain, he himself would now be heard and regarded. He went boldly up on deck, and as Mr. D., came up offered his hand, saying, "Good morning, Mr. D." It was refused with the reply "Have you forgotten the insult of last evening to an English Officer, Mr. Binney?" "Come, come, Mr. D., this has gone far enough; walk with me," and drawing his arm by a gentle force within his own, they walked the deck for more than an hour. Soon after, Mr. D., came to Mrs. Binney, who was sitting below at the door of her cabin, offered her his hand, and when she took it, burst into tears, saying, "Mr. Binney said you would, but I could not believe you would touch my hand." She had little opportunity to speak, as he had himself a great deal to say. He pledged himself there and then to touch no intoxicating drinks till he reached his father's house in England; and said that if he had had any one to talk to him while in Burmah, as Mr. Binney had done now, he need never have been sent home for his health. From that moment Mrs. Binney had a charge. To read with, talk to, interest, and keep him from other influences was not a small task for an invalid. She had earnestly asked the Lord to give her some work for him on board the ship, but did not dream of the way in which her prayer was to be answered. But the Captain's anger was aroused. He had sacrificed a great deal to keep on good terms with the young military officer, and now, he had lost not only the respect of others in doing it, but even that of the young gentleman himself; he urged him to drink "moderately" and brought ridicule to bear upon him. Mr. D., was weak, and as yet there was little evidence that he had sought strength from above, but he was seriously alarmed for himself, and leaning on a human arm. The mate had acknowledged to Mr. Binney, that one night there was no one sober enough on board to manage the ship, and seeing their danger, he had pledged himself to drink nothing intoxicating during the remainder of the voyage.

On the second morning after the talk with Mr. D., Mr. Binney met the Captain on deck, and said pleasantly but seriously,

" Good morning Captain, I had a walk with Mr. D., the other morning, which I think has done him good. I am anxious for a little conversation with you, and that it may not attract attention will you join me in my morning walk?"

" No, sir, I want no preaching, and will not hear it ; if you have anything to say to me, we will have witnesses."

To this Mr. Binney gladly assented. The chief mate and Mr. D., were called, and one or two seamen lingered near. Mr. Binney then rehearsed without interruption, the story of the voyage, acknowledging all that had been kind and good, of which there had been much, but showing him that he had neglected the proper care of his provisions till we were almost starving; that he used wine, beer, and even brandy to a degree that few

men could bear without being intoxicated, and that he
had nearly been so more than once; that he himself had
no protection when life was in danger; and that he allowed
or caused animals such as monkeys, and a young bear
to be so teased and tortured, that neither his wife nor he
could stay on deck to witness it, though they could not
escape the cries of the poor creatures. All this was
done, he thought, to spite him for faithful performance
of duty. He had now gone so far, that he was sure of
being able to take the ship from him by reporting him
to the proper authorities at St. Helena. This he said
he was resolved to do, unless there was a decided
change in his conduct. He showed him at the same
time from "The Marine Laws of Great Britain," which
he held in his hand, how completely he had forfeited
his right to the ship.

A wonderful change was effected. Mr. Binney was
really the master on board, and though he treated every
one with studied respect, his wishes were consulted on
every occasion. The poor little monkeys and all the
animals, with an instinct which was wonderful to see,
seemed to recognize him as their benefactor. Though
he never petted them much, they would follow him
about and walk the deck by his side continually, ready
to lie down by him when he should be seated.

Fortunately, the reformation which had been effected
was not long tried; the wind proved favorable, the Cape
was rounded, and the trade winds took the ship without
further trouble into the beautiful harbor of St. Helena.
Seventy vessels of different descriptions went in about
the same time, all more or less disabled, by the gales

20*

which they had encountered, except the "Sutlej" and the American ship "Arab." On arrival, the Captain kindly took Mr. Binney to the American Consul, the venerable Mr. Carrol, who at once invited him, with Mrs. Binney, to make his house their home while they stayed at St. Helena. Here, with Mr. Carrol and his two accomplished and amiable daughters, they found rest and a home indeed. Here they also were greeted by Mr. Wells, who had come out nearly seven years before with them in the ship "Charles" as supercargo. He was now one of the owners of the "Arab," in which he was returning, with his lovely young sister from Calcutta. He introduced his old friends to the Captain of his ship, and arrangements were soon made for their return in the "Arab;" and in order to make it comfortable for them Mr. Wells gave up his own cabin. There was another fine large ship in harbor, and Mr. Binney being very reluctant to subject Mr. Wells, whose health was a good deal impaired by his residence in Calcutta, to so great discomfort, applied to the Captain for a passage. He said he had several vacant cabins, and wanted passengers, but would not take Missionaries at any price. The next day he dined at Mr. Carrol's, with the Captain of the "Sutlej," who spoke of his former passengers in such high terms, that he offered to take them at a mere nominal price; but their friends of the "Arab" would not give them up, and so three days after landing at St. Helena, on the morning of September 2d, they were on their way to Boston, under very favorable circumstances.

The two or three days at St. Helena were full of interest. As soon as it was known that Mr. Binney was at Mr. Carrol's, Mr. Janish, the pastor pro-tem. of the little Baptist Church, called and requested him to preach for them at 7 P. M. It was then past mid-day, but the news spread, and the chapel was filled with men and women hungry for the bread of life. At the close, almost the whole congregation pressed round him, asking him to preach again the next evening, to which he gladly consented. It was with great difficulty that he was able to leave the island so soon. They were eager to have him stay with them till another good opportunity for returning, recommending the salubrity and healthfulness of their " sea-girt isle," and assuring him, that his expenses would be duly met. Mr. Carrol joined in the request and offered a home ; but Mrs. Binney needed medical treatment, and they could not safely remain.

When Mr. Binney went on board the " Sutlej " to bid the sailors " good-by," the warm, hearty " God bless you," " We shall always thank the Lord for this voyage," " Pray for us," from many lips, seemed an abundant reward for all the discomforts and perils endured. While at St. Helena Mr. and Mrs. Binney were taken by a gentleman of the island, in his own carriage, to visit the house built for Napoleon, but which he never occupied, as he died before its completion ; also to see Napoleon's tomb, then empty, his remains having been carried to France a short time before. They also visited the grave of Mrs. Sarah B. Judson, which possessed a far deeper and tenderer interest for them. It was in a sweet, quiet resting-place ; but seemed very lonely, so far from all she had loved in either hemisphere; but her gentle spirit would doubtless have chosen it rather than the "rough ocean bed" in which Dr. Judson had now already been laid. Such were the thoughts expressed to each other; so difficult is it to make the unseen the real. Their fellow passenger of the "Sutlej" kept with them everywhere while on the island, and, with a Bible as a parting gift, they left him with sincere regret, but not without hope that they would meet again with great joy. And here the record is gratefully made that a few years since, when last heard from, he was not only honorably discharging his duty as an officer in Her Majesty's Service, but most loyally serving the "King of kings."

The passage from St. Helena to Boston had few incidents to record. Everything was pleasant; a small but airy cabin; a good table and willing assistants; the Captain gentlemanly and kind; the seamen competent and obedient; the discipline firm, but not obtrusive; passengers most agreeable, and the weather for the most of the way fine. Mr. Binney brought out his books and commenced his old way of employing his time at sea. He had not unpacked his books which he brought from Maulmain before; and with the exception of some little reading aloud to his wife, sick and alone when he left her, he had no heart to read. Now he was happy. One very large element in causing the difference in the two parts of the passage, was that there was no intoxicating drink seen on board the "Arab." One Saturday morning the Captain told the passengers they might make everything ready for landing in Boston the next morn-

ing. On retiring at night Mr. Binney remarked that he
had never seen a ship in such perfect trim. The small sa-
loon looked like a lady's best parlor, and all that scour-
ing, painting, and "tidying up," could do, had been done.
Before morning, however, all learned by a new experience
that it was not well to "boast of to-morrow." A severe
gale struck the vessel suddenly, the Captain put out to sea
for safety, and a succession of head winds kept them
there. There was confusion, sea-sickness, and a good
deal of discomfort; but though greatly disappointed, all
were patient and thankful for preserving mercy. Twelve
days later the little "Arab" came into Boston harbor
safe and sound, looking as if she had never seen a gale.
Friends were anxiously awaiting her arrival, and even
Mrs. Binney's doubts as to whether they would meet
with a warm "welcome home" soon vanished. The
first greeting of the Foreign Secretary was, "This is
most providential; we need you here, Mr. Binney;" and
many afterwards echoed the sentiment.

CHAPTER XIV.

PASTORAL LABORS NORTH AND SOUTH.

1850–1855.

AFTER a few weeks spent in Boston and vicinity, with Mr. Binney's relatives and friends, and with Dr. Pattison, then Professor in the Theological Seminary at Newton, they went to New York for medical advice and treatment for Mrs. Binney. At the same time Mr. Binney spent two or three months in New York and Philadelphia laboring in behalf of the Foreign Mission cause. Their home while in New York was with the Rev. Edward Lathrop and family. Mr. Lathrop, now so well known as Rev. Dr. Lathrop, of Stamford, Connecticut, was a member of the Baptist Church, in Savannah, while Mr. Binney was its pastor, and although he was but a small part of the time in Savannah, they had been brought into close and tender relations, and it was pleasant to these two men of kindred spirit thus to meet again, though in new and quite different relations. The one was no longer a student struggling with difficulties, but a successful pastor of a large city church; whilst the other had relinquished that prize, and, like his Master, had humbled himself and become poor, that others might, through him, become rich; but the same

236

mind that was in Christ Jesus was in them both, and they were "mutual helpers of each other's joy." In Philadelphia, his home for a few weeks was in the genial, hospitable family of the Rev. Dr. A. D. Gillette, then a pastor in the city. He had never met Dr. Gillette before, but a long acquaintance was not necessary to the formation of a friendship which was ever afterwards a source of great happiness to Mr. Binney.

As the cold weather came on he found the exposure of preaching every Lord's Day in a new pulpit, and often two or three times a day in different pulpits, too trying for his throat, and was admonished that he might have to desist from public services altogether, unless he could preach under more favorable circumstances. He therefore accepted an invitation from the E. St. Baptist Church at Washington, D. C., to supply their pulpit for a few months. As he was still hoping to return to Burmah, he would not have entertained any proposal for a permanent settlement. That winter in Washington was an exceedingly pleasant one to both Mr. and Mrs. Binney; the health of the latter was somewhat improved, and Mr. Binney loved to preach to appreciative audiences, which he uniformly commanded. He formed that winter some pleasant acquaintances, which not only made him richer in personal friends, but exerted a decided influence upon his usefulness while in America, and subsequently in Burmah. J. S. Bacon, D. D., was then President of Columbian College, and he and his interesting family attended the E. St. Church. Most of the Faculty, with the students, attended also. Mr. Binney and Prof. Wm. Ruggles, LL. D., were thrown much together, and a warm, personal attachment was formed. Then commenced Dr. Ruggles' deep interest in the Foreign Mission work, especially in the Educational part, as inaugurated among the Karens of Burmah. As is well known by all who have been interested in the details of that department of labor, he bestowed very liberal benefactions upon its various organizations so long as he lived. Other members of the Faculty became his admirers and friends, and were loved by him in return to the very close of life. Under date of March 12th, 1851, Mr. Binney wrote from Washington the following letter to the Rev. S. Peck, D. D., Cor. Sec. of the A. B. M. Union:

DEAR BROTHER:—You have doubtless been expecting for some time to receive some intimation of our future course. Under other circumstances it would have been my duty long since to have written you, but I have not known what to say. At no period since I left Maulmain should I have been able to speak with much encouragement about our return to Burmah. The state of Mrs. Binney's health, which induced us to leave, has never allowed us much hope of returning. She has now been home sufficiently long to afford something of an indication of our future prospects, and though we hope she may, under favorable circumstances, live with some degree of comfort and usefulness, we cannot see that it would be duty for us to return. Her health is not essentially improved. She is somewhat stronger so long as she makes little exertion, but the least excitement or fatigue prostrates her; so we have at length decided that we ought not longer to think of resuming the work in Burmah. I wish, therefore, to ask that my relation to the Mission may be dissolved. I intend again to become a pastor so soon as God may open the way, in which relation I hope still to be useful to the cause of Foreign Missions.

I think I need not say to you with what pain we have contemplated leaving our labor for and with the Karens. Their mental and moral capabilities, their rapid improvement, and the blessing of God so richly resting on every consistent effort in their behalf, have been enough to repay any sacrifice ; and their · grateful attention and devotion have bound them to us by ties not easily sundered. On the whole, however, our duty is plain. May God be gracious to them and make for them suitable provisions.

In communicating this to the Executive Committee, please give them my best thanks for all their sympathy and co-operation while in the Mission, and for their cordial welcome home again, with assurance that

I am very truly yours and theirs,

J. G. BINNEY.

When this decision was known, the E. St. Church began to look to Mr. Binney as their future pastor. Most of the leading men, even those who had not been accustomed to act in concert, came to him expressing their desire that he would allow his name to be brought before the church, and a meeting was held unknown to him for the purpose. Through some misunderstanding the meeting was adjourned, and the subject of choosing a pastor not even mentioned. A day or two after, the fact came to his knowledge. It looked like a want of harmony somewhere. Though he had no reason to suppose there was any difference of opinion, with regard to himself, still it might lead to that, if it did not already exist, and he acted with promptness. The following letter will explain itself.

"WASHINGTON, 1851.

TO THE CLERK OF E. ST. BAPTIST CHURCH.—DEAR BROTHER : When first invited by you to Washington, I had not determined to remain in this country, and consequently could not think

21

about a settlement. I was glad, however, to accept your invita-tion to spend the winter months here, which gave me a tempo-rary sphere of usefulness in a milder climate. The future, I was willing to leave to him in whose hands I cheerfully leave my all.

When, a few weeks since, I decided not to return to Burmah, I stated that much, not supposing any formality with the church on the subject necessary. Having heard before, from what I supposed every part of the church, the kindest expressions, I was willing the church should make any proposal desired, and was prepared to give no unfavorable interpretation to what might appear to be the will of God in the case.

I was not aware till last evening of your meeting on Monday night. I should exceedingly regret to be even the innocent cause of any difficulty about me. It was never supposed possi-ble that I could be a party man, or accept a party vote, or con-sent to remain in a church divided about myself. On the con-trary, it has thus far been, by the grace of God, my happy lot to be always a healer of breaches and a restorer of confidence and peace in the church. I could not remain in Washington to do otherwise.

I hasten, therefore, to inform you that it will be necessary to make some other provision for your pulpit after next Lord's Day. With this please present to the Committee for the 'Supply of the Pulpit,' the assurance of my kindest regards and of my strongest desires for their comfort and usefulness, individually and col-lectively; and I shall not cease to pray that the grace of our Lord Jesus Christ may be ever with them and the whole church, and send them speedily a pastor after their own heart.

Very affectionately yours and theirs in the gospel,

J. G. BINNEY.

P. S.—I ought to state, I have had no communication with any person on this subject. The state of the case was learned only by a remark or two in the family at the tea-table."

The following Lord's Day Mr. Binney closed his ser-vices for the E. St. Baptist Church. While the congregation had greatly increased, and the church had been considerably quickened, there had been few conversions. This fact led to serious heart-searchings on his part, and the sermon was calculated to produce the same effect in the church. The parting was solemn and tender.

The next morning found Mr. and Mrs. Binney on their way to New York. This arrangement was made chiefly that Mrs. Binney might be near her physician, and Mr. Binney was sure of finding work for the Master there, while waiting the further development of Providence.

During the remainder of the spring and early summer Mr. Binney supplied various destitute pulpits in New York City, as from week to week invited. Early in July, he received a letter from the church in Elmira, New York, asking him to supply their pulpit the following Lord's Day. He had no engagement, and the country was inviting, so he gladly accepted the invitation. The New York and Erie Railroad, which had not long been opened, afforded some charming scenery. The place itself, at this season of the year, was very attractive, and the people hospitable and cordial. His heart went out to them in return, and they all had a "good time." He promised to be with them the Lord's Day following, and hastened back the next day to his wife, whom he had left very unwell. The church did not wait, however, for him to visit them again, but called a meeting, and agreed to invite him to a permanent settlement with them. They requested him, in case he could accept their invitation, to bring Mrs. Binney with him,

so that he need not return to New York. He accepted
their call, and as soon as she was able to bear the journey, he assumed the pastoral office among them. He
was very candid, and told them that the first winter
might affect him as it had done before, take away his
voice ; but he was willing to make the trial, hoping that
there would be no unkind feeling should such prove the
case. His fears were realized, and even as early as the
following November he was beginning to suffer from the
climate. His old bronchial troubles returned, and he
did not hesitate to let some of his Southern friends
know that he was likely to be compelled to seek a
Southern climate. He soon received an invitation to
"come to Augusta to spend the winter." This, under
the circumstances, he declined to do, but it led to a correspondence which resulted in the acceptance of a call
to become their pastor.

He was in Elmira about six months. His stay was
too short to accomplish any very marked results, in his
way of working ; but it was admitted by all that he left
the church working together more harmoniously and
systematically than when he began his labors with them.
There had been a considerable addition to its members
by letters, and he had the great joy of baptizing from
time to time new converts and receiving them into the
church. The church and community were appreciative
and kind, and Mr. and Mrs. Binney were happy. The
six months' residence with their kind brethren and
friends in Elmira formed an exceedingly pleasant episode
in their lives.

An incident which occurred a short time before they

left may furnish a useful suggestion to others. Mr. Binney had called together the deacons and leading members into his study, where he laid before them his invitation from Augusta, and the probability of his acceptance. That they might understand his motive fully, he told them, what he had before carefully concealed, that he had received invitations to visit three different city churches since coming to Elmira, and that he had also been written to concerning several professorships, to all of which he had refused to listen. But this call to Augusta seemed to offer him a sphere of usefulness where he might reasonably hope to remain. They assured him that no one who knew the circumstances could blame him for leaving them so soon. He then left the room to speak to a person who desired to see him. On his return, one of the deacons said to him:

"What will you do with this furniture, Mr. Binney? We understand the furniture in the room is yours."

"Yes; I must send it to the auction rooms and take what it will bring. I suppose there is not enough for a sale here."

"Well, we have already sold it for you, conditionally, while you were out. Brother A. will take the book-case; Brother B., the chairs, and so on; as to the carpet, it is on the floor, and your host must take that; but never mind *who* takes the furniture; if you can give us your bills so that we may know what you paid for it, you can just let the things stand where they are till you leave."

A few days after, when he did leave, the money for the furniture was handed him with tickets for the

21*

through train to Augusta. They said to him as they put these in his hands, "We did not quite like the looks of this, paying you to leave us, but we do not know the custom of the Southern churches, and whether they propose to meet the expenses of your journey. If they do not, it would of course come out of your own pocket; and if they do, this addition will not come amiss just now."

He assured them the Augusta Church would take good care of him. But this token of their regard was pressed on him; and coming at the parting hour, when he would naturally be sad and depressed, it was very cheering.

For the second time, he was accepting a pastorate in Georgia, when scarcely able to take the journey, and with a wife still more feeble; this time, however, they were not going among strangers, but knew that a warm welcome awaited them. In truth, it must be recorded, they had a yearning desire to go South; they felt in going back to Georgia, though not to the same church, that they were going among friends. On arriving at the depot in Augusta, the first person that greeted them was old Marcus, Dr. Turpin's coachman, the same who had driven them on the unfortunate evening of the overthrow into the ditch.

"Well, well, Marcus, how are you? After all these years you are looking as young and hale as ever."

"Yes, Mr. Binney, a good master and mistress, and light work have kept old Marcus in pretty good condition; and I reckon you have been serving a good Master too, or you would never have got back here safe again;

though you both look a little worn, as if you might have had hard work. Well, there is a person over there looking after your trunks, and my orders are to bring you at once to my old master and mistress, who will think the time very long till they see your faces."

This was a specimen of the warm greetings which awaited them on all hands. When they left the North the snow lay deep on the ground; and here, after only three days of travel, vegetation was covering its face, and roses and fruit trees were in blossom. The air was balmy, and Mr. Binney after a few weeks was a new man.

On the last day of February, 1852, he was publicly recognized as pastor of the Church. Rev. W. T. Brantly, of Athens University, preached the sermon; Rev. H. O. Wyer, of Savannah, addressed pastor and people, and Rev. W. I. Hard, of the Augusta Church, gave the right hand of fellowship. Mr. Wyer's address was eloquent and touching, and brought vividly to mind scenes of thrilling interest in which they had formerly been associated. A short extract is given.

You remember, my brother, when in the last public assembly in which we ever met, I turned away from you with an overflowing heart, sorrowing most of all that I should see your face no more. You remember, I was among the brethren of your church who could not see it to be your duty to leave us; but seeing your face set towards Jerusalem, and that you heard a voice we could not hear, we bowed with submission, saying, "The will of the Lord be done." The pillar of cloud by day and fire by night went before you and stood by you, during your sojourn in Burmah, where you were a blessing to many. It has been lifted up and brought you safely back to us, and we rejoice in that our

eyes are again permitted to behold you in our midst. To charge
you to be faithful to the trust committed to you, would be inde-
corous in me. We all feel, your feet once planted in our midst,
your labors are commenced. Lift up your eyes, my brother, and
behold these whitened fields, here you will find ample scope, in
promoting the interests of the Redeemer's cause, for all the rich
and varied qualifications which you bring to the work. Your experience as a pastor ; your power and eloquence as a preacher ;
your critical Biblical knowledge ; your enlarged knowledge of
mankind, as seen in the poor and degraded, as well as in the
highest walks of life—all will but enable you the more successfully to gather here souls into the kingdom.

You remember, my brother, when in Savannah, you once expressed to me the opinion that there was no place where you
could do so much for your Master. Others thought so too.
Mysterious was the providence that took you from us. You are
now placed in a similar situation, with richer qualifications for
successful labor. God has been mindful of his people here, and
we look with confidence to see his work accomplished through
your instrumentality.

Much more that was kind was said, and he then addressed the church.

Under such circumstances, Mr. Binney commenced his
pastoral work in Augusta, and God blessed and prospered him in a wonderful degree. The church co-operated with him, backsliders were restored and sinners
converted; and though Mr. Binney was obliged occasionally to obtain help for a single sermon, yet the bronchial affection, which was always like a drawn sword
suspended by a hair over him, had never given him less
anxiety since he left Savannah in 1843. Mrs. Binney's
health was steadily improving. All this was interpreted
to mean that God designed them to make Augusta a

permanent residence. The old parsonage was put in good order for their use, and furnished pleasantly and comfortably. Once more they had it in their power, as in former days, to receive their friends, both Northern and Southern, to their own home. The congregation had so rapidly increased that applicants for pews were obliged to be refused, and the church was contemplating an enlargement. In the meantime, other influences were at work, and he was embarrassed somewhat in interpreting them. The Executive Committee in Boston found it very difficult, even impossible, to supply his place suitably in Maulmain; and they, as well as some of the Karen missionaries in Burmah, were in constant correspondence with him; but he did not see it to be his duty to return to Burmah. Under date of March 23d, 1852, a short time only after his resignation, he wrote the following letter to Dr. Peck, which will show his state of mind:

My Dear Brother:—Yours of February 4th and March 5th were duly received, and would have been immediately acknowledged, but for the intention soon to answer them. The answer has been delayed solely because I did not know what to say. Never has my heart been more affected in behalf of those without the gospel, and never have I felt more interest for the Karens than during the past year. The importance of the place assigned me has appeared the greater to my mind by long and careful reflection, at a distance from the field.

There are, it is true, difficulties in the way of my return, which I have not mentioned, because a prior reason has really governed my course. I left Burmah on account of Mrs. Binney's ill health, and that alone has been sufficient to keep us at home. Such was really my position until invited to the South again. With a term of five years, with Mrs. Binney to return in two to five years, if necessary, the resumption of my work in Burmah was quite possible; and had the proposal come in time, I should seriously have thought of an immediate return, other things favoring, as I doubt not they would have done. But before any intimation of these views of the Executive Committee had reached me, I had committed myself to the church here; and my recognition had been arranged, so that I could not stay the process. I am now here. The people have received us with great confidence and affection, and their expectations are awakened. Can I leave them? Much as my heart has longed for such a quiet field of labor, permanently, I would not remain here for any merely personal interests. I know I am not my own. I wish to be and do only what is pleasing to God. But is it right so to disappoint this people? Would that please God? At present I can only say, that I do not know. I cannot say either Yea or Nay. I could not in any case leave before another Fall. By that time God may shed more light upon my path than I now see. In the meantime, if you can otherwise suitably provide for that department, that, of itself, would fully decide the case.

With best regards, affectionately your brother,

J. G. BINNEY.

Again, a few months later, he writes the Secretary as follows:

The truth is, I have made but little progress in thinking upon this subject. I do not mean that it gives me no thought. Far from that. It is seldom out of my mind many hours at a time. No other point has so many of my thoughts or so much of my anxiety. I wish to do right, so as to please God, and to be as useful as possible in the cause of Christ. So far as health is concerned it may now be assumed that there would be no difficulty in our going for five years; Mrs. Binney having full permission to return sooner, if desirable; beyond that, to be subject to the providence of God.

When we think only of the work to be done, of the Mission work among the Karens, or to the Karens themselves, our whole heart pleads to be there at once; we ask no more important sphere in life. But when we think of other things, of which you are not ignorant, we instantly exclaim: "If it be possible, let this cup pass from us"! Yet it might be our duty to drink that cup. But the great difficulty still remains, the effect of those things upon usefulness. Here my whole life tells for all that it is worth. Others wish to increase and make the most of my influence; will it be so there? I cannot afford, I have no right, to throw away a large part of what little I am and have. You see my difficulty in part.

As will be seen by the above letter, there were in Mr. Binney's mind obstacles in the way of his return besides health, but they were eventually so far removed, that he ventured to write his letter of acceptance of the proposal of the Board in June, 1853. He felt that the great question must be settled; it was affecting both his health and usefulness. The letter requires no special notice; accompanying it was a personal one to the acting Secretary, Edward Bright, D. D., in which he says:

The welfare of the Church has demanded a little delay. Questions of grave importance were before them, which might have been seriously affected by an untimely presentation of my decision. Their church edifice is being enlarged and improved. The money is subscribed and the work begun. I now hope all will be well with them.

His letter of resignation to the church was dated July 9th, 1853. Though not demonstrative, it is suggestive of suppressed expression of sorrow.

DEAR BRETHREN:—Early in June, I expressed to you my decision to enter again the mission work in Burmah, which must necessarily sever my relation with you as your pastor. As this is your last regular meeting before my departure, I seek this opportunity formally to resign my pastoral charge. In doing this, allow me to say, I have been influenced by no dissatisfaction with my present position, either for happiness or usefulness. In this church I have felt no want of confidence or affection, and it is with no ordinary pain that I leave you; but after contemplating the subject with much care and prayer, I think I could not retain a good conscience should I refuse to make the sacrifice required of me. The peculiar circumstances and wants of that Mission demand immediate and effective efforts for a native ministry, and God in his providence seems to lay upon me an imperative duty to resume that work. Painful as it is to sunder this intimate and endeared relation, and trying as are the circumstances through which we must necessarily pass, we feel that the grace of our Lord Jesus Christ will be sufficient for us and for the Church. We feel assured you will not forget us at the throne of grace, while we are so long subjected to the trials and perils of the sea, nor while in that far off land.

Accept my warmest thanks for the kindness with which you have regarded my labor, and the affectionate and respectful attentions which I have so uniformly and to the last received. Be assured, no distance can make us forget you ; and the recollections of Augusta will ever be to us a comfort in that land of strange men and things ; our prayers shall still be for you and your children, that God may ever give you his richest blessings.

Affectionately your brother,

J. G. BINNEY.

All needed preparations for the passage had been quietly made in their own home. As soon, therefore, as the resignation had been given, they disposed of their furniture and all appertaining to their cheerful home, and left for Boston to spend the short time before sailing with relatives. Difficulties and misunderstandings had for some time existed in the Mission, and a deputation consisting of S. Peck, D.D., the Secretary, and J. N. Granger, D.D., of Providence, authorized to act with the same powers as the Executive Committee had been sent out. The first letters from the deputation arrived soon after Mr. Binney reached Boston; they were of such a nature that they caused him to waver. No one had felt more desirous that more direct preaching should be done in Burmah than he; he had been the first to awaken a deeper interest in the minds of the Committee, as well as in Burmah, on this subject; but he contemplated no changes which would prevent his carrying out his views of education, which he had fully laid before the Board, as already given in this volume.

He mentioned his fears in a letter to some one of his Augusta friends. The Church at once caught at the possibility, after all, of his remaining at home, and promptly called a meeting and invited him, if such should be the case, to return to them at once. As an evidence of the earnestness of their desire, they offered to add several hundred dollars to his salary. This he had never expected or wished, but it was gratifying as an expression of esteem. The time of sailing drew nigh. The Committee assured him in a written communication that they had no doubt but he would be sustained in carrying out his views, especially with regard to the Theological School. His goods were put on board the vessel and the prospect was fair for another voyage in a sailing ship round the Cape.

Mr. Binney went into Boston, accompanied by Dr. Pattison, to complete some little preparations for sailing the next day; Mrs. Binney stayed at her brother's to

22

give the last touches to the work there.   On the return
of the two brothers from the ship they called in at the
Mission rooms.   The mail had arrived from Maulmain,
and all the letters from the deputation were read.   Their
purport was such that Mr. Binney retraced his steps to
the ship, ordered everything that belonged to him to be
taken off, and the next morning wrote to Dr. Bright,
Corresponding Secretary for the Home Department:

I have received your kind communication respecting the
action of the Executive Committee and the outline of the plan
for the reorganization of the Karen Theological Seminary.   I
need not say that I have given it a very careful consideration.
For the Theological Seminary itself, the plan is a good one.   It
clearly shows the desire of the Executive Committee to meet the
necessities of the Karen churches as well as to answer an engagement with me.   I do not see, under the circumstances, how
they could have done more or better.   Such a manifestation on
their part has made me anxious to comply with their wishes in
returning to Burmah.   Still the difficulty is not removed.   I
have from the first been influenced more by the consideration of
a general prospect of usefulness growing out of a concurrence of
favorable indications, than by any peculiar features of the case.
    You will more fully appreciate my difficulty by considering
the position I occupied on deciding to return.   When I resigned
my relation to the Union as their missionary, it was because I
had no reasonable promise that Mrs. Binney's health would
allow her permanently to live in Burmah.   You afterwards proposed my return for five years.   The question now before me
was, Can I in five years do in Burmah sufficient to repay what
must be lost at home if I comply with this request?
    You know how careful I was to ascertain all that might affect
this question; not whether I could be useful merely; nor whether,
if I should remain abroad ten or more years, the balance would
be in favor of my return, but whether I could reasonably believe
that would be the case in five years.   I should, indeed, be wil-

ling and expect to remain longer, if not providentially prevented; but my judgment could promise nothing beyond that short time. Mrs. Binney's health is too precarious. That I could do so much in five years seemed doubtful; but on the whole it seemed so much like it, that I preferred to risk a failure, rather than assume the responsibility of declining your appointment. The grounds of promise were, in part, that I could commence my work at once, to carry out the plan then approved, with some years' advance from my previous efforts, particularly in the Normal School; that in this I should have every facility for working from the first; that I should have the hearty co-operation of all concerned, both at home and in Burmah; and that, therefore, no time would be lost in decision and correspondence, but my whole time might be devoted to the one work. Hence I supposed it possible to do in five years enough to warrant the breaking up of all my plans, relations, and influences at home.

It will occur to you at once to see how great uncertainty is now thrown over every one of these points on which I relied. It is not necessary to mention other considerations, nor to enlarge on these; the position of everything is either changed or made uncertain. I am, therefore, constrained to the conclusion that it would not be right for me under these circumstances to enter the foreign field. I am aware how difficult it may be for some to appreciate fully my position; but I am myself compelled to act from six years' experience in the work, from an intimate acquaintance with the bearings of all these things on my influence and success. It was at first but a trembling decision; now the greatest considerations are made to reverse that decision, with little room for the shadow of a doubt.

Please accept for yourself, and present to the Executive Committee, my warmest acknowledgment for the kindness I have received in the consideration of this matter; they have gone as far under the circumstances as I could possibly expect. I fully appreciate their position, and am far from feeling that the failure is from any want of disposition on their part either to meet their engagement with me or to provide for the wants of the Karens. I regard the whole change as a part of God's providence, teaching me my duty with a clearness that will enable me hereafter to work at home with an approving conscience.

I ought perhaps to add, I have not the first unpleasant feeling toward your Deputation to Burmah, for any part they may have had in leading to this result; not only do I highly esteem them as men and brethren, but am thankful for the ability and fidelity with which they have performed their work in Burmah. Deeply as I regret the application of certain principles in education to the Karen Mission, it is perhaps better even than to do nothing, to break up the influence under which the Mission has so long suffered. I have not for some years had so much confidence as I now feel. It is my earnest prayer that God may enable you wisely and effectively to meet the great crisis of the Mission.

As ever, affectionately, your brother,

J. G. BINNEY.

Under the same date, he writes his acceptance of the conditional invitation he had received to return to the Augusta Church. While not wholly freed from anxiety as to the work he had left in Maulmain, he was relieved of the weight of personal responsibility with regard to it; and his elastic spirits resumed their normal state, and he indulges in expressions of great happiness in view of resuming the pastoral work. " This change," says he, " enables me to give up the foreign field with an approving conscience, while my heart retains all its interest for the Mission and the men who conduct it." He was absent from Augusta a little more than two months, just an ordinary holiday during the excessive heat of summer.

Mention has been made of an increase of salary on his return, which he had neither expected nor especially desired; he had all he needed. The incidents connected with this increase furnish one of the many illustrations which he experienced in life of the truth that " He that watereth shall be watered also himself." On leaving Augusta, as on leaving Savannah, he was greatly interested in securing a suitable successor. His predecessor, the Rev .Wm. T. Brantly, was then a Professor in Athens University; and Mr. Binney was anxious to see him in the pastoral work again, and named him to the church as being most desirable for them to obtain. All would have been united in him, but doubted if he could be persuaded to come to them, as the same reasons, to some extent, which induced him to resign still existed. Mr. Binney thought it worth the trial; and to assure him of their earnest desire, he advised them to offer him a larger salary than—they had ever given.

"As your pews rent now," said he to them, " you can do it, and it will show your appreciation of his services."

They thought that money would be but little object, as he had already an ample salary, and besides was not one to be eager for money.

" Certainly not; but he will probably be influenced by such an evidence of your appreciation."

" But," said they again, " we cannot do that, Mr. Binney; it would be unjust to you, and an implication that we should not like to make."

He assured them that he had never thought of that; and said that if they could secure a good pastor by it, he hoped no consideration of that kind would hinder them. When they asked him to come back to them, they mentioned this proposed increase of salary " as an

evidence of their appreciation which he would not fail
to interpret rightly."

On reaching Augusta, Dr. Turpin's carriage was
again in waiting, and his hospitable family were ready to
give him a hearty welcome; but another family were
also waiting anxiously their arrival. Mr. and Mrs. Benjamin Chew had recently parted with their eldest daughter, by her marriage, while their two younger daughters
were away at school. They were lonely, and wanted Mr.
and Mrs. Binney to take their large empty rooms, and
occupy the empty seats at their table; they must not
go to housekeeping again till rested, and one year must
be kept free from all domestic care and expense. They
were glad of the rest and the cheerful home; one year
passed rapidly away, and no change was allowed; they
remained under this hospitable roof till they were
obliged, nearly two years afterwards, to leave Augusta
altogether.

Although Mr. Binney returned to Augusta in good
health and spirits, yet, on resuming his work, it was
evident that the excitement and anxiety through which
he had passed, had somewhat weakened the general tone
of his system; at the same time the chronic affection of
the throat became so much worse that he often preached
with great pain, and his naturally fine voice was losing
much of its sweetness and power. For this reason,
several institutions of learning, supposing he might be
compelled to leave the pastoral office, had their thoughts
turned towards him. He was not actually elected to
any position for some time, but merely addressed "to
know if he would entertain a call of the sort." He de-

clined for some time, and kept everything of the kind a profound secret, for the sake of the institutions concerned, and especially that the church might not be disturbed by such rumors.

In the summer of 1854, however, he was appointed President of the new Theological Institution at Fair-mount, near Cincinnati, Ohio. This was done without having previously consulted him. He was interested greatly at the time in its success, and would probably have accepted the invitation but for a letter from one of the professors to Dr. Pattison, expressing some fear lest Mr. Binney would not be willing to co-operate with the men on the ground, and might be inclined to act too independently.

Mr. Binney wrote to his brother-in-law in reply:

I do not blame the Professor. He has had influences enough to awaken his fears, and he does not know me. I should not hesitate were that the only difficulty in the way, but that must be viewed in relation to the character of the work to be done. The work at Fairmount is new, and is not to prosper without much energy and decision of purpose somewhere. I should be ashamed not to take my share of the hard work, but the very elements of character essential to success as its leader would be likely to nourish suspicion now existing. I could not engage energetically in the work thus hampered. I rather regard the whole matter as an indication of Providence that I am to remain where I am at present. God will, doubtless, open some door when the time comes that I must relinquish preaching. Proverbs, iii. 5–6 has been my motto ever since I entered the Lord's service, and it has never failed me. I do feel that he has richly blessed me. Events, at first regarded as adverse, have, in almost every instance, proved introductory to my increased welfare and usefulness.

Another subject has given me anxiety. Mr. T. resigns at Savannah. The Committee of the church to procure a pastor have offered me the place with the hope of reuniting, if best, the two churches. That little church offers me $2000. If my throat would allow, I probably should feel it my duty to return to them, though I should be deeply grieved to leave Augusta, but I think I could do for Savannah what no other man could do, and much of their present trouble is in consequence of my having left them. I shall D. V. visit them in October and see what I can do for them. The yellow fever is now in Savannah and Charleston, and a few cases have been reported here; our people are getting alarmed; it is now only August, and about the worst month of the year for that disease is yet before us. Do not be anxious about us; we are in the best possible position for such a time. For us to live is Christ; still it is gain for us to die and be with him. We ought not, therefore, to be anxious about the fever. We can do our duty and trust the Lord.

Soon after, the yellow fever did make its appearance in Augusta; and one who has never been in like circumstances can scarcely imagine the panic. It was like being on board a burning ship, every one thought of his own safety and of those dependent on him. In two hours after it was known that two deaths had occurred nearly simultaneously in different parts of the city, every one who could do so was fleeing for his life.

Mr. and Mrs. Binney happened to be both engaged that morning in the back part of the house, and saw nothing for an hour or two of what was transpiring on the street, when a servant came rushing up saying, "Why I thought you had gone too, everybody has gone!" Sure enough, not a conveyance was to be had of any kind. The city authorities were removing all who were unable to go themselves, and every private carriage had left with its owners A friend two miles from the city had said to Mr. Binney the Sunday before, "If the yellow fever appears, take a carriage and come with Mrs. Binney to us at once." ·He succeded in getting a man to take a note to this friend, who immediately sent his carriage for them. The next morning Mr. Binney returned to town and caused it to be generally known, that from 8 A. M., till sunset he would be in town ready to visit the sick and dying of whatever class or denomination. One other pastor remained till he was taken himself, and then Mr. Binney remained alone. The Baptist Church was opened for service every Lord's Day; and, though some protested, it was well filled. There were enough, obliged to remain, who gladly came to listen to the words of one who spake as a dying man to dying men. Many heard the words of life who before the next Lord's Day were numbered with the dead. In a letter to his brother Jonathan of this date, he says:

I will do all I can for E. If I live, you may rely on me for fifty dollars in November, and the same in March. I have no money by me now. Such is the state of things in our city that I should not know where to get even fifty dollars. I have been all the morning seeking nurses and servants for the sick, and this afternoon I am to bury the dead. Juliette is about two miles from here with kind friends, and I go there at night, but through the day my place is with the sick and dying ; still I feel easy. Be sure that in life or death all will be well. God knows best what to do with and for us. Pray much for us.

Toward the close of the season, slight frosts having already appeared, and but few cases of the disease re-

maining, Mr. Binney decided to stay out of town altogether, unless sent for.   On the very day that his decision was made known in town, he himself was taken
with the fever.   Both he and his friends had been in
readiness to treat the case promptly should he need it
He was mercifully brought through the fever, and was
about again in a short time, but the effects of the whole
season upon him increased his inability to preach regularly.   The next winter the church gave him the means
of securing an assistant.   Young Boardman—now the
Rev. Geo. D. Boardman, D. D., the distinguished pastor
of the old First Church in Philadelphia—came at his
request and spent the winter months in Augusta, ren-
dering him considerable assistance..   The church expressed their readiness to employ permanent assistance
or a colleague, that he might not leave them, but he felt
himself still too young a man to do but half a strong
man's work, especially, if in some other department he
might do full service.

Augusta had special attractions for him, and he came
slowly and reluctantly to the conclusion, that a necessity of leaving them was laid upon him.   His labors
had been greatly blessed, and although at no time had
there been any remarkable revivals, as in former pas-
torates, yet the work resembled a regular succession of
showers and sunshine, enriching and vivifying the face
of nature, and causing the earth to bring forth fruit in
its season.   Dr. Brantly, in the article from which we
have already quoted, says of his success in Augusta :

There, as in Savannah, he soon attracted a large and intelligent congregation, and in a short time it became necessary, as

during his former charge, to add to the accommodations of the
house. His power in the pulpit was always rather that of a
teacher than a herald, and his missionary training tended still further to the education of this characteristic. But in Augusta he found
every Sunday many pupils delighting to sit at the feet of such
an instructor. A distinguished jurist of the state, a Presbyterian,
said to me, on learning that Mr. Binney had resigned his charge,
"Mr. Binney has had only a short career among us, but it has
been a brilliant one."

In his letter of resignation to the church he says,

Most sincerely can I repeat to you every expression of confidence and affection at any time before made. Few pastors have,
in the same time, had so little to annoy, and so much to make
them happy, with the people of their charge.

CHAPTER XV.

1855–1858.

AT the Annual Commencement of Columbian College, June, 1854, The Trustees and Faculty conferred on Mr. Binney the Honorary Degree of Doctor of Divinity, "In consideration" they say, "of your able and successful labors in the Christian ministry, and of the love, which you have manifested, and the efforts which you have made, for the promotion of sound Scriptural learning; hoping that this token of respect, coming from those who know and appreciate your character and course, will prove acceptable to you and contribute, in some small degree at least, to your usefulness." With unaffected simplicity he thanks them, saying, that this expression of esteem, so unexpected, and coming from the source it did, could not but give him pleasure.

On going to Elmira, in 1850, he found the people, both in Elmira and vicinity, universally calling him "Dr. Binney." As the degree had never been conferred upon him in any other way, than by that somewhat uncertain authority, Public Opinion, it was exceedingly unpleasant to him ; and he publicly requested those who regarded his feelings to call him by the only name to which he was honestly entitled. But it made lit-

262

tle difference; the habit was formed, and there it was his common appellation. In Georgia, he was always called "Mr. Binney;" and when the Degree was conferred, except in very rare cases, the title was never used. "You will always be Mr. Binney to us," they said, "and we cannot bear ever to call you anything else." He loved to have it so, but it is believed he had no conscientious scruples in the matter, looking upon this much as he did the title of "Reverend;" personally, it was of little importance.

The following winter, Rev. Dr. Bacon resigned the Presidency of Columbian College, when the Trustees, in connection with the Faculty, showed the sincerity of their profession of esteem by electing Dr. Binney to fill the place thus made vacant. He left Augusta and delivered his Inaugural Address at their Commencement, June, 1855, and at once entered upon his work in the interests of the College. How much he did directly to improve the finances of the College, is not so well-known to the writer. G. W. Samson, D.D., then the esteemed pastor of the E. Street Church, and afterwards his successor in the College, did more in that direction. Dr. Binney was, however, in correspondence with men of means, known for their interest in education, during his entire stay in Washington, and that not without considerable relief to the existing needs of the College; but Southern men felt it too little a Southern Institution to invest largely in it, and Northern men felt it too much a Southern Institution, for them to do much. Both North and South, however, were anxious that such an Institution, at the Capital of our country, should take a high stand. That his accepting this posi-

23

tion, was an encouragement and a stimulant, in making it what all desired, there is no doubt; while all freely admitted that everything which came within his province was conducted with the most rigid regard to economy, consistent with the conditions of success. His chief labors were given, however, to its internal condition. He endeavored to raise the standard of scholarship, and to so conduct the discipline of the College as to render this possible.

The discipline had been very gentle, to say the least. under the former amiable regime, and considerable pains had been taken, unfortunately perhaps, to let it be known that Dr. Binney was a "strict disciplinarian." As has been seen, this was true in his church government, but it has also been seen that no pains or labor were thought too great to save the offender, not only to the church, but from public reproach. But *how* he was to be strict, probably never occurred to them to inquire, and the students were naturally arraying themselves to act on the defensive. His Inaugural Address met with great favor on all sides, and the students were prepared to give the new President their respect. He had a happy faculty of not seeing all the little failures or foibles of his pupils or subordinates, and for a while they were beginning to think there must have been a mistake after all in the rumor. He certainly treated them as if he thought them gentlemen, and not schoolboys, and the tide was setting strongly in his favor, when, unfortunately, the Faculty and students came into collision on an old question in which the latter had invariably carried the day. They had a habit of cutting the benches, desks, and even the pillars, with their pocket knives, thus disfiguring the College building.

When Dr. Binney entered upon his office, everything was made "as good as new;" but he was told that very soon the process of mutilation would be repeated. He called the young gentlemen together, talked the matter over with them, and finally assured them that in view of all he had seen of their gentlemanly conduct, he felt great confidence that they would co-operate with him; and that should any one of their number be so rude and thoughtless as in any way to mar the beauty of the building, the general opinion would be so strong against it as to bring the offender at once to justice. For a time everything went on well, but at length one, bolder than the rest, cut an ugly figure on one of the front pillars. Without comment it was repaired, and then the students in session called upon to say who should "foot the bill." All agreed upon "the one who cut the pillar," but no one was ready to acknowledge either that he himself had done it, or that he knew who had. The President then gave the offender the opportunity to declare himself by writing or otherwise, to pay the bill, and receive forgiveness without exposure. After a while, no confession being made, the slight expense was averaged on all the students and paid without reference to their bills sent home. But soon the case became serious. It was evident that more than one had determined to try who were stronger, the Faculty or the students. Expensive repairs had to be made, and outlays were averaged and now charged in their bills. Then letters from parents began to come in, and a great deal of correspondence resulted, but the culprits were finally exposed, not by the help, however, of fellow-students, and made to pay the charges themselves, which put a stop to the mischief altogether. It would have been a very unpopular thing after that to repeat the offence.

Some months after, there was another combination which was the cause of considerable trouble, and for a few days threatened to empty the College of students. This, also, by the aid of a united Faculty, was satisfactorily settled. The great firmness of the President convinced all that he deemed strict obedience to law more essential to the welfare of the College than the attendance of any number of students. To close the College he believed to be more honorable to it than to have its halls filled with students who would not submit to its laws. His calm and firm attitude, and his evident concern for the real welfare of the students, were not without their just influence. He was gratified by the conviction that the larger portion of the students would in future consider *obedience to law no degradation.* There was no further trouble in the discipline of the College, save such minor incidents as so frequently occur from the thoughtlessness and inexperience of youth.

In regard to his position afterwards, an extract from an article written soon after his decease by the Rev. Dr. A. J. Huntington, then a Professor in the College, and now an able Professor in the University, tells the facts in a few words. *Only* these few words are given here, because the whole article will be published further on in the work. He says: " Nor was his post at Columbian College less inviting. The Institution was rising under his judicious administration. He was held in profound respect by the Trustees, the Faculty, and the students, as well as by the community in general. His relations with all were of the most pleasant kind."

But though Dr. Binney was so happy in all his relations in Washington, his mind was not at ease. Eugenio Kincaid, D. D., one of the oldest and among the most honored missionaries of Burmah, was then in America, and spent much time with Dr. Binney in Washington, urging his return to the field. Dr. Kincaid had not severed his connection with the Missionary Union and attached himself to another organization, as several others had done; but he was anxious that Dr. Binney should go out *independently*. He thought this would relieve the Executive Committee of the Missionary Union, financially, of a heavy burden, unite all the missionaries in the work of Theological Education, and thus harmonize all interests. Dr. Binney, under some circumstances, might have thought this a good plan, on account of the low state of the Mission treasury at the time ; for he had known by experience, how hard is the task of making bricks without straw; but he never entertained for a moment, the thought of placing himself in a position of even seeming antagonism to the regularly organized society for carrying on the work of Foreign Missions in behalf of the Baptist Denomination at the North, and thus, so far as his influence went, weakening the cause. Any proposal made by brethren to send him out independently was considered by him as supplementary to the work of the Missionary Union, and in harmony with its main de-

23*

sign. It was soon seen that the brethren in Philadelphia who were ready to send him out were prepared to act in connection with this body. He received earnest letters from his brethren in Burmah, who made no conditions with him, urging his return. Dr. Kincaid acquiesced in the proposal made by Messrs. Bucknell, Jayne and G. McIntosh, to sustain Dr. Binney, *through* the Missionary Union, though he would have preferred independent action. If the "voice of the people is the voice of God" then, Dr. Binney was called of God to leave his delightful home and work in Washington and return to Burmah. The religious denominational press, both North and South, echoes the sentiment of the paper which emanated from the rooms at Boston under date of October, 1858, from which the following extract is taken.

In 1853, a correspondence was opened with Dr. Binney, having reference to his return to Burmah, and he was nearly on the point of embarking, when he discovered in the doings of the Deputation some things which he regarded as unfavorable to his plan of action, and he declined the service. From the time that Dr. Binney left till now, that Seminary has been in charge, first, of Mr. Vinton, then of Dr. Wade. The students have at no time been numerous. Owing to a lack of harmony among the missionaries, pupils have not been forthcoming from all the Missions. Many have been retained in their fields, preaching a portion of the year, and gathering, during the rainy season, under the instruction of the resident missionaries. This method has not been without its advantages; but the conviction has been growing that the Karen Theological School must be better sustained and made to do the whole work for which it was established.

During the past year, urgent appeals have come from Burmah, for the return of Dr. Binney. The Executive Committee have deeply felt the desirableness that this demand should be met; but, in the embarrassed condition of the treasury, they have till recently been restrained from action.

. Months since, a few liberal and earnest friends of missions in Philadelphia made overtures to Dr. Binney, then President of Columbian College, in the District of Columbia, to go out at their expense, as an independent laborer, and give a few years to the work which he had left unfinished. After the late meeting at Philadelphia, it was understood that Dr. Binney was disposed to go, and would prefer to go in connection with the Union; also that his friends in Philadelphia, who had been negotiating with him, preferred to contribute for his support, through the treasury of the Union. After a careful, fraternal correspondence, and a frank interchange of views, the preliminaries were adjusted to mutual satisfaction. In the meantime, fresh letters were received from Burmah, *written at the very time when the Board and Union were in session*, in May last, that delightfully facilitated the consummation of a result that has been widely desired. Among the communications, were letters from Dr. Wade, one to Dr. Binney, urging his return, and another to the Executive Committee, requesting his appointment, and offering to resign the School at Maulmain to his care, and to work with him, or in any other department, as may be thought best.

Thus the proposed action of the Committee was opportunely relieved from all embarrassment, and accordingly on the 30th of August, Dr. Binney was unanimously reappointed a missionary of the Union, and Principal of the Karen Theological Seminary. His outfit and salary for five years are provided for, by the pledges of three worthy brethren in Philadelphia. It is anticipated that the Seminary will be located at or near Rangoon, perhaps occupying the premises at Kemendine. The design is, that this shall be the one Theological School for the Karens north of the Tenasserim Province, and, if possible, of the whole Karen people.

From the great unanimity with which the missionaries, both those who abide by the Union, and those who have left it, have urged the return of Dr. Binney, strong confidence is cherished that he will unite the missions around his school, and make it the means of restoring that harmony for which thousands have prayed. The Committtee regard all the steps which have led to this re-appointment as indicative of special interposition and guidance from above. To them, the hand of Providence is distinctly visible. Nothing apart from the divine promises has for a long period, inspired them with so much hope.

If Dr. Binney shall be permitted to re-enter the field which he so well understands, and to prosecute for a few years the work for which he is so eminently qualified, it may rationally be expected that our Karen Missions will have a prosperity, surpassing all that has hitherto been witnessed. The latest intelligence shows that among the Karen churches are a larger number of promising candidates for the ministry, than are found in all the Baptist Theological Institutions in the United States. To train those young men for their important work is a service full of hope for perishing thousands, perhaps millions. Many of our present readers will live to see great things done in Burmah. That Empire is yet to be reckoned among the Christian nations. God has already a great people there and he will have a greater. Let us trust him, hope in him. He says, "For a small moment have I forsaken thee ; but with great mercies will I gather thee. In a little wrath I hid my face from thee for a moment; but with everlasting kindness will I have mercy on thee, saith the Lord thy Redeemer." Let us hold steadily on, giving and praying, and when we shall have passed through the needed discipline, we shall have occasion to say, "Lo, this is our God, we have waited for him ; he will come and save us."

While everywhere it was hoped and expected that this action would unite conflicting elements, and the opinion was expressed that the co-operation and encompassing influences by which Dr. Binney would be surrounded were full of promise for Burmah, the friends of Columbian College expressed their regret in the strongest language, that he should feel it his duty to leave them. At a meeting of the Trustees of the College, the following resolutions were passed.

Rev. Dr. Binney having tendered his resignation as President of the College, from a deep conviction of his duty to resume the labor of instruction among the Karens in Burmah :

"*Resolved*, That in accepting his resignation, the Board acquiesce in what seems to be an arrangement of Divine Providence.

"*Resolved*, That as our intercourse with Dr. Binney during his connection with the College has been one of uninterrupted harmony, satisfaction, and pleasure, we cordially reciprocate the feelings of confidence and esteem expressed in his letter of resignation.

"*Resolved*, That in parting with Dr. Binney, not only does the College lose a truly efficient and valuable officer, but the cause of education one of its firmest and most valuable friends.

"S. C. SMOOT, Secretary of Board."

Of this meeting and the resolutions adopted, a leading Washington paper speaks in the following terms :

Dr. Binney's loss will be deeply and seriously felt by the friends, patrons, and pupils of the College, as it is by his brother-officers and the Faculty. At a meeting of the Trustees, held September 3d, the resolutions which accompany this letter were drafted by Rev. G. F. Adams, the Chairman of the Committee. Neither these, nor any other resolutions, however framed, could express the respect and attachment manifested for Dr. Binney, when the sudden announcement that he felt it his duty to leave the College for his old field of labor, was made. Every consistent effort was employed, to urge upon him the claims of the College; but every mind at last acquiesced in the conviction, that God had called him to go to the Karens.

Dr. Binney, it is expected, will leave Washington about the 30th of September, visiting Baltimore and Philadelphia, among other places, before sailing for Burmah.

Many Christian hearts will invoke blessings on him and his companion during their ocean voyage.

CHAPTER XVI.

1858–1863.

WHEN Dr. Binney left New York for England, his plan was to take one of the fine passenger sailing ships, known as "Green's Ships," leaving London for Calcutta twice a month. This arrangement, would have brought him to Rangoon in April, and given him time to make preparations for the opening of his school at the commencement of the rains. But, being detained in London by the misfortunes of fellow passengers, he found himself a "little too late." When he was ready, the last vessel of the season had just sailed. The Missionary Union had not yet felt able to send their Missionaries by the overland route. He had advocated the wisdom of so doing before he left home; and, as his case was a peculiar one in many respects, it had been proposed to him to take that route; still, though he was receiving his support wholly from rich men, who were as generous as rich, he would not do anything that his brethren generally could not do. So, he took the best sailing vessel he could find for Calcutta. She was heavily laden, and consequently he had a long and tedious passage. His friends had supplied him with a

272

collection of new and choice books, and these helped to pass the time not unpleasantly; very mercifully, he did not anticipate the trials before him.

. On arriving in Calcutta, one of the first persons he met was the Rev. Dr. Duff, that remarkable man and devoted missionary of the Free Church of Scotland, now of world-wide fame. He had just returned from a visit to the Missions in Burmah, and almost his first words were:

" Brother Binney, I cannot tell you how my heart has been, and is, burdened for you. I know, I suppose, the whole history of this movement—of your work, your sacrifice, and the motives which have led you to make it; but it is, I think, a vain oblation. You will not be received in Burmah."

Dr. Binney thought perhaps he did not know the earnest desire which had been expressed by nearly, if not all, the Karen missionaries and the Karens, for his return to his old work; and told him briefly the reasons he had to believe that all would work well with him.

"Not as a missionary of the Union," said Dr. Duff. "But," he kindly added, " if any man can take up this work successfully, you can. Nothing, so far as I know, has ever been said against you personally."

At the same time Dr. Binney received from Mr. Ranney, of the mission press, the following note of welcome, and the only one he did receive; though Dr. Stevens had written kindly, the letter had failed to reach him. This, though cordial, was not cheering:

DEAR BROTHER BINNEY:—In anticipation of your possible arrival in Calcutta before another Rangoon mail goes, I acquit myself of a pleasant duty, by sending you a brief note of welcome back to your old scene of labor and trial; and yet not the old place, as, in the world's progress the old place has become antiquated, and too dilapidated for profitable occupation. Though they did not know that, in America, and it is said you are to pitch your tent either in Maulmain or Rangoon. Our lamented Brother Vinton was always at headquarters, where he had a clear vision of the field, and before the world of Baptists could look through *his* glass and see as he saw, he moved headquarters to Rangoon.

You are not going to Newton, to set yourself down in the comfortable nest, among the flowers and foliage of your own cultivation in former days; instead of which, as I understand it, you intend to locate in the Kemendine jungles, where all is primitive as the minds upon which you are now to operate; where the tall trees keep out the sunlight; and where the undergrowth of jungle will require all the leisure you may get while digging the jungle out of the native mind.

Well, I am glad you are coming. You have counted the cost, and, I have no doubt, have well ascertained the point of duty; and as pleasure and duty do not always go together, and as you have well learned this fact by experience, you will perhaps feel less the sacrifice of stepping out of the College at Washington into the Karen jungle. We anticipate no small pleasure in you and Mrs. Binney being added to our little social circle. Accept both for Mrs. Binney and yourself a very hearty welcome back to Burmah.

While in Calcutta, a letter was also received from Dr. Warren, then our Foreign Secretary, in which he says:

Since you left, we hear all sorts of stories about the reception you will meet with in Burmah. But I am resolved to judge nothing before the time, and shall hope all things, and despair of nothing till I hear you say "give up the ship." If *you* cannot make an arrangement with the brethren, then who among us can?

Please do not think of turning homeward, but set up a standard in the kingdom of the soul. Converts are multiplying in Toungoo and Henthadah, and there will be work enough for you.

· Before leaving Washington, soon after hearing of the death of his old colleague, the Rev. J. H. Vinton, Dr. Binney wrote the Rev. Dr. J. Wheaton Smith, of Philadelphia, in this manner:

Brother Vinton is not there. You can hardly estimate what the cause of Christ among the Karens has lost, by the death of this good man. I assure you, should I ever return to Burmah, my work will be a different matter from what it was with his cooperation. The first night after receiving this intelligence, I could not sleep, and until now I cannot think of it, but with pain, such as I never felt upon the death of any other man.

His anticipations were more than realized on his arrival in Rangoon. He missed his fraternal welcome. He had loved him and been loved by him, and largely through Dr. Binney's influence the Missionary Union had invited him and others back to their old places, the Union to ignore the past. So soon as this was known, Dr. Binney wrote to Mr. Vinton, in terms which show the confidence and esteem that existed between them, as also between other brethren who had left the Union.

My heart is glad. After I left Philadelphia yesterday, I was informed that measures were adopted which promise peace and success to our Mission. Dr. Sears, Dr. Anderson of Rochester, Judge Harris, Dr. Lamson, and others led off, and ably supported important changes; and one was, on motion of Hon. Mr. Duncan, instructing the Executive Committee to invite back the missionaries.

Now, my dear brother, don't delay. If they invite you back, accept the invitation without any reference to the past. Were I

24

in your place, I would simply answer, " Dear Brethren, I accept, with my whole heart, your invitation to restore my relation to the Missionary Union; and trust the past may be sanctified to our good and the promotion of our Master's cause."

Nothing further is, in my opinion, needed. You know I would not advise this, if I did not think it safe and best. I fear nothing but doing wrong. Give my love to Brethren Brayton and Beecher, for I do not know where to address them; and say to them, that if they are invited back, as they will be, they must not hesitate. May God direct us all.

The following circular preceded him to Burmah :

To the Missionaries in Burmah, with the native Pastors and Churches. .

BELOVED BRETHREN : The Executive Committee of the American Baptist Missionary Union have re-appointed the Rev. Joseph G. Binney, D.D., a missionary and the Principal of the Karen Literary and Theological Institution. To this act they have been moved by a conviction of the desirableness of his services in that field, and also by the repeated and earnest entreaties from many of you, that he might return and resume the work in which he was formerly so useful. Five years ago he would gladly have acceded to the expressed wishes of the Committee, and joined you in Christian labor; but he was restrained by obstacles which he regarded as likely to interfere with his success. Happily, those obstacles no longer exist, and he is now on the eve of his departure, assured of the confidence of his brethren in America, and anticipating from you a cordial welcome.

The Committee have no disposition, as they have no motive, to conceal the fact that Dr. Binney's appointment this third time has been made under a new class of circumstances, and with unusual stipulations, and is therefore, in some of its aspects, a departure from past usage. This may seem to demand an explanation ; but for the present the Committee would fraternally intimate that they find themselves required, by plain indications of Providence, to reëxamine, and revise with care, some parts of their missionary policy, having reference especially to a greater simplification of the treasury department, a fuller recognition of the parity of the foreign and the home laborers, and an adjustment of the whole system upon a basis that shall accord more perfectly with the light furnished by more than forty years of varied experiences. You will, therefore, be pleased to regard this case, not as an exception that is to remain indicative of a special preference, but as a step taken under the pressure of providential circumstances in a given direction, and foreshadowing some changes which may hereafter be proposed for your consideration.

The Committee in the mean time are desirous to facilitate, as they may be able, the important service intrusted to Dr. Binney; and they take it for granted that his enterprise, coördinate with yours, will be regarded by you all with special favor, and that you will unite with him and with them in earnest efforts for its vigorous and successful prosecution. They do not pretend to arrange the details of his service. Much is committed to his known experience and discretion. You can aid him largely in his work, as he can essentially aid you in your respective departments. May he and you have grace to labor together, congenially and effectively, for the evangelization of Burmah.

The Committee are far from supposing that everything desirable in the Educational Department can be done by one teacher, or by one Institution; but we have the impression that the Missions in Burmah will best promote their own interests and the general cause, by concentrating for the present, as far as practicable, the work of Theological instruction in a single School. And, while they say thus much, they do not forget that more or less of the missionaries may find it, as heretofore, both desirable and advisable to impart Biblical and other instruction to native assistants during the rains. Recognizing fully all fair exceptional cases, they cordially commend Dr. Binney and his plans to your kindest consideration, with the prayer and the hope that there may be, throughout the entire field, harmony of views, and a generous ·co-operation.

The Committee regard it as an issue to be contemplated and sought by all concerned, that the Institution shall be made so much an object of interest to the Karen preachers and churches, as that they will, at no distant period, make it their own, and assume its entire support. For every reason the Committee desire such a consummation, and they respectfully commend the thought to your serious reflection, and solicit your wisest endeavors to render it practicable.

With affectionate esteem, your brethren and fellow-laborers,

J. G. WARREN, *Cor. Sec.*

BOSTON, Nov. 2d, 1858.

On the evening of Dr. Binney's arrival in Rangoon none of the Karen missionaries met him. After tea, with the Ranneys and Stevens in town, he took a gharry, and he and Mrs. Binney, though all was new and strange to them, went out to Kemendine, two miles away, alone. He learned that Mrs. Vinton was expecting them at her house. She received him with evident embarrassment, and lost no time in telling him that a paper had been drawn up and signed by all the Karen missionaries, except Dr. Wade and herself, asking him to go on to Maulmain, or at any rate not to stop in Rangoon. She had at first intended to sign the paper—indeed, she had urged that it be written—but had finally changed her mind ; and pupils were coming in from the Rangoon District, some of whom had waited in town a whole fortnight for his arrival. Dr. Wade's pupils were ready to come over in a body as soon as they heard of it.

That night to Dr. Binney was literally a sleepless one. He must either comply with the request of his brethren or stay where he was. The sun arose, and he was still undecided what to do. The Karens began to come in before he could dress; and these, his old and tried friends, no sooner saw his face among them than all *their* suspicion vanished. To them he made no allusion to the trying circumstances in which he was placed. They told him "they had prayed him back," and he believed them.

At the breakfast table, the letter of which he had heard in Calcutta, and the evening before from Mrs. Vinton, was handed him. He put it in his pocket, fully intending to read and answer it. But such a communication demanded time, of which he could not command a moment until night. Then he was exhausted, and even ill, from want of sleep, the incessant talking of the day, and the extreme heat. The next day was Sunday. He had not preached in Karen for nine years, but was overjoyed to have the opportunity again, and his tongue was loosed, so that he spoke as if he had been in constant use of the language. He was already in the harness, and went on with his work. Preparations to receive the pupils had to be made in haste. The rains were well begun. His own dwelling-house was covered with a roof, and partially enclosed, but had no windows, doors, partitions, or even properly laid floors. He had purchased in Calcutta all the furniture actually needed, and the vessel by which it would come left before he did. It was expected daily. So, with a borrowed bed, a few chairs, and a table, they moved into the one partially enclosed room, and opened the school. The twenty-eight Karen pupils came over from Dr. Wade; from their dearly loved "Teacher and Mamma," to whom they had been as children, they came *to* strangers and

24*

among strangers. Dr. and Mrs. Binney were overwhelmed with cares, and had little time to converse with them and less means for making them comfortable; but as they afterwards said, "they were able to see that they were much more comfortably provided for than the Teacher and Mamma." On the second Lord's Day, Dr. Binney preached a sermon to them from the words: "The joy of the Lord is your strength." The notes of this sermon are found among his papers, and to this day frequent allusion is made to it by those who heard him.

He explained to them the circumstances under which the text was spoken, and its meaning. In a few words he gave his own experience of this joy; that though he had left an inviting work, shared with beloved and esteemed associates, and surrounded by every comfort, he had done it for his love for him who, when on earth, had not where to lay his head; for the love of him who had suffered even unto death—that we might live. He told them that it brought him into close and loving fellowship with the Master, and he counted it great joy thus to be honored by him; that this joy made him very happy, so that he was able to reckon these as among his best days. Then he entered into detail, naming the trials through which they too were passing, especially that many of them were among strangers and homesick. They did not yet know the heart of their Teacher even; that he was sympathizing with them, and doing all in his power to make them comfortable; and they must see, if they would consider, that his own family was more uncomfortable than they. Then he told them of the tender, loving sympathy of Jesus, and that not a hair of their heads could fall to the ground without his notice. If they had come from any worldly motive, he had no word of cheer for them; but if they came from love to Jesus, from the simple desire to prepare themselves to serve him better, then, in view of all his precious promises, they might joy and rejoice; though they now sowed in tears, they would reap in joy. His sermon so encouraged their hearts that they were greatly affected at the time, and never afterward were disposed to complain, or even to feel homesick.

, But all this time the letter remained unanswered. His silence, and apparent ignoring of it, led one of the brethren to address him on the subject. His brief reply did not satisfy the brother, and he-wrote again. The first two letters have not been preserved, but the two which followed show their character, and also the state of mind which led Dr. Binney to the course he took.

Rev. D. L. Brayton writes under date of June 7th, 1859:

DEAR BROTHER BINNEY.—I have known you more or less for nearly thirty years. I have always loved you for what I believed to be your candid, open-hearted, upright course. I have always looked upon you as quite above, and far out of reach of, every thing like littleness or intrigue; and—what is more than any thing else, and all things else combined—I have had and still have unbounded confidence in you as a Christian brother. Now, if this confidence can be reciprocated, I should like to have—if convenient to yourself, at an early hour—some conversation on matters deeply involving, as I think, the interests of Christ's kingdom among these Karens. If you have no objection to such a conversation, I will meet you at your house, or any other place most convenient to yourself.

If our views can possibly be brought to harmonize, it will be a matter of very great consolation.

Affectionately yours,

D. L. BRAYTON.

To this most fraternal letter Dr. Binney prepared and sent, before the day was ended, the following reply.

MY DEAR BROTHER BRAYTON.—In answer to yours of this morning, allow me to say, I believe there has been far too much talking, explaining, and arguing, respecting missionary work. If brethren have confidence in each other, it is not needed ; and if there is a want of confidence, it certainly will not be produced or increased by any such course; as the past, at home and in the field, already clearly shows. With this impression I decided to come back, resolved not to spend my time or strength in continual writing or talking. I was assured on every side, that the Karens both needed and wished for my labors, and that my missionary brethren had confidence in me. I came to work for the Karens; and already have my hands and heart full, with my time so fully occupied that I have yet had no opportunity to provide even common comforts for my family. I have sixty-seven students looking to me for instruction and for many other attentions. Everything has to be obtained anew, or fitted to circumstances. I have been in Rangoon only twelve or thirteen days, after an absence from Burmah of nine years, but my classes are formed, and I am already engaged in my recitations.

Still, I will gladly meet you, simply to talk together as Christian brethren. Be assured, you will find me the same Brother Binney as formerly, and ready to reciprocate any and all confidence that may be placed in me. We will meet, if you please, to-morrow evening at 7 o'clock. Please interpret every word in this and my other note as designed to express only such feelings as our Master would approve between brethren.

And believe me, ever affectionately, your brother,

J. G. BINNEY.

The paper, inviting Dr. Binney to leave Rangoon, was never formally answered. Several of the brethren had already requested their names erased, though not in time for it to be done before he received it. He was well in his work almost before he himself was aware of it; and as every brother expressed only the kindest feelings toward him personally, he deemed discussion unnecessary and impolitic. He thought, as he said to Mr. Brayton, that "too much had been said already." As the sequel proved, harmony was best promoted by silence and fraternal co-operation in all good work. The brethren all, sooner or later, accepted the invitations to return to the Missionary Union.

The question will naturally be asked, "What was the cause of this want of harmony among the Missionaries?" Especially will the inquiry be made, "What was the cause of alienation from the Missionary Union?" It is not proposed to go into detail in answering these questions, but only to glance at the principal causes.

In the early history of the Mission, there was little of what since has been termed "Missionary Policy." Two or three brethren, isolated by a voyage of months from their brethren at home, were all the world to each other, and were entrusted with funds to spend as they saw fit. The interests of each were nearly the same, and if little differences arose, as there might arise in the family relation, yet the ties that bound them to each other were so strong, that these differences were easily adjusted. Soon, however, it became very different. As their number increased, and each had to some extent a different department, it was necessary to apportion the means accordingly. Each station was made independent of other stations, but the appropriations were made by the Executive Committee at home, *to the station*, and not to each individual worker, and the money given to the worker, not wholly as he felt he needed to use in his work, but as the majority of the brethren of the station thought he needed. This naturally would seem the wisest way, but practically was attended with difficulties. If a brother desired an appropriation for repairs on his house or for any department of Missionary Work, a majority of one could prevent it. This proved a strong temptation to a brother to act on the principle, though he might not avow it, "if you will vote for me, I will vote for you;" and if a man was independent enough not to do so, it was sometimes thought he suffered for it. But would good men so act? That was, in part, the point at issue. The Karen Missionaries were in the minority, and complained that their interests were often disregarded. Mr. Binney found this feeling; he did not create it; but he strongly advocated separate organizations of the Burman and Karen Departments. This he did, partly because of the existence of this feeling, but chiefly because he thought each must better understand the claims of its own special work—than the other could. Moreover, he believed that if there were no vote to be feared, advice and co-operation would be sought more frequently and largely. All the meetings were held so far from the Karen Department as to involve much time and expense to attend them. He also thought, that to narrow the responsibility would make it more deeply felt. Though several letters are found advocating the division so far as the distribution of funds is concerned, not a word is seen anywhere imputing blame to a brother. It is doubted, whether such a word from his pen, could be found either on that or any other subject, in the archives of the Union. When the Karen Mission, at their earnest and united request, became independent of the other Department, the appropriations were made directly to them. In Maulmain, they being a small body, were in a very similar condition to the first Missionaries. It was productive of greater harmony of action, while this state of the Mission continued.

With regard to the alienation from the Missionary Union; the relation between the Missionaries and the Union was considered by many not to be "fraternal," but that of "employers and employees." This feeling was increased by the sending out of a "Deputation" in 1853, empowered to act for the Executive Committee without referring anything back to them. If a Deputation entrusted with so much power were desirable, Dr. Binney thought that two better men, perhaps, could not have been selected, than Drs. Peck and Granger. They came, hoping to make crooked things straight, and to restore harmony where there was disaffection. Instead of the expected result, parties were formed—Deputation and Anti-deputation. Several of the brethren left the Union; others were even more aggressively opposed to the measures inaugurated than those who did leave; while some co operated with the Deputation, thus making themselves antagonistic to the brethren who did not.

As has been seen, Dr. Binney felt that he could not return to Maulmain to carry out the circumscribed work thus planned for him, and he left the Mission quietly, doing nothing to embarrass the Board, but working for them in all possible ways. He felt that, "if the work planned for him was all that the Executive Committee needed, they had men enough to carry it on without him, and he could do more good at home." He was so silent on the subject, that little excitement was produced either at home or in Burmah, by his refusing to remain.

When the brethren at home and in Burmah, were ready to give him the privilege of doing all he thought he could do for the elevation of the Karens and the perpetuation of the work, no personal sacrifice seemed too great to accomplish this. He came to Kemendine from Washington for that purpose, under the legitimate control of the Union, his best friends and friends of the cause, so preferring to work, but in harmony with *all others.*

There was, however, another serious obstacle in his way. On the annexation of Pegu, in 1852, Mr. Vinton, his former co-worker, removed the headquarters of the Karen Mission to Rangoon, which then had become the Capital of British Burmah. He took up a considerable tract of land in the suburbs of Rangoon, at a place called Kemendine, at a merely nominal price. It was a little out of the business part of the city, but was accessible by boat. Commanding the river view and air, it was a very desirable location.

It was entirely uncultivated, but partly by aid of

friends in Burmah, and chiefly by friends at home and the Missionary Union, the ground was prepared and buildings erected for Mr. Vinton's dwelling, and for school purposes. An expensive brick chapel was also erected, though not completed, by contributions mostly secured by Mrs. Vinton in America. It was called "Francs' Chapel," facetiously so at first, but afterward this was adopted as its real name, from the fact that the first contribution made for it was a five franc piece, given by a poor woman. All this was done while Mr. Vinton was a missionary of the Union. The Executive Committee of that body, considered it their property, to be used exclusively for the purposes of the Mission. There were misunderstandings, and there was much and prolonged discussion. Mr. Vinton was overwhelmed with cares and work, organizing and visiting the Karens scattered through the jungles. In the mean time the Karens, not having been able to attend to their crops during the war, were starving in consequence. Mr. Vinton brought hundreds of them to Kemendine and fed them. In this good work he received help from English friends, and to some extent from friends at home. While thus pressed with cares and anxieties, his business accounts became confused, at least. Correspondence did not succeed in bringing order out of confusion. America was a long way off; mails were slow; and it seemed next to impossible to get all these debatable matters settled satisfactorily.

On the eve of embarking, the Executive Committee had asked Dr. Binney to try and bring about an amicable understanding, and gave him full power to do this

25

in his own way, promising to abide by his decision. This was known in Kemendine. Suspicions were awakened that this authority to act might result in wrong to Mrs. Vinton and the Karens; the one, widow of a brother- beloved, and the other, dear to him as his own children, as was shown by all he had given up and done for their sake.

These suspicions, however, were soon set at rest. He called for books and papers and oral explanations; and worked upon the subject long enough to become well convinced that the whole business had become hopelessly entangled. He wrote to the Board, saying, that were the money involved in the case his own, he would relinquish all claims; not on the ground of justice,—that he would not attempt to decide,—but on the ground that the whole property would be used for mission purposes in the hands of a Karen Society, and independent of any organized body beside. He therefore advised, in the interests of peace and for the good of all concerned, that controversy should cease, and the Karens or their advisers be allowed to take the whole. This was done without a dissenting voice from the Committee.

For the purpose of making this explanation, we left Dr. Binney, only a few days after his arrival in the country, with his large school, to be cared for, and no comfortable provision yet made for self and family or school. It was a busy, anxious time. Carpenters had to be overseen, recitations heard, mostly by Dr. and Mrs. Binney; for the head teacher of the school at Maulmain was not able to come; and the others, young and unqualified, were his only assistants.

According to the custom of the country, the cook-house must be at some distance from the dwelling. The whole place being a dense jungle, the native servants were afraid of robbers, who were always prowling about, and would not stay. As many as ten or twelve servants were procured, one after the other, and paid each a little in advance; still they were continually leaving, and Mrs. Binney, with the aid of some one of the pupils out of school hours, had to attend to the cooking. This, with the care of the sick, and classes to be heard daily, was quite too much for her, and she suffered constantly from fever. All suffered, more or less, from acclimatizing in the jungle under such unfavorable circumstances, but Mrs. Binney the most severely.

Such was the beginning of the work. Four years thereafter passed away with no remarkable or sudden changes, but with steady improvement in every respect. Dr. Binney's relations with his brethren were pleasant, and the school was getting back to its former state. The leading man, Pah-poo, whom he had prepared so well to be his assistant in Maulmain, returned to him. The younger teachers became more competent to help. The dwelling-house was completed, and comfortable; roads were made; and the grounds graded and taste-fully laid out. Flowering shrubs and plants were taking the place of forest trees and jungle growth. But this transformation was not wrought suddenly by any magic wand, as we shall see hereafter.

At this same period the Missionary Union was undergoing a severe ordeal at home. Few of its active workers of to-day have any adequate idea of the trials through which it was then passing. A few years before, the Baptists of the South were dissatisfied, and withdrew to form the Southern Baptist Convention. Some sympathized with the action of the Southern brethren, and thought the division was caused by the unnecessary scruples of brethren in the North. Many more thought that the Missionary Union, which was formed after the separation, had not been sufficiently bold and aggressive in its declaration of anti-slavery sentiments. They originated a new organization, called "The Free Mission Society," through which they sought to express their views and carry out their principles. They also desired that more freedom of action should be granted to missionaries than heretofore.

Many of those who had been strongly attached to the Union were disturbed by the attacks made upon it, and confused by the discussion that arose. Funds for the work which the Union had to provide for came in too scantily, and Dr. Binney and others were embarrassed. His salary, it is true, was secured by the three brethren from Philadelphia; but the school was larger than the Executive Committee had expected, and its expenses were met with great difficulty. Dr. Binney obtained help for completing his dwelling-house, putting up an inexpensive school building, grading and making a road to the public highway, grading and improving the ground in front of his house, in this way. There was at the time an unusually large number of pious military officers and business men in Rangoon, who greatly desired stated religious services on the Lord's Day, and asked Dr. Binney to conduct them in "Francs'

Chapel." They even formed a little church. They had been accustomed to have regular preaching by some one of the missionaries, but without any thought of recompense. Dr. Binney candidly made known to them his wants, the pressure of his work, and all his circumstances, and told them, also, that he would preach to the poor for nothing, but neither the Bible nor reason required him to do this for rich professing Christians. If, according to their ability, they would give of their temporal substance, he would give according to his ability in spiritual things. The proposal met with a prompt and cheerful response, and the Theological Seminary Compound at Kemendine soon became comfortable and pleasant, and, in that early and unimproved state of Rangoon, noted for its neatness and beauty. Socially, too, there was an improvement. Those who attended his preaching on Sunday evenings naturally wished to pay him social attentions. Others wished to visit him occasionally for religious advice and instruction; but this would embarrass his work, and place him in the position of the pastor of a small church. He could not spare the time from his Karen work, but told them that every evening at half-past six he took tea with his family; if any would come in *then* he would give them a cup of tea and spend an hour or more, according to circumstances, on any evening, Saturdays excepted. This brought him into contact with many good Christian friends, and was a slight relaxation to him. If they did not leave at eight o'clock, he always left them and retired to his study, to prepare for the next day's recitations, and they expected him to do so.

25*

In the meantime, though he was compelled to gather much of the straw for making bricks, yet the bricks were made. The friends of Missions at home were writing encouraging letters also. Dr. Warren, the Foreign Secretary, wrote as follows:

The Executive Committee have watched your progress with constant solicitude, being well aware of the magnitude of the undertaking and the difficulties which must meet you at every step. As you well know, so many and so great were the obstacles to be met and overcome, that, but for the manifest, and I may almost say unexpected, indications of Providence, favorable to the design, they would hardly have ventured on the measure of sending you abroad. They relied very much upon you; your experience in that sphere of labor; your knowledge of the field, of the native character, of your missionary associates, and all troubles past and present, with their causes and results. No man was better qualified than you to detect the tendencies of things here and there, at home and abroad; and none could calculate better than you the chances of success or failure. Brethren on both sides of the water were very anxious to have you go. You were willing to go; the Committee were more than willing to appoint you; they would with you, venture on the Lord, and see what he would bring to pass. The whole undertaking was, in a sense, of the nature of an experiment; and, I may say, as the sense of the Committee up to this time, it has resulted better than they expected. They are satisfied, and more than satisfied, with what God has wrought through your means. And if it should prove in the end that not all you had hoped in relation to the School should be realized, the incidental benefit of your being at Rangoon will be a compensation for all toil and sacrifice on your part. You do not need to hear me say this, but it is in my heart to say it, and I will not refrain.

But while there was so much to encourage him, in

common with other of his missionary brethren he had
much that was unpleasant to meet during the progress
of the war in this country. The small congregation to
which he preached every Sunday evening was composed
largely of British army officers, who hailed with joy every
reverse which the forces of the Government met. Most
of the respectable merchants and business men of the
place took the same side, though they manifested less
bitterness. The local papers were filled with misrepresentation and abuse. His situation was a very trying
one. For awhile he kept up the same friendly intercourse, and patiently explained the actual state of things,
seeking to enlighten all who came to him, and these were
not a few. But every mail brought more or less matter for controversy, and this took too much time and
strength from his legitimate work. He finally frankly
stated this, and declined to converse on the subject.
Then he was invited to lecture before "The Young
Men's Literary Association" on "America's Civil War."
He did so, announcing his theme to be "The United
States of America. In their present efforts, ought they
to have the sympathy of other nations?" The community of Rangoon were invited, and all classes, especially those for whom it was purposely designed, came
out to hear. It would be impossible to give here even
an analysis, which would do it justice. Though the small
building was densely packed, and all suffered greatly
from the heat, yet during an hour and a quarter they
listened eagerly with no sign of impatience. This lecture, although his views differed very widely from those
of a large number of his hearers, did not alienate his

English friends; on the contrary, respect for his moral courage, was repeatedly expressed.

Even in the most trying days, when everything was new and uncomfortable about them, their home had been made very sunny by the presence of an adopted son, a fatherless nephew, who came with them from Washington. He was of an age and disposition to make little deprivations, having the charm of novelty, an actual pleasure; the unconventional and free life which he enjoyed, turned all difficulties into adventures; and, with a devotion unsurpassed, he made himself very essential to his mother, and his society was to both a well spring of joy. When he had to be sent to America for better advantages of education and business, it made the home very desolate. Though always chary of complaints, Dr. Binney would almost daily say, " How we do miss the boy !"

But hardly had time, which makes all such losses seem more endurable, a fair chance to work a favorable change, when he was called upon to bear a loss which indeed brought desolation to his home. Mrs. Binney's health had suffered a good deal, from their first coming to Kemendine, but her naturally elastic temperament had kept her up. She had never been obliged to abandon work, and neither she nor her husband were fully aware of her real state. On attempting to arise one morning, she found one of her limbs quite useless, and soon any attempt to move was attended with so much pain, that she was obliged to keep her couch for a long time. Under good medical treatment the suffering was partially alleviated; but after fifteen months trial of all that could be done in Burmah, the decision was, that she must have medical treatment in a favorable climate. That *she* must go home was certain, but what was *his* duty? He felt very reluctant to allow her to go on alone in that helpless state, but on the other hand he was very unwilling to leave his work just at a point, where all past labor and sacrifice might be lost.

The Executive Committee had written him that the Rev. C. H. Carpenter and his wife were on their way to Rangoon, and that Mr. Carpenter had been appointed his " Assistant for the present." But he was a young man, unacquainted with the country and language; and on his arrival could only afford a prospective relief. As soon as it was known, however, that Mr. and Mrs. Carpenter were in Calcutta, Mrs. Binney decided the question which he seemed unable to do. She would go without him, and he must return the following year. This decision he accepted. Then the term of his actual engagement would be ended; the School would be established; Mr. Carpenter fairly started in school work; by that time also, Mrs. Binney would have thrown aside her crutches as useless, and would never be subjected to a tropical climate again. ·With words like these he cheered her, and at the same time kept up his own courage.

Three days after she left Burmah, May 12th, 1863, Mr. and Mrs. Carpenter arrived. Dr. Binney welcomed them gladly, gave a part of his house for their dwelling, and did all he could to introduce them to their work. His letters by every mail were cheerful, and full of hope for the work, and for the ability of his assistants. He was counting the lessening days of separation, when a letter came from the Executive Committee, saying, that, while deeply sympathizing with him in his separation from his wife under such trying circumstances, they felt constrained to ask him not to return at the expiration of his five years, but to stay one year longer; at least until the Seminary should be secured upon a permanent basis.

He did not need the Executive Committee to show him the great desirableness of such a course; but he was reluctant to leave his wife longer without his care; and felt that he could not propose it, nor answer in the affirmative, until he received her consent to do so.

Papers from Rev. Messrs. Carpenter and Smith, for a while his able assistants in the Seminary, and the latter his chosen successor, are inserted here. Though alluding to after times, yet they have reference chiefly to this period.

FROM REV. C. H. CARPENTER.

My acquaintance with Rev. Dr. Binney began May 12th, 1863, the date of our first arrival in Rangoon. He was looking out for us, and welcomed us most cordially to his home and a share in his work.

Only three days before, Mrs. Binney had sailed for America in very precarious health. He felt her absence keenly, and was constantly anxious about her. Nothing but a stern sense of duty to remain by the Seminary until the new hands should become somewhat familiar with the work would have induced him to make the sacrifice of sending her home helpless and alone. He was far from well himself, but his cheerfulness was uniform, and his sense of God as an ever present help seemed to be strong and abiding. In his times of greatest weakness and pain, he often would speak laughingly of his body as a refractory old mule, that required the whip.

Most of his time was spent in his study and class room, but at the table and in our daily walks on the verandah after dinner, his conversation was most interesting and instructive. He took a genuine interest in our progress, both in the language and in the knowledge of the Karen people; and he was always ready to draw upon his long and varied experience for our benefit. The view of mission work and the principles of education which he set forth at those times were invaluable to us and will never be forgotten.

The war in our country was then in progress, and none watched the course of events with intenser interest than he and the other missionaries· in Burmah. While Dr. Binney evidently retained his old feelings of warm regard for his numerous friends and acquaintances at the South, his convictions and his sympathies were on the side of the Union. His country was the whole country.

In common with other Americans abroad at that time, we had to endure the unfriendly remarks of not a few of our English neighbors. One of these gentlemen, a genial and learned man, but an avowed infidel, called repeatedly to see Dr. Binney, during one of his ill-turns. He expressed the hope that he might cheer him up; but Dr. Binney was firm in his refusal to see him. "A man who hates my country and rejects my God can do me no good."

The impression that Dr. Binney made upon all was that of a *manly* man. Beyond most men that I have known, he adhered rigidly to what he conceived to be his duty. He did not go beyond his province, and interfere with the work of other men. He was capable of giving a stern rebuke, but it was always to the offender in person. During the two years in which we lived together as one family, I cannot recall a single word spoken in disparagement of his brethren. He had kind words and kind words only, concerning all. At the same time his regard for all the proprieties of life was perfect.

His work in Burmah was that of an Educator. He did not

believe that the schools of the mission should be restricted to probable candidates for the ministry, and he was decidedly in favor of teaching some of the children of the native Christians English. At the same time, he was himself a rare preacher, and his life work was the training up of native preachers, and we have never had a missionary, probably, who magnified the preacher's office more than he. Burmah, in his judgment, must be won for Christ by preaching; but the conquered territory must be held, and its resources developed, by a thorough and extensive system of Christian schools. While in after years I was compelled to differ from his views in some points of detail; his views on education in the main have long since become my own, as in fact they are the views of nearly all Christian missionaries in India.

He had the true teacher's regard for his pupils, and he watched the subsequent course of his graduates with great interest. It was pleasant to see the warm welcome which he gave them, as they came back from time to time to visit him, and the interest with which he recalled old times and questioned them with regard to the progress of the Lord's work at their hands.

Many have felt deep sorrow at the removal of Dr. Binney from the scene of his earthly labor, but none will miss him more or mourn for him more truly than the Karen pastors and preachers who studied the word of God with him. In common with myself, they will ever cherish deep respect and affection for his memory.

August 15, 1878.   C. H. CARPENTER.

FROM REV. D. A. W. SMITH.

RANGOON, June 3d, 1879.

MY DEAR MRS. BINNEY: You know that during your absence in America, in 1863, '4' and '5' Dr. Binney was for a time an inmate of our household. From October, 1864, to February, 1865, the date of his return to America, we had the rare pleasure of meeting him two or three times daily at our table. His table-intercourse I consider a bright spot in our sunny domestic life. I used often to think, at the time, that a record of Dr. Binney's table-talk would possess a rare intrinsic value. I should *now* consider it, if I had it, a precious and invaluable memorial.

We used to listen—the pleasure was shared with us by Mr. and Mrs. Carpenter—with the deepest interest to Dr. Binney's narration of incidents in his pastoral life in America, and in the early part of his career as foreign missionary. In connection with these incidents, he would give us his views on various subjects, in which we had a common interest, and all in so impressive and forcible a manner, that we would sit almost spell-bound.

I cannot forgive myself now for not having taken more pains to preserve at least an outline of these table utterances.

I am sure, anything that I can recall with distinctness, you would be glad to hear, even though it be a repetition of what you have often heard yourself from his own lips.

Speaking about ministers' salaries, Dr. Binney remarked once, that a pastor was entitled to a living equal in comfort to the average of his church-members. If pastor of a church, the members of which are mostly poor, he should cheerfully share with them their poverty, and be poor with the poor. As pastor of a rich church, however, he is not bound to poverty, but on the other hand should claim a support which would enable him to live as comfortably as the average of his flock. His own self-respect should not allow him to ask for less; his parishioners' self-respect should not allow them to give him less. In preferring such a claim, too, the pastor would be consulting the truest interests of the church he served. If I remember rightly, Dr. Binney said that he had himself been poor with the poor, and rich with the rich, and that he felt that he was in the line of duty no less in the latter case than in the former, and that his happiness was no less in the former case than in the latter.

With regard to its being always the duty of the foreign missionary to intermit or forego his parental obligations, Dr. Binney seemed to feel and always spoke very strongly. Nobody excepting the parents themselves are bound to bring up their children, while hundreds and thousands share equally with them the obligation to preach Christ's gospel to the perishing heathen. The prevailing Christian feeling at home condemned the prac-

26

tice of throwing missionary children on the charities of the Christian public; and, at the same time, demanded it. Missionaries who *left* their children were condemned, and missionaries who remained behind to care for their children, no less so. Dr. Binney thought the time had come for the churches and ministers at home to realize that the command to evangelize the heathen world was distributive, while the parental·obligations were personal and, for the most part, untransferable. Consecration for life to the Foreign Mission service, involving, as it seemed to do, the rupture of family ties and the disregard of parental obligations, deterred, no doubt, many who would prove eminently efficient workers, from engaging in the Foreign Mission enterprise. No man has a right to say, for himself and beforehand, where he shall be "for life"—whether in the home field or the foreign field. Such a predetermination, on either the home or foreign side, involved a dictation to Providence, which could not fail to be mischievous in its tendencies. Both home and foreign workers should be more flexible in their plans, and allow for a healthy interchange of home and foreign service. Such an interchange would be a mutual benefit to both the home and foreign work, bringing each into more intimate relations to the other. Of course, it was not incumbent upon *every* home pastor to have engaged in foreign service, nor would it prove the duty of every foreign worker to have a limited service in the foreign field. Let God marshal his own forces to suit his own infinite wisdom, while every soldier stands ready with his "here am I."

But I shall tax even your indulgence, I fear, if I run on in these reminiscences. Let me close by saying, that we feel it a rare privilege to have known Dr. Binney in the unguarded intercourse of home-life, and it has given me great delight to recall and, for a few moments, to live over again, those pleasant months of the autumn of 1865.

　　　　Very sincerely yours.　　　　D. A. W. SMITH.

CHAPTER XVII.

PERMANENT SEMINARY AT RANGOON.

1864—1865.

HE remained in Burmah another year, during which time, finding it impossible to procure a deed of the lands at Kemendine, and a favorable opportunity occurring for purchase elsewhere, the Seminary was removed to its present beautiful location. He had, under date of February, 1864, received full authority to go forward, purchase lands, and erect buildings suitable for the uses of a Seminary. Ten thousand dollars, less exchange, were to be placed at his disposal, which, " With what he had on hand, would be sufficient to begin with." This he had especially requested, as ready money would enable him to buy at an advantage. The manner of the purchase was so characteristic of the man, that it should not be omitted. Dr. Kincaid had co-operated with him in trying to obtain a deed or permanent lease on the site at Kemendine, and was kindly interested in looking out for a new location. He returned from town one afternoon about four o'clock, and informed Dr. Binney that certain premises, which Dr. Binney was well acquainted with, were for sale, and could be purchased at an incredibly low price for ready payment. He stated that there were competitors for the purchase, but they had not " cash in hand."

" Go right back there, Brother Kincaid," said Dr. Binney, "and secure the refusal of it."

" I am very tired," replied Dr. Kincaid. " I have had nothing to eat since breakfast. There is no need to go now, for no more business will be done to-night. Offices will be shut before I can get back. But I will be on hand at the opening of business in the morning and secure it, if you are decided that it is best to do so."

Dr. Binney had been ill of fever all day, and was in bed, the fever passing off and perspiration issuing from every pore; but he sprang up, ordered a pony to be brought, and was hurrying on his clothes before Dr. Kincaid perceived his intent.

" What are you going to do, Brother Binney?"

" I am going to see Mr. ———, and secure the refusal of that estate before I sleep. To-morrow will be too late for us."

Dr. Kincaid most good-naturedly replied :

" Well, well, if one of us is to go to town to night, I shall go. I will do this cheerfully, in order to relieve your mind; though I am quite sure it is not necessary."

A few hours later he returned with the report that if the money could be handed over the next day, the deeds would be given, as the owner wished to embark at once for England. The next day the two brethren went together. They found that they had been none too quick in doing the work, as several hundred rupees more had been offered for the refusal. But they secured the property, and others were disappointed.

Temporary accommodation for dormitories and school-rooms was soon put up, and the Seminary removed. In the mean time, Rev. D. A. W. Smith, who had been sent out a few months before to the Burmese Department, was transferred to the Theological Seminary, so that the prospect for its future cheered Dr. Binney's heart greatly. He was especially pleased with the new premises, containing seven and a half acres of land, two large, fine dwelling-houses,—one of which could well accommodate two families,—with good out-houses, needing only the erection of buildings for native teachers and pupils and a Chapel, for school purposes and worship. The location was well described by Rev. Mr. Carpenter in a paper prepared for another purpose.

The present location of the Karen Theological Seminary is in every respect pleasant, and adapted to the requirements of the school. Whatever changes may be made hereafter in the limits of British Burmah, Rangoon will in all probability remain, as it is now, the only convenient station for a General School like this; and of all the eligible sites in Rangoon and vicinity, the one now occupied cannot be surpassed in adaptation to our wants. It is remarkably healthy. It is at a convenient distance from the town. It is near enough to the other Mission Compounds for all friendly intercourse, and far enough removed to prevent all danger of friction.

Professor Wm. Ruggles, LL.D., of Columbian College, pledged at once the funds for the erection of a good chapel. But our country was then in its worst struggle for even a national existence, and it was a remarkable fact that in the midst of it all, our benevolent operations were carried on with so little embarrassment.

26*

Just about this time, however, Dr. Warren writes Dr. Binney.

In my last, I expressed a fear that the national currency would depreciate still further, occasioning a further advance in the cost of exchange. My fears have been realized; gold selling now at $2.50, or thereabout, and exchange ranging from $2.60 to $2.70, more or less, and no one supposes the highest point has been reached. I need not tell you what effect all this must have on our operations abroad. I had a month ago made up my mind that we could pay two dollars for one, and go through the year without incurring a heavy debt, but I must confess the present state of facts looks discouraging. It would not surprise me if we should be compelled virtually to suspend remittances and leave you and the brethren with you, to take care of yourselves as best you may. If it were a business operation, we would stop at once ; but knowing that the whole enterprise is of God, and has his vast resources pledged for its success, we may expect help to arise from some quarter.

This state of things led Dr. Binney to defer the erection of permanent buildings till exchange was more favorable. Thus it came to pass, finally, that Dr. Ruggles' munificent gift for a chapel went to another department of Educational effort for Karens, not, however, without the approval of both Dr. Ruggles and Dr. Binney himself.

He was also pecuniarily embarrassed. All that he possessed was invested in the State of Georgia. He not only failed to receive any interest, but banks failed, and he supposed himself to be left without a cent, and that at a time when others were dependent on him. He was obliged to relinquish the cherished expectation of giving his adopted son a liberal education, and yielded to his desire of going into the army, though a mere boy, while he himself shared his little salary as best he could with others.

His health, too, was becoming seriously impaired, and he was constrained to bring matters as speedily as possible to a state in which he could prudently leave them. The Executive Committee, hearing of his failing health, urged his speedy return. Dr. Warren wrote :

I saw Mrs. Binney week before last. Though suffering much, she is still herself, fully so ; and I tell her she will recover and go back to Burmah. My plan is to have you to call in Dr. Wade to take your place at the helm for a time ; come home and recruit : and then, a couple of years hence, both go back as good as new. It is worth while to make considerable outlay to secure five years more service for such workers.

His letters continued to reach his wife by every mail, full of details of his work, notices of particular pupils in whom he was interested, and the progress of the young people in the language. He was constantly saying,

Do not be anxious about my health. I tell you every thing, as you do me. To-day you are at ———. My heart follows you, and is with you everywhere ; if you listen, you will hear its whisper ; or if you do not, you will feel its throbbing. At any rate it is there, even if you fail to hear or feel it ; it is lovingly, prayerfully with you.

He did not think best to call Dr. Wade to his help, but with Mr. and Mrs. Carpenter making good progress in the language ; Mr. and Mrs. Smith doing the same, though having entered the work a little later ; and with native teachers, prepared to do a great deal, he left Rangoon, early in March, 1865, to join his wife in Philadel-

phia. He wrote her his time of sailing, his plan of spending three days in Paris, and the time when he would
arrive in London, if prospered. Mrs. Binney was then
staying in the family of Wm. Bucknell, Esq., Philadelphia, to whom she read this letter. They were interested, and fixed in their minds the fact that he was
already on his way and would be in Philadelphia some
time early in May. Mrs. Binney, being familiar with the
journey, fixed decidedly in her own mind the very day
when he would be with her. When the morning of
that day arrived, she saw in the early paper that a
steamer of the Cunard line, bound for New York, had
been telegraphed off Halifax. She then said to Mr. and
Mrs. Bucknell, that she thought her husband was in that
steamer, and would probably reach New York about the
time when she was reading the paper; and that she
hoped soon to receive a telegram. All looked as if they
almost thought that her mind had lost its balance. It
seemed to them that so many things might occur to prevent his making every connection; and, moreover, as this
was his first visit to Paris, they believed he would not be
content with a stay of three days in that city. She, however, was sure that nothing but sickness or something
entirely beyond his control would detain him, but having no reasons which she considered convincing to
others, she kept very silent, seating herself where she
would hear every voice at the street door, and interesting herself in the morning news. This was a few days
after the assassination of America's beloved President,
and the papers were of thrilling interest. Persons were
passing in and out the front door for two hours, but no

telegram came; at length Mrs. Bucknell kindly urged Mrs. Binney to come to her room. "If a telegram came," she added, "you will know it all the same, and if it does not ——" Before she could finish the sentence a boyish voice was heard at the door.

"Is Mrs. Dr. Binney here? I have a telegram for her."

Mrs. Bucknell kindly did what Mrs. Binney found herself unable to do,—opened the envelope and read— "Just arrived. Health improved. Take the next train for Philadelphia."

Friends knew not at which to marvel most—Dr. Binney's success in reaching New York from Rangoon at the earliest possible time, or Mrs. Binney's absolute confidence that he would do so.

CHAPTER XVIII.

EIGHTEEN MONTHS AT HOME.

1865—1866.

ON his arrival in Philadelphia, it was very evident, that if he was not then very ill, he had been so. He looked at least ten years older than when Mrs. Binney had left him in Rangoon, two years before. His bent figure and uncertain step told a story which his pen had withheld. He was cheerful and happy, and did not seem at all conscious of his own condition. He was emaciated to a degree that made it seem impossible for him to keep up, yet his face was full and his eye bright, and no one out of the intimate circle understood how changed he was. He went on to St. Louis to attend the Annual Meetings of the Missionary Union, but was able to attend only a single session ; much of the time being confined to his bed with vertigo and headaches. Friends called, and he refused no one, so glad was he to meet them. Afterward, he went to Alton for a few days to visit his brother-in-law, but was obliged to decline most of the many invitations to preach, address Sunday-schools, and the like. His wife hurried him back to Philadelphia, where they retired at once to the country, took board in a nice farmer's family, near their friends, the Crozers, in Upland, and *rested*. Plenty of cream and good fruits and vegetables, with freedom from all responsibility and care, began after a while to bring back his flesh and strength; but not till the bracing autumn weather came was he able to bear any unusual excitement. He supplied the vacant church at Upland occasionally, and gave himself little thought for the morrow. It seemed very improbable that he would ever go back to Rangoon. Indeed, he had for a long time been decided, that Mrs. Binney's strength should never again be taxed as it had been, and he had great doubt as to whether she could bear the climate, even under the most favorable circumstances. At that time, though Mrs. Binney's general health was nearly, if not wholly, restored, she had not so recovered the use of her limbs as to walk independently.

But, as the cool weather of autumn came on, and he began to feel stronger, he could not be idle, and was seriously considering what work he could do, that would tell most upon the interest of the cause for which he lived. The Home Mission Society just at this time was working in Richmond, and his former relations with the South, his knowledge of Southern people, both masters and servants, led the Committee to invite him to go to Richmond, in order to see what he could do there. His mission was a very indefinite one, though it was expected he would do something specially for the colored preachers of Richmond and vicinity. A large school was in progress in the "Old First Church" (African), and several excellent ladies were working in it with zeal and success. Hundreds of children and adults were already able to read the word of God for themselves, and every one who could read was furnished with a Bible. The Old African Church had not been without faithful pastors. Dr. Ryland, the mention of whose name among the colored people "was like sweet ointment poured forth," had labored faithfully for them. Some of the members were found, who, as soon as they could read the word for themselves, were prepared to take classes in the Sunday-school. The large day school and the Sunday-school presented very inspiring scenes. A man was appointed, by the Home Missionary Society, to superintend this work, and especially to act as pastor of the church.

It must be confessed, however, that the place was one exceedingly difficult to fill, and the need had not been fully met. It was perhaps too much to expect that any man on such a mission would be received with great cordiality, the very first winter after the close of the war.

Dr. and Mrs. Binney on their arrival, took apartments in a Southern boarding-house. He called on the pastors of the city, and told them his mission, that his first work would be to call together the colored preachers of the city and vicinity, and teach them in the evenings; as they all had to earn their daily bread for themselves and families, probably he could not, for a while at least, establish a regular school. All the pastors were very cordial; though much had been done for the colored people, now that all obstacles were removed, it was thought, that they should receive different instruction. They expressed the greatest confidence in the wisdom and kindness of his plans. Several ladies called on Mrs. Binney, and the civilities were promptly returned; but they were shut out from much intercourse with the people. The colored people not only would not come freely to them, but they would not have been allowed to do so. In some other respects they were not pleasantly situated. Ex-confederate officers and ladies, full of politics, were at the same table, and often, as might have been expected, bitter things were said. This kept Dr. Binney not unfrequently from the second course at dinner. He felt that he could afford to bear a good deal, and it was natural that the company would discuss these things among themselves. He frequently had very pleasant conversations, but at the table made it a point to be silent on political topics, hoping to keep others silent also. But strangers would come in from time to time, and introduce such subjects.

It happened one day that Mrs. Binney went down to dinner before it was brought in, and something was said which led her to make a remark rather unfavorable to the Southern mode of doing domestic work; but she immediately begged pardon, saying, she probably would do the same way under the same circumstances. One of the ladies responded:

"Do not beg *our* pardon, Mrs. Binney, for anything. How it is possible for you and Dr. Binney to hear the things you have often heard at this table, and remain silent, I do not know. No Southerner could, or would, do it; yet one only needs to see Dr. Binney to know that he is not a coward. It is his self-control, which exceeds everything I ever witnessed."

27

"He has, it is true, great self-control," Mrs. Binney said. "Doubtless, his naturally fiery spirit has needed and received a good deal of discipline. But you must remember, we can afford to bear a good deal from you; we have had a severe contest, and we are on the victorious side. It would be rather ungracious, under the circumstances, to get angry, and reproach you, because you chafe a little."

One of the most intelligent and amiable of the ladies present replied:

"You are right, Mrs. Binney, and it is *possible* if the case were reversed, that we should do as you do; but I fear we should not. At any rate I think it would be more considerate and dignified, on our part, to say less on political subjects at table, where your rights are the same as ours."

Thenceforth they were treated with great respect and courtesy, and the table was a more agreeable place. Dr. Binney did what was in his power to make it so, and the company were pleased to draw him out on topics of common mutual interest. Still, the old objection to his location in the boarding-house remained. The colored people had not free access to him, and Northern friends came and went, and he had only a passing call, sometimes not that. He was able, however, after awhile to secure rooms and board with the Superintendent of the colored schools. It was a change which facilitated his work, though it involved, especially to his wife, a loss of social intercourse.

Dr. Binney while in Richmond, made an effort, to establish a Central School, similar to the one he had in

Rangoon; not merely for Richmond, but for Virginia, and other States as well. He wished it to be a school where not only preachers should be taught the Bible, but where they should receive a literary and scientific education, sufficient to make them intelligent men and capable of leading the colored churches. He knew very well that this was needed, whether in Burmah or America. He found no difficulty in enlisting the sympathies of men, North and South, but needed the co-operation of men of means to carry out his plans. He had commenced negotiations for a large building in Norfolk, but could not at once complete his plans, which had reference, not only to the present, but the future. In the meantime he saw men coming forward to do the needed work; if not exactly in his way, still, to do it; so he went on instructing his preachers, and preaching the gospel himself almost every Lord's Day.

The members of the Old First Church boasted that they had the cream of teaching and preaching in the city. On Lord's Day mornings, church and yard would be packed until there was no longer standing room. Not a white person, except the Teachers and perhaps some Northern visitors, would be seen in the crowd, but all were usually quiet and orderly. Sunday evenings were the great occasions, and sometimes there would be considerable disorder in the crowd that gathered about the church.

Strangers visiting Richmond came to see how colored people conducted their meetings by themselves. Shouting, singing, stamping, and hand-shaking of the most emotional kind characterized these meetings, and they would often be held till a very late hour, breaking up amid a good deal of confusion. As they would crowd the pavements and talk and laugh loudly, it was not always pleasant to meet them. Dr. Binney in his evening class talked this over with the preachers, trying to show them how much more respectable and Christian-like a quiet manner on the street would be, and especially how desirable it was that their meeting should be dismissed at an early hour, and the people go quietly home instead of disturbing the slumbers of people for a mile each way from the church, at a late hour at night, by boisterous talk and laughter.

This was delicate ground to tread upon; especially as he seemed to be on such friendly terms with the white pastors of the city; the freedmen had sometimes been encouraged to show their independence, but Dr. Binney reminded them that there were laws of good breeding which no man could violate with impunity. Gradually his influence prevailed with pastors and preachers.

Whenever invited, he would preach on Sunday evenings. Such visitors then as came merely to see a curious show were disappointed, and would sometimes ask that the people might have a little prayer meeting afterward, but the preachers had independence enough to urge their congregation to leave the house. On one occasion, Dr. Binney had been preaching one of his most earnest and solemn sermons, and the immense audience had honored him by silence. At about nine o'clock the congregation was dismissed, and

walked home very quietly, conversing, if at all, in subdued tones. Some gentlemen, citizens of Richmond,
met the colored pastor of the church, who was among
the last to come out, and saluting him kindly, asked,

"What can be going on among your people? They
are all so quiet, and talking in whispers. Something
must be concocting."

"No, no, nothing evil. Just, Dr. Binney has been
preaching to us to-night, and we all feel solemn-like."

"Pray, who is this Dr. Binney that is making such a
revolution in the old church?"

"Well, you just come and hear for yourselves. I will
be bound you will be thinking about yourselves too.
You come and hear, and if you go away talking much,
then I give it up."

The next Sunday, they came, stood in the yard with
the crowd till the sermon was over, then retired quietly,
saying to one of the preachers :

"Well, it is a pity, you should have all this preaching
to yourselves. I think it would do us white people
good too."

"Yes, master, I dare say you could have your share.
Dr. Binney likes mightily to preach to either whites or
colored people."

Nothing really discouraged Dr. Binney with regard
to the establishment of such an Institution as he earnestly desired for the colored people. He saw that it
would take time, and felt sure of ultimate success; but
as has been intimated, he hoped the work would be
done without him. The winter had set him up. He felt
like himself again. He had had very uphill work during

27*

all his years in Burmah, and just as he was prepared to enjoy somewhat the fruits of his labors, had been called away. Mr. Carpenter, the senior in the Theological Seminary, had kept him well informed of the progress of the School, and always wrote, hoping he would be spared to return. His name was kept on the Seminary Catalogue as its President, and Dr. Warren had written as if expecting he would recruit and go back. When he was leaving Rangoon, Dr. Warren wrote to Mrs. Binney in the following strain:

Dr. Binney has been placed in a very trying position, and, I must say, he has met it nobly. May the grace of God be sufficient for him even to the end! I hope he will live yet many years, and, after recruiting with you a while at home, return with you to his chosen work and field.

About this time a very earnest appeal had come from Burmah for more men. Mr. Beecher was sick and about to leave Bassein, and the Karen pastors had written to the Missionary Union, requesting them to take back the field and send them missionaries. This was a very important event, and moved him greatly. Henthadah was appealing for a man to be sent there. All these circumstances combined made him desirous to return to his old place in the Seminary. This desire was not expressed in words; but Mrs. Binney became quite sure that, but for fear of her health, he would be glad to go back. She dared not make the suggestion. She was not certain whither the path of duty led, and feared to err. Her sufferings had been so great in Burmah as to make her shrink from their possible repetition. But

she waited for clearer light on the way. Things seemed
to be coming to a crisis in the providence of God, and
she quietly awaited its leadings. The Home Mission
Society was anxious that Dr. Binney should decide to
pursue certain measures for the establishing of a School
for the colored preachers, and this important sphere of
usefulness, that was then awaiting his decision, would be
lost if he delayed long. In talking this over with his
wife, he dropped this incidental remark:

" If all hope were given up, of your being able to live
in Rangoon, with no more to do there than you would
have here in connection with an Institution, I could
decide this question at once."

" If you really desire to return," replied Mrs. Binney,
" I should not be afraid to go back, provided Mr. Carpenter or Mr. Smith be permitted to remain with you."

" Then I will write to Dr. Warren a confidential letter,
to know if the Committee would think that the best way
of furnishing men for Bassein."

The letter was on its way in a few hours, and Dr.
Warren replied, by the first mail after its reception,
speaking only his own mind:

If you and Mrs. Binney have that measure of health which
will warrant your return to your work among the Karens, nothing
could be more desirable. It would do good in every way, both
here and there.

More in a similar strain followed, and he spoke of the
appeal from Bassein especially:

These things look providential. If you go out this fall, either
Mr. Carpenter or Mr. Smith could take hold of the Bassein field.

These brethren are both doing well in the Seminary, and have come to look upon it as their work, and might perhaps be reluctant to give it up, even for the Bassein field ; but either of them will readily give place to you, I should suppose.

At the next meeting of the Executive Committee, the appointment was made. Dr. Warren expressed great pleasure at the result of the " confidential letter intended as a feeler," rather than a proposal, and Dr. Murdoch, then Assistant Secretary, wrote his first letter to Dr. Binney, which was followed in after years by a great many of a similar spirit. He said :

Permit me personally to express my great satisfaction at the proposal for your return to Burmah. You can do there, by the blessing of God, what no other man is qualified to do so well, while the work in this country may be carried forward by other hands."

Dr. Binney stipulated that they should take the overland route, and asked that Mrs. Dr. Stevens, then in America and about to return to Burmah, might accompany them. This the Executive Committee had already proposed ; and thus ended, or nearly so, the former plan of sending the missionaries round by the Cape of Good Hope.

CHAPTER XIX.

AGAIN AT RANGOON.

1866–1867.

THE journey was in every respect pleasant, and did much to establish his health. He met a cordial welcome on all sides. The Karens had heard of his interest in the Freedmen, of the crowds who flocked to hear him preach, of his desire to see a Seminary established for the colored preachers, and they were making up their minds that he would never return. Mr. Smith on hearing of his purpose to resume his place in the Seminary of Rangoon, hastened to Henthadah to take the place made vacant by the removal of Mr. Thomas to Bassein, where he was already, like a magnet, drawing all the Christians to his aid. Mr. Carpenter, too, was burning with zeal for the "regions beyond," and asking permission to open a new field. In this desire, Dr. Binney thoroughly sympathized, but he had come out with the expectation of having one of the young men *at least* to remain with him, and felt, that, in order to make progress in the work, so much was essential. Just at the close of the war, too, exchange was so largely against us, that the Board found it almost impossible to keep up the old stations, and he thought it unwise, for the sake of plowing and sowing new fields, to neglect those already prepared for a harvest, and so allow the seed to fall back into the ground for want of reapers. The Executive Committee thought so too, and Dr. Binney entered at once upon a new department of the work, preparing and printing books, and fully expecting and believing that the time was not distant when he could give up his place to Mr. Carpenter. The next year Mr. Thomas's health compelled him to leave Bassein, and try, as a last resort, a voyage to his native land. Bassein was again sorely bereaved. Hardly had they dried their tears for the loss of their devoted and beloved teacher, Mr. Beecher, when Teacher Thomas must leave them. Not only were the Karens distressed, but his Missionary brethren generally felt deeply afflicted. Dr. Binney grieved, with others, that he was losing so faithful and genial a co-worker, but saw, also, that this involved the loss of Mr. Carpenter to the Seminary.

After a painful and wearisome passage, Mr. Thomas reached New York on the 8th of June, 1868, just three days before he was called to his heavenly home. The Foreign Secretary, in announcing his death to Dr. Binney, asks,

Who will fill the place thus made vacant at Bassein? Under the circumstances, we must have the best man we can obtain. Brother Carpenter's name is mentioned, but with great reluctance. Call together the brethren at once, and let me have the result of your best deliberations.

On the 26th of October following, a telegram was dispatched from Boston, which reached Rangoon the

27th, saying, "Carpenter transferred to Bassein, Smith to Rangoon." This being the first telegram ever sent to the Mission from Boston, it produced a profound sensation, independent of the changes which it made.

Mr. Carpenter left at once for Bassein. The Karens, of Henthadah, found it hard to submit to so summary an edict, and were anxious to raise the money on the spot and send back their protest by the telegraph, but were persuded that it would be better to write fully and deliberately, which they did. Mr. Smith left his post reluctantly also, but came to Dr. Binney's help early in the February following. He kept up as far as possible an oversight and general interest in the affairs at Henthadah, and in one of his letters to the Board, he says :

I sometimes have as many as a dozen letters from the Henthadah field in a single mail, besides frequent visits from the pastors of churches. My heart has often bled on account of the remoteness of the station and my inability to follow up cases of interest.

He only remained in Rangoon one year, and then returned to Henthadah, in accordance with his own desire, and to the great joy of the Henthadah churches, but this left Dr. Binney again alone. He had, however, a very well prepared native Faculty, and his health was good. Though greatly disappointed, he girded himself to the work.

After Dr. and Mrs. Binney's return to Rangoon in December, 1866, up to this time, Mrs. Binney had never taught a class or rendered other important assistance in the Seminary.   It had not been necessary while either Mr. Carpenter or Mr. Smith remained, but her health had so improved, that she ventured to call a class of a dozen fine, promising young women to her, and was giving her time and strength to preparing them for teaching at their various stations.   All the expense incurred, in this work, was met by Mrs. Bucknell and a few members of her family.   Before Mrs. Binney left America the last time, Mrs. Bucknell had urged on her to spare no pains or needed expense for Karen girls, as she would like to be *her* co-worker, as Mr. Bucknell had been a co-worker with Dr. Binney.   This was a very congenial labor to Mrs. Binney, and she could not dismiss at once the first class as fully prepared as she desired it to be : and so was for awhile unable to render her husband any assistance.   As soon, however, as these girls were sent back to their stations, Dr. Binney found ample occasion to call upon his old assistant, and she never failed him again, except in cases of severe illness, while he remained in Burmah.

Dr. Binney was not a voluminous correspondent. His life was too busy and earnest to allow him to write many letters, yet he never neglected the claims of duty, and when his heart was touched, his pen was ever ready. Under date of April, 1869, he wrote his old friend, Wm. Bucknell, Esq., of Philadelphia, a letter which will serve a double purpose, a specimen of his tender sympathy, and a deserved tribute to the memory of a woman o rare consecration to the service of her Lord :

MY DEAR BROTHER BUCKNELL :—We sometime since learned that Mrs. Bucknell was quite ill, but hoped the changes she was making would wholly remove the tendency to the lungs. From a letter just received from Dr. W——, I am led to fear that you have cause for serious anxiety. We know that God's ways are not as our ways; still we trust that faith and prayer, with the aid of such means as you have at command, will, with God's blessing, save a life we deem so needed in the church, and in the circle in which you move. You can hardly imagine how seriously, in this far off place, any immediate danger to Mrs. Bucknell affects us. We have had reason to esteem and love her, not only for what she is to us, but for what she has done and is doing in our Master's work. If her strength fails and her system is undermined, we know the cause; she was overworked. Her solicitude for her country, her sympathy for her countrymen, and her interest in behalf of the future salvation of men drew upon her energies more than her constitution cauld bear. During our late war no class of persons did more good or at a greater expense, than those ladies, who, in the spirit of Christ their Master, exhausted their energies in providing for the physical, mental, and religious wants of those who stood in the breach, and fought for us.

You know, my dear brother, that your dear wife took no small share of that anxiety, work, and suffering upon herself; and added to it incessant labor for the fatherless and destitute; all taken into her very heart. Without doubt, her present malady had its origin there. I trembled for her, while we were enjoying your hospitalities. Her heart seemed so full of sympathy for every good work, and yet I feared she had not strength to execute her wishes. More than once I was on the point of urging her to abate her efforts for the temporal good of men, and even for their soul's salvation, feeling sure she could not last to work so, long; but she was so sincerely in earnest, her whole heart seemed so thoroughly engrossed, that I could not bring myself to the task of trying to cool her heart's impulses. She was working for humanity and in her Saviour's name; and I hoped that her recuperative power might equal the strain upon her strength.

But while we are engaged in our modes of thinking, God has his own counsels to be fulfilled; and they are always wise, always gracious toward his own children. It may be his inten-

28

tion to take your dear wife to himself. In my selfishness, I trust it is only to prepare her for greater usefulness in his cause. In either case, I know that she and you will alike submit cheerfully to his will.

I need not tell you how constantly we think and speak of you, nor how earnestly we pray our Heavenly Father soon to remove all these fears, and to restore her to perfect health again. We feel that one very near and dear to us is afflicted, even to apprehension ; but, my dear brother, let us not forget that she is dearer to our Lord and Saviour, and he will govern every change, in his infinite wisdom and in his immutable love to her. Please tell her how much we both love her, and how earnestly we pray for her, that the Saviour may verify to her own soul's experience every one of his precious promises. For yourself, my dear brother, I trust you have strength equal to your day. You know the way to the throne of grace. The Lord Jesus will never leave, never forsake us. I trust you feel all this in your present experience.

It is not to be inferred that Mrs. Bucknell's interest in those outside her home made her unmindful of its duties or its enjoyments. Whether in the relation of wife, mistress of a family, hostess, or friend, she seemed to neglect nothing that could contribute to the happiness of others. In less than a year from this time she was called to her reward. Dr. and Mrs. Binney never ceased to feel her loss, as a friend and co-worker.

Dr. Wade, after the death of his wife in Tavoy, in October, 1868, had come to Rangoon and found a home with his old friends, Mr. and Mrs. Bennett. They being compelled to leave for a time, on account of ill-health, Dr. Binney most cordially invited him to come and make his home at the Seminary. Dr. Wade had previously expressed a desire to "identify his last days with the educational work at Rangoon!" From the first acquaintance of these two men there had been mutual respect, confidence, and affection; and now, in Dr. Wade's solitary old age, Dr. Binney felt very tenderly toward him, and anxious to alleviate his solitude as far as possible.

He had hardly been a month in the family, when it was ascertained, that a cancer had fastened itself upon a part of the lower jaw, caused by irritation, produced by wearing a plate improperly fitted. Both Dr. and Mrs. Binney in inviting Dr. Wade anticipated a considerable addition to their already exhausting cares and labor, but they also looked forward to great happiness in the society of one so ripe for the better land; but when the suffering, protracted and intense, through which he must pass came up so unexpectedly before them, their hearts melted within them. Mrs. Binney's memorandum shows how they were afflicted.

Dr. Maynard has pronounced the soreness in Dr. Wade's mouth to be a cancer, which must eventually prove fatal. Dr. Wade seems to have anticipated the decision, and received it calmly, only saying, after the doctor left, "My dear sister, I would not have dared to come to you had I known what I was bringing." I was taken so entirely by surprise, I could not reply, but stepped into my husband's room and told him all. He at once arose and followed me out, and in the most quiet, tender manner, took Dr. Wade's hand, saying, "This my dear brother, is a very serious thing to you and to us, but I am glad you are here. The Lord has ordered it wisely, and in great mercy. He will help us all through with it. He will not forsake us in this our time of need. We will try and help you to bear it, and afford every alleviation in our power. You believe me when I tell you that I am glad you are *with us*, don't you?" All shed a few tears of mutual sympathy, and went to our rooms to cast our sorrows on the great "Burden-bearer." Dear, dear Dr. Wade, how he misses his wife now!

He lived fifteen months longer, each month increasing the intensity of his suffering and his helplessness, until nature could hold out no longer, and he "fell asleep." For a twelve month before he died, Dr. Binney gave an hour, between eight and nine o'clock, every evening to him. With what interest did the dear sufferer look forward to that hour! The very moment the clock struck he would go into the study, a room adjoining his own, and, though they may have met several times during the day, twice always, yet they would shake hands, and make a few kind inquiries before beginning the subject of conversation for the evening. In this, Dr. Wade always led, unless there was a special reason for reversing the order. He kept little memorandums for these subjects, often days in advance. They were sometimes experimental, sometimes doctrinal; not infrequently would they dwell upon the employments of heaven, bordering perhaps upon the imaginative, but both clung with great tenacity to the necessity of having a "thus saith the Lord," in matters of belief. Mrs. Binney usually spent this hour upon a little couch in the room, often as an interested listener; though broken rest and freedom from the necessity of doing anything for the dear invalid made an hour's sleep more refreshing, sometimes, than even such rich converse.

When the clock struck nine, then again would come the hand-shakings, the good-nights, and earnest wishes for refreshing sleep; for freedom from pain; for the pre-

sence of Jesus, in the weary wakeful hours, if such were
to be. These were every night repeated, with no manifestation of fatigue or formality, but with the same
fervor, as if it were the first night of care. This was a
great tax upon Dr. Binney's powers, after a hard day's
work in a tropical climate, but the occasions were very
rare when he was obliged to disappoint Dr. Wade; no
personal gratification ever led him to do it.

At last there came a night when the beloved sufferer
was brought in upon a chair, his feet so swollen as to
be useless, and his breathing so difficult that he could
converse but little.

" Talk to *me*, to-night, Brother Binney," he said, " I
cannot talk."

" What shall I talk about, my dear brother ?"

" Tell me of the wonderful love—tell me, of the
ground of hope."

And he did tell him the "old, old story of Jesus and
his love." He told it to him " slowly" that he might
take it in, and commended him to his Lord in prayer.
As the clock struck nine the dying saint, sensitive to
the last lest he should intrude, beckoned his attendants
to take him back to his room ; Dr. Binney as usual assisted. When they reached the door, he bade them
stop, then looking around, said in broken sentences,

" I shall never enter this room again ; all these precious seasons are past; I cannot leave without thanking,
you for all the time, and for all the comfort, you have
given me here." He wept, and this distressed Mrs.
Binney, which he perceived. " Oh ! but these are not
tears of sorrow, but of joy. What mercy is this, that

28*

one so unworthy should have such perfect confidence
and sympathy in this hour, when heart and flesh fail!
May God reward you both when your turn shall
come!"

Then he was carried to his room, prepared for bed,
and placed tenderly in it, never to leave it again long
enough to be dressed. A few days after, Dr. Binney
stood by him for the last time, holding his hand and
praying with him; and when he left him for a moment's
relief the patient sufferer said :

"Bear with me, if you can, till I pass this dark valley.
I see the light beyond; the way is very sharp, but it
will soon be over. Stay with me."

Such leaning, even as a child upon its mother, all
through his illness to the last moment, mingled with
manifest respect, was an unconscious yet manifest tribute to the character of Dr. Binney.

After the last sad offices had been performed by his
Missionary brethren for this servant of the Lord, whose
life had been one of rare consecration and success, the
house seemed desolate indeed. Dr. Binney's work, however, had accumulated ; and, without a day's relaxation,
he hastened to perform it. Mrs. Binney, too, had a new
work laid upon her. Dr. Wade had worked upon an An-
glo-Karen Dictionary for two years; continuing it as he
was able even down to within a few days of his departure.
He had reached the letter M, but without any revision,
when he called Mrs. Binney to him and asked her to
take it from his hand and complete it. She hesitated to
assume so great a work, but Dr. Binney seeing Dr.
Wade's anxiety lest his past labor should be lost, en-

couraged her to promise him to try and do her best to carry out his wish. Dr. Wade placed funds at her disposal for a copyist and for the printing. This encouragement, which Dr. Binney had given his wife to undertake the Dictionary, made him very anxious to render it as easy as possible for her, and to this end he assumed many little unaccustomed cares.

Now they were again alone, cheerfully working together; she still having some classes which he disliked to teach and for which the native teachers were not competent; he helping her when the exact meaning of a Karen word was difficult to define in Karen, and required research, and often continuing the work when she had retired to rest.

Dr. Wade's sufferings had awakened their deepest sympathy, and when he was removed, they sorrowed for the removal of a faithful fellow-laborer, and a loving Christian brother; but they were comforted by the knowledge that one whom they loved so much was forever freed from pain and with the pure and blessed, where he had so longed to be. They were deeply impressed with the solemn admonition they had received, to work while the day should last. Thus various causes combined to make them perhaps unconscious of the great exhaustion they had experienced.

Only a few weeks of this earnest, happy labor had passed, when Mrs. Binney was again brought very low, this time "nigh unto death." Again was Dr. Binney called upon to care for, to comfort and sustain; and bravely did he perform the duty allotted him. By the blessing of God upon good nursing, and the most skilful and devoted medical treatment, she rallied, but was not able to resume her work. In this time of trial Dr. Binney received another kind letter from his faithful friend, Mr. Bucknell, urging him to take Mrs. Binney and come home at once to recruit.

"I can not leave, but Mrs. Binney must accept the kind offer; and, as the rains are about to commence, she will not delay, but soon be on her way to America." Such was the reply sent by return mail; and although she was most reluctant to leave him alone again, he was strong in his conviction that it was wisest and best for both that she should have a decided change. She therefore yielded again, and with only a few hours preparation, embarked for London on her way to America.

It was arranged when she left that she should be absent a year; and Dr. Binney wrote her to be sure to remain till her system had time to fully recuperate. She was absent, however, only eight months, and returned in greatly improved health.

When she met her husband, a single glance showed her that she had not come a day too soon. Evidently her going had been an expensive one to him, for he had grown in appearance many years older. His cheerful home being restored, his health soon improved, but the successive trials through which he had passed, and his unremitting labor, left indelible marks. He never recovered the old elasticity again.

Had it pleased the ever-wise and loving Father to lessen his trials then, he might probably have rallied so far as to have had still some years of happy, successful work; but such was not his plan.

While Mrs. Binney was in America, contributions were given her, largely by personal friends, to complete the sum necessary for the erection of a building for the accommodation of " The Rangoon Baptist College," but recently established. The location had been fixed at Rangoon by the Executive Committee, and Rev. C. H. Carpenter was placed at its head. This relieved Dr. Binney, as he thought, of all further care or responsibility relating to that department of education ; but hardly had this object been secured, which his brethren had unitedly asked him to attempt, when Mr. Carpenter requested the Committee to allow him to return to his former field of labor, Bassein, and take the College with him. This measure pleased no other Karen Missionary ; but other places were consequently proposed, and local influences were so great, as to lead the Committee to inquire into the " expediency of abandoning all attempt to establish a College anywhere." Dr. Binney saw the work, which had once before eluded his grasp, again coming to nought. He felt that it would be a final failure, if he failed now, and he could not yield the point without a desperate effort to save it. He was also about to erect a Chapel for the Seminary, and had the daily routine of the School upon his hands. He felt too much ; thought too much ; wrote too much ; and suddenly, without a moment's warning, he sank under it. One side was paralyzed. Though incapable of continued thought, he took in the situation at once. "This," said he, "is the beginning of the end." Under good medical treatment, however, he was up and about again, drove out occasionally, and began

" to set his house in order." He called together a few Karen friends for counsellors, laid the case before them, and drew up a paper for subscription to the Chapel. The Karens contributed liberally, and, with a little assistance from the European residents, and a small appropriation from the Board at home, he soon erected a neat and suitable building, which served the double purpose of Church and School.

His physicians now urged entire cessation from thought and care, as well as a change; but he felt the necessity of preparing for a successor, and worked on by proxy so long as possible. His plans were all designed to promote the future good of the Karens. Their present and future welfare lay very near his heart, and he could not consent to spare himself. With unremitting zeal he still labored on for a few months longer, when, a second stroke affecting the other side, compelled him to desist.

CHAPTER XX.

FINAL DEPARTURE FROM RANGOON.

1876.

THE Committee made such efforts as they deemed practicable to relieve him, and the Rev. John Packer was sent to his aid, but still his labors and time were imperatively required for the College; he was urged, however, to leave all and come home at once. The invitation of the Committee had been preceded by one from Mr. Bucknell, who for the second time asked him "to return at his expense." Dr. Binney desired his medical attendant to call for counsel the best adviser the profession in Rangoon could furnish, and before they entered into an examination of the case, he said to them:

"Gentlemen, I charge you to deal candidly with me. I am neither afraid, nor unwilling, to die. I do not think it seemly, at my time of life, with the hopes I cherish for the future, to be playing hide and seek with death, dodging him at every corner. I would fain meet him face to face as a Christian man should do. Indeed, I do not look upon death as an enemy; but death means the end of my service here. I have a little work which, even with very feeble health, a year or two

333

would enable me to perform, but would be much more difficult for another to do. I hope that a little entire rest would enable me to finish it by and by, *where I am.* Still, if you think this cannot be, for the sake of another year or two of work, I would be willing to make the change, provided there is a reasonable prospect of that being accomplished."

After much conversation with each other they told him very candidly, that he could not live three months, unless disease was arrested, and that they thought there was a prospect that a long sea voyage would give considerable alleviation. They said nothing of mental labor. The decision did not satisfy him that it was best to go; "considerable alleviation" might involve protracted suffering, with none of the comforts of home; yet his work would not be accomplished. "Quiet was what he needed—not excitement." He took a little time to consider, but finally could not settle the matter. He would greatly prefer to remain; but the bare possibility that he might be restored to complete his work, with the fact that another's happiness was concerned, made him hesitate. He left it to his wife to do as she thought best. To decide any matter, great or small, alone was a responsibility to which she was unaccustomed, but she knew what *he* would do were the case reversed. He would leave no means untried to procure "alleviation," were he well and she the sufferer. She at once wrote to a friend in Rome, making all needed inquiries as to the desirableness of that city, as affording quiet, comfortable winter quarters, where his mind might be diverted without being excited, and at a reasonable expense for living. In the meantime, she set about making preparations for a public sale of furniture and everything they owned in the world, except their personal wardrobe, holding herself ready at any moment, by day or by night, to act as nurse and helper in the closing up of personal business and the necessary preparations for leaving the Seminary.

Not only was the Chapel to be finished, and its business settled; but there were daily interviews with the teachers, at which he would become exhausted, and require help to get through. The Lord's Day before he left Rangoon, the Chapel being sufficiently advanced for public worship to be held in it—indeed, the hall for worship was completed—he was helped by his native teachers, one on each side, to walk over to it and to preach what was at once the dedication sermon and his farewell to the pupils and numerous Karens assembled. He surpassed himself. "I have not sought yours, but you," was his theme. A brief review of his labors among them, and for them, with his grateful testimony to their co-operation and appreciation at all times, together with a few words of counsel for the future, closed the affecting scene. One of the missionaries whose privilege it was to be present said at the end of the service: "This is a fitting close to such a life-work as that of Dr. Binney."

After the services, he was carried to his bed, and strong apprehension was felt that he never would have strength to leave it again. But he was able the following week, with Mrs. Binney and a good Karen attendant, to embark for Rome, where he hoped to acquire strength

29

which would enable him to bear the excitement he must meet in returning to his native land.

Before he left his house, when the luggage had been sent on board, and the carriage was waiting to convey him to the steamer, Mrs. Binney, with several of his Karen friends, went to his room where he was resting, to inform him of it, and to assist him out. He completely broke down at the commencement.

"Yes, dearest, the carriage is waiting to take us from the last home you and I will ever have together. How much better, instead of voluntarily taking ourselves out of it, had we waited for the Lord to call me to himself —to my Heavenly Home?"

"Perhaps it would have been, since you feel so; but we sought his direction, and acted according to the light we had. Can we not trust him now, and go forward cheerfully?"

"Yes, we will; bear with me, I am very weak."

He soon composed himself, and never again expressed regret at the course taken.

He was hardly out to sea, before he felt stronger, and on his arrival in Calcutta the improvement was very great. All the way to Rome, he was cheerful and attentive to the comfort of his wife and the young Karen, both of whom were very sea-sick. On the French steamer, every one was charmed with the "old gentleman on deck," as he was called; and nothing could exceed the politeness shown him in little kind and thoughtful attentions. It was difficult for him to go up and down, and he stayed on deck, from early morning till late at night. So conscious was he of every day's gain, that on his arrival at Naples he had a great dread of landing, fearing that on land there would be a relapse. But this fear was not realized. Between three and four months in Italy passed rapidly away, and on the whole he improved decidedly in strength, and especially in his ability to walk. Nearly three months were spent in Rome in quiet lodgings. The effects of this long rest were in many respects very favorable. The city abounds in objects of interest; and he went out from time to time sight-seeing as he felt able. He was pleased and interested with what he saw, though he did not seem to enjoy it as it had been hoped that he would. Had he been well and strong, it would have given him intense enjoyment to look upon the objects in this city, so full of memories of by-gone centuries. But his mind dwelt more on the future than on the past; more on the subjective than on the objective.

The Sunday evening Conferences at the Rev. W. C. Van Meter's, he enjoyed very greatly, when he was not called on to speak. He was nervous in regard to any public effort, and would often say,

"I look so well that people will hardly believe me unable to help to make the meeting interesting."

He loved the Conference, and repeatedly expressed his belief that the successful effort to keep open a place of that kind, where all visitors, from any part of Christendom, who loved the Lord, could meet and speak to one another, was well worth all the expense incurred.*

---

* Mr. Van Meter was sent out by the American Baptist Publication Society, as a Bible and Sunday-school Missionary to Rome. These weekly Conferences were established as an incidental part of his work.

Those who did not truly love the Lord were not infrequently invited by their friends to attend, and were deeply impressed. It was good to be there.

A short time in Florence, followed this pleasant sojourn in the " city of the seven hills," and then he embarked from Leghorn for New York, stopping at all the principal ports of Italy and Sicily; touching at Gibralter, Cadiz, and Valencia; and arriving at their destination May 23d, 1876. This kept him at sea, about six weeks, and although the steamer, designed for trade rather than passengers, was a good deal crowded, and the passengers not generally congenial, yet he enjoyed every day, and often regretted that he had not embarked for a longer passage.

CHAPTER XXI.

SURVEY OF HIS WORK IN BURMAH.

AT this period,—the final leave-taking, the closing up of his work in Burmah—it may be well to take a cursory review, and bring before the mind, in a more succinct form, the character and extent of his labors there, though this be done at the risk of some repetition.

When first invited to enter the Foreign field, it was, in the language of the Committee of the Board of the Baptist Triennial Convention for Foreign Missions, " to establish and conduct a school for the training up of a native ministry among the Karens." He was also " expected to unite with his brethren, in inaugurating a system of general education among them." This was the work to which he was called, and to which he strictly adhered.

After one year of close application to the language, preaching, however, nearly every Lord's Day in English to the English-speaking community, he commenced his school in Maulmain, then the capital of British Burmah. The school was commenced with thirteen pupils. The characters of these, with the peculiar circumstances under which they came to him, their eagerness to learn, and the subsequent career of these men, have been too fully described to need farther notice.

The Old Testament had not yet been printed, neither had the New, except in detached portions. The language had been reduced to writing but a short time previous by Dr. Wade. There were no Text Books, or nearly none, for his use. The instruction was almost entirely oral.

These preachers—for such they already were—were taught the way and word of God more perfectly; and all were instructed in Arithmetic, Geography, Astronomy, and even a little Natural Philosophy, and anything else which he found time to teach, and which he deemed necessary to the enlargement of their minds, and to their better understanding of the character of God as revealed in nature or in grace. As soon as the Bible was printed, it was taught systematically and connectedly, so dividing it that the whole should be gone over in the three or four years course, more or less critically. A few simple rules of interpretation were, as far as possible, explained and enforced.

A day in Maulmain may serve as a specimen of his work. He usually rose at five o'clock, took a hasty cup of tea, and perhaps a bit of dry toast, donned a working suit, and by the ringing of a gong summoned his pupils together for an hour or two of physical exercise. When Mr. Vinton's school was in session, he with his young men often united with them. With tools in hand, he directed them, and worked with them, in draining and grading the large compound, the making of roads, planting of hedges, shade and fruit trees, and flowering shrubs; and in keeping the ground generally clean and tidy. These were often merry times, when a passer-by might imagine, from the shouts and laughter, that some new play had been introduced on the Mission compound. Thus, while health and cheerfulness were promoted, an unsightly jungle was made attractive. Then a gong called all to breakfast, and to necessary preparation for the school-room. Less time was given to private study than in later years, as there were no Text Books for the purpose.

From nine till twelve, and again from one to four o'clock, he gave to teaching. A portion of each lesson consisted of dictation, which the pupils wrote down for study and for review the next day. He seldom was with his pupils less than five hours each day, and often more. After dinner the pupils worked an hour again, in which he sometimes engaged, and at early lamp-light an hour was spent in worship, reading, singing, and prayer, which, while in Maulmain he conducted, or at which he assisted.

He usually spent about two hours after tea in preparation for the next day, or in personal conversation with his pupils, as there was need or desire. This habit he kept up all through his connection with the Seminary, of considering one hour of the twenty-four sacred to the teachers or pupils if they desired assistance or advice, or if he desired to see them especially for any reason.

Some of the pupils, for years, brought their wives and little children with them when they came to the Seminary; and these had to be cared for in sickness as well as in health, which was often a very onerous duty. Accounts had to be carefully kept and much correspondence conducted, in all of which for a long time he had little assistance, except such as Mrs. Binney could render. It will readily be seen that, in such a climate as that of Burmah, his position was no sinecure ; but it is not recollected that he ever complained of either the character or extent of his labors. Being done for Jesus, they were elevated and elevating, in his esteem.

The reader who has followed his history thus far needs not here to be told of his reasons for returning home in 1850, of his remaining from Burmah nearly nine years, of his resuming his work in 1859, at Kemendine, near Rangoon, rather than at Maulmain.

Here he had emphatically to begin anew. He had, also, more advanced scholars, and of a more promising age. The work of education had considerably advanced at the station schools. Dr. Wade had sent him a fine class of young men, but his assistant, whom he had with great pains prepared for service in the Seminary, could not be induced to come to Rangoon. A class of three or four fine young men, selected with one exception from Dr. Wade's best pupils, was formed; and the work of training them for assistants commenced; and though they taught as fast as they learned, yet the extra labor was considerable. This daily routine differed little from that in Maulmain, except that he was obliged to preach more in Karen, and for a time he added the care of a small English church and congregation to his Karen work, for which service he received enough to aid in grading roads and bringing the grounds into fine condition. He added considerably to the curriculum of study, and gave more attention to the preparation of text books. A work on

Systematic Theology, and another on Sermonizing, were prepared for the press. A Vernacular Grammar for the use of the Seminary was prepared by Dr. Wade at his special request. A work on Mental Philosophy, and another on Moral Philosophy, were nearly completed, and used in the school. He gave considerable time, also, to a volume of Transferred Terms with Karen definitions—something in the form of an encyclopædia for his own future use and that of others in preparing books. This, finally, grew into several volumes, but has not yet been printed.

His labors here were excessive. Probably no man could for many years have sustained them. He broke down, and in 1865 left the Seminary in charge of Messrs. Carpenter and Smith, not then long in the country, and returned home. The Seminary during his last year was removed to Rangoon City.

After two years rest and recuperation he resumed his labors. As has been seen, Mr. Smith went at once to Henthadah; and a year later so pressing was the demand that Mr. Carpenter went to Bassein, and Dr. Binney was again left alone without the aid of any American Missionary; but Mrs. Binney resumed the place in the school which she had in Maulmain and Kemendine. He had, too, a well-trained corps of native teachers. These, with a little oversight, kept the well-cultivated place in nice order, attended to the boarding department, kept the account of daily expenditures, attending to the sending out of classes, and the school routine generally. He discontinued any regular English preaching, and only took turns with three of the teachers in Karen preaching. He also had for one year the assistance again of Rev. Mr. Smith, who, however, returned to the pressing claims of his former charge.

He had never deemed the discipline of the Seminary difficult, but now it was so perfect that there seemed to be none. The machinery worked with so little friction, that it apparently ran itself. One of the last terms he ever spent in the Seminary, he boasted, that for the entire term he had never reproved a teacher or pupil. It must be confessed, however, that the last week of the term came very near depriving him of this boasting. Having more than eighty persons on the place, it was not easy in that climate to keep all departments in perfect order. The culinary department, with that part of the compound contiguous, was in charge of one of the younger teachers; and as he had a good deal to do toward the close of the term for his classes, he had neglected his duty in regard to it. Mrs. Binney, thinking her husband had not noticed it, suggested, as they were about taking an evening drive, that they should drive in the direction which would take them through that part of the compound. He drove, however, out of the usual gate, saying as he did so,

"I do not wish to see that part of the compound just now. You can hardly imagine how nervous that little matter has made me to-day. There has been no occasion for reproof during this entire term, and I am unwilling, just at its close, to make those fine fellows a marked exception. I hope they will manage it some way before night of their own accord."

During the drive he was silent and evidently anxious. When he came back in sight of the compound he perceived that every member of the Seminary, young and old, was at work. He turned back and drove half an hour longer, and then came in through the gate which a little time before he was unwilling to pass. Meeting the teacher who had neglected his duty, he spoke in terms of commendation of the state of his charge.

A few days later in taking leave of the graduating class, and of the other pupils for their vacation, he thanked the entire school for their uniform regard to his wishes, which had been so perfect that he had not had occasion for a word of reproof during the long term. The teacher above alluded to arose instantly and with a smile said, he objected to the phraseology of the Teacher's commendation. He thought he should say, " there had been no reproof administered " rather than that "there had been no occasion." He remembered an occasion for reproof, not many days since, which only the Teacher's forbearance had prevented. All looked as if they understood it, but no reply was made.

During the latter part of his life in Rangoon, much time and labor were given to the establishing of the Rangoon Baptist College. Knowing the importance of educating the young, he began early to work in that direction, as has been seen by the history of the Karen Normal School in Maulmain. He afterwards made several tentative efforts, and as these failed, he quietly awaited the action of others. When his brethren, however, under the leading of Rev. D. L. Brayton, asked him to make one more effort for establishing a School for Higher

Education in connection with the Theological Seminary, he gladly accepted the invitation, though for reasons which have been named elsewhere, it was thought desirable that the two institutions should be contiguous, yet they were entirely distinct in their character and control,—the Seminary having no more control over the College than the College over the Seminary. The College was, like the Seminary, a General Institution for all the stations alike, and for the education of Christian youth, without regard to their future calling. It was hoped that young men from the College would enter the Seminary, and so prepare for preachers and pastors; but if they afterwards became clerks, or merchants, or timber dealers, or engaged in any lucrative calling, there was to be no claim further than upon any other Christian man. It was believed to be as important that there should be intelligent and prosperous business men to support the work in Burmah, as that there should be preachers. He worked for the College, with the same spirit and intent that men work in this country for Academies and Colleges, feeling that if in the technical sense, this was not Mission work, it was exceedingly important Christian work, which sooner or later, would need to be performed, and which it was exceedingly wise and desirable to begin as soon as possible.

At this point it may be well to revert to the plan for education in Burmah which Dr. Binney desired to see fully and successfully carried out. He had a strong personal attachment to Martin B. Anderson, LL.D., President of the University of Rochester, whose life-long devotion to the cause of education peculiarly fitted him to discuss intelligently and wisely all the educational questions which the work in Burmah suggested. The result of these discussions, Dr. Anderson gives in the following letter, presenting Dr. Binney's views and his own on this important subject.

FROM MARTIN B. ANDERSON, LL. D.

ROCHESTER, N. Y., May 24, 1880.

MY DEAR MRS. BINNEY:—It was only two days ago that I learned that you were preparing a memoir of your late honored husband. This brought to my mind very many reminiscences of conversation with him, regarding the duty of American Baptists to provide a comprehensive educational system for the members of our mission-churches in the East. His opinions on that subject were very decided; and they seemed to me to be eminently just. His experience as an educator had been acquired both in the East and the West. He had given more profound and thoughtful attention to the subject than any man whom I have ever met. He was also a man of unusual breadth, solidity, and clearness of mind. I accepted his views so far as I understood them, also, because they commended themselves to my own judgment as a teacher and a student of history.

I write to you now simply to make the request, that in the Memoir you are preparing, you will give a full, frank, and decided expression to Dr. Binney's views regarding the education —both secular and theological—which he thought best adapted to the Christian population of Burmah.

⸱ I am aware that there are serious differences of opinion on this subject: One class of conscientious and intelligent men insist that the education of our Eastern converts shall be conducted in their vernacular tongues, and that the English language shall be excluded from the courses of study in all the mission-schools. Dr. Binney, if I understand his views aright, believed that the higher education should be conducted through the English tongue, and that instruction in this language should be begun so

30

early as to give pupils such a facility in English, that the higher departments of science and literature could be profitably and easily taught through it as a medium. ‘ I do not know that I represent adequately his views; but such is the impression left upon my mind.   They seem to me now so well adapted to promote the well-being of our Eastern Christians, that I hope most earnestly that you will be able to give them adequately to the public.

The work of our Eastern Missions is vastly more comprehensive than ordinary Christians suppose.   It is nothing else than the creation, among a heathen, semi-barbarous, and ignorant population, of the most advanced type of Christian civilization.   This at least ought to be the ideal which we should hold before our minds, and for whose realization we should constantly labor.   The foundation of this great work must be laid in the preaching of the gospel, in the translation of the Holy Scriptures, and in the formation of a distinctively Christian literature.

But this is not all.   The cultivation of the moral and religious nature of man should be carried on simultaneously with the highest practicable development of the intellectual powers. Christianity must ultimately lay its hands in India, as it has in Europe and America, upon the entire moral and intellectual life of the people.   What, through great sacrifices and long years of labor, the Baptist Denomination has accomplished in England and America, should be aimed at in the East.   We may not reproduce the same courses of study in the East which we adopt here; but there must be a high Christian education made available for our converts if we would do for them, relatively to their situation and capacity, what we are doing for our people at home. Without a comprehensive and vigorous system of education, that shall keep pace with the growth and demands of the intellectual life of our converts, their churches will become superstitious, the ministry feeble, and the brightest intellects in our Eastern churches will be rapidly drawn away from us.   The fact that we were compelled to remain a century behind other religious denominations in establishing institutions of liberal learning, was one of the bitterest results of the persecutions which our fathers suffered. Let us not blindly follow, in the East, the course which our fathers were obliged to fall into, through the legal disabilities under which they suffered.

The question arises, "Can such an education as our Eastern converts require, be communicated through their vernacular languages?" My own impression is, that it cannot. History is full of illustrations of the fact, *that semi-barbarous peoples have almost universally received their education and culture through the languages of nations who were educated and civilized.* Roman literature and the philosophical elements of the Roman law came from the Greek mind through the Greek language. The education of the Middle Ages was accomplished through the medium of the Latin tongue. The study of the Roman law furnished almost all the moral and scientific elements in the codes of Europe—England included. What Greek literature was to the Roman; what the Roman literature and language were to the barbarians of Western Europe,—the English is, relatively, to our converts in the East. It comes to them freighted with the intellectual accumulations of all the past. It brings to them the terminology of spiritual religion, of the science of mind, and the science of God. It brings to them the complete circle of the moral and political sciences, in systematic form, couched in exact and sharply defined terms. It brings to them, also; the entire circle of the sciences conversant with material nature.

If I understand the matter aright, it will be utterly impossible to translate typical treatises in these various departments of knowledge, without an infusion into the languages of the East, of an enormous addition of scientific and technical terms, adopted from the languages of the West. As our missionaries speak the English language, they must, should they make this attempt, borrow from their own mother-tongue. The English language became scientific by borrowing enormously from the Latin and Norman French. The vocabulary of law and science all over Europe is Latin and Greek. What these languages have done for Modern Europe, the English language must do for our Eastern Christians. It is not necessary for the mass of these peoples to learn the English language; but their preachers and teachers, and moral and political leaders, must be trained in English, or their education will be inadequate and narrow.

The Government of Great Britain has absorbed a portion of Burmah, and in all probability will soon absorb the whole. A great advantage will be given to those young Burmans and Karens who are able to speak the language of the people, who—after making all allowance for maladministration—have brought to the East the blessings of stable government and just and equal laws.

We may be certain, if this education is not offered by us to our native Christians, that it will be brought to them by others, and with it the fatal gifts of rationalistic or hierarchical error.

Excuse me for having said so much. I began this letter with the design simply of asking you to develop fully your husband's views on this vast subject of providing an education for our converts in the East. We have aroused their intellects by the gospel of Christ. We must provide for them a high education, imbued with the principles of that gospel whose elements they have received into their minds and hearts.

Dr. Binney deserves the title of the " Pioneer Educator of our Missions in Burmah." He brought to that work a mind of rare endowments, natural and acquired. These mental qualities were combined with an unselfish and Christ-like devotion to what he believed to be to the best interest of these converts to our faith. It seems to me that you owe it to your husband, to the Christians of the East, to the American Baptists, and to the Christian world, to develop your husband's views on the subject of this letter.

I trust you will excuse me for the almost imperative earnestness with which I have written. The letter has been drawn out by my sense of the importance of the subject, and by my personal reverence for the opinions and character of a great and good man.   Very truly yours,

CHAPTER XXII.

STARTS AGAIN FOR BURMAH, LAST DAYS.

1877.

HE spent the following summer—after a few weeks in Philadelphia, at Mr. Bucknell's — with his friends, at Upland, mostly as a guest in Mr. Samuel A. Crozer's family. The country was very charming, and everything that friendship and hospitality could devise was done to make him happy, but time hung heavily. He was not able to engage in any employment which presented itself at home. Every department of work in this country was attended with a degree of excitement, which his poor wearied brain could no longer bear. He longed to be among the Karens, where he felt that, in his own way and time, he would carry out some incompleted plans. The autumn and early winter were spent in Boston with his relatives; and though he enjoyed his visit greatly at times, the cold weather was unfavorable; his nervous excitement, alternating with great prostration, increased, and about mid-winter he returned to Philadelphia, where he spent the remainder of the season. In the spring, he was able to go on to Washington, D. C.; Dr. J. C. Welling, the President of Columbian University, had invited him some months before to do so, and to come to his house, but he had not seen any time after his return when his strength was sufficient for it. Early in May, however, he made preparations to accomplish this cherished purpose; he bore the journey well, and was able to meet his old friends once more with great joy. Mrs. Binney had looked forward to this with much apprehension. The associations connected with his work there, with all he had abandoned in leaving it, and all the trials since undergone,—though indeed mingled with great and distinguished mercies,—she had feared would be too trying in his enfeebled state. All his old friends were considerate and kind, and though there was no lack of respect, yet he felt more than ever, the change which had come over him.

"When I was here before," said he one day to his wife, "I could work more hours in a day than any man on the ' Hill,' and not feel it. My example was an inspiration here. No man ever heard me complain of hard work. Now, I can do nothing. They all show plainly that they pity me."

"They all show respect and kindness."

"Yes, they do, but it is very hard for me to give up. This rebellious spirit must be very displeasing to God. I think I ought to be the happiest of men. I am overwhelmed at times with the sense of God's distinguishing mercies. But there is so much to be done; and I feel able to work—and yet—I can't—I am tethered."

Still his visit was very gratifying, and he remembered it with great pleasure.

He went from Washington to Providence, Rhode

Island, and attended the Annual Meeting of the Missionary Union in that city in May, 1877. He entered into all its plans for enlargement with the most intense interest, especially for the establishing of the mission in Upper Burmah. He longed to be with his old pupils and to encourage them to engage in this, to them, foreign field. He was anxious to speak more fully on this point, but exercised great self-control, and said but little; still, that little was so manifestly from an overflowing heart, that it told upon the audience. He could not, however, refrain from telling in a few words his experience as a pastor, in interesting his people in Foreign Missions, and his manner of doing it. Several brethren afterward asked him to write down what he had said and allow it to be published for the use of pastors, but that was quite impossible for him to do.

When the effort was made for the extinction of the heavy debt, which was embarrassing the Committee greatly, his whole soul went into it.

"Oh," said he, "if I had the power in the pulpit which I once had! but I dare not trust myself to go beyond private conversation, nor to attempt very much even there."

After the meeting a friend expressed some surprise that he had pledged himself for so large a subscription. Invalid as he was, he might need it for personal comfort.

"Yes," he replied, "if no one gives to Foreign Missions, except those who can give without calling into exercise faith and trust, very few would give. There are a few who are honored with large means; but if they do not give till they feel it somewhat, they do not probably give according to their ability. I, for one, cannot afford to withhold the Lord's due. No, no;" said he in the most emphatic manner, "I never saw a true Christian who made anything by that. I prefer to trust him, rather than my own devising."

The following summer was spent with Mrs. Binney's sister, in the quiet, pretty village of Warsaw, Wyoming County, New York. For awhile the change seemed so favorable, that he began to entertain strong hopes of a return to Burmah. Indeed, he had never fully abandoned all hope of so doing; and accordingly wrote the Foreign Secretary, that he would be prepared to go early in the ensuing autumn.

He did not in this matter act inadvisedly. In May, after his return from Washington, his physician, Doctor Wm. W. Keen, of Philadelphia, was surprised to see him so well. He had never given the slightest encouragement to his hope of being able to return to Burmah, but "Now," said he, "Dr. Binney may live ten years." He consulted also his brother-in-law, Doctor S. W. Pattison, a man of great experience and skill in such cases. After a careful examination, he said it seemed to him quite probable that the sea voyage would do him much good, and perhaps enable him to accomplish what he so much desired, and what was so desirable to be accomplished.

The Rev. D. A. W. Smith, the new President of the Theological Seminary, had written to him, saying, that if he could return, and was able to undertake anything more than to carry his books through the press, it would be a great help to him if he would give one hour daily to the senior class, on his own books, which would require but little labor in preparation.

He was very eager to be once more at work in Rangoon, and did not for a moment doubt that it was the wish of the Executive Committee to have him there. But when the subject of his return was brought before the Committee, some of them doubted the propriety of his return. The doubt arose solely from a consideration of his years and infirmities. They were fearful that he would be compelled very soon to return to this country again. They were all, as Dr. Murdock wrote to him, "Inspired * * * with the sincerest love and veneration for him;" and, finally, a vote was passed making the appropriation needed for his return. The letter announcing this action of the Committee also informed him of the hesitation on the part of some of its members, and stated what was their only reason for doubting the propriety of his return.

The perusal of the letter placed him in a peculiar position, the delicacy of which some perhaps would not readily appreciate. Although the appropriation had been made, and he was anxious to go, yet he could not feel entirely willing to return to Burmah while a respectable minority of the brethren of the Committee doubted the expediency of his doing so.

An extract from a letter written since his decease by Dr. Murdock, who fully appreciated the strong points of his character, will serve to throw some light upon his state of mind.

Dr. Binney was clear-sighted and very decided in his views of the policy to be pursued, but when the Executive Committee failed to enter into his views, he surrendered the matter to those who had a right to decide, without a reproach or even a complaint. There was a spirit in him so magnanimous and gracious in this particular, that he ought to be held up as a model to all missionaries. He knew alike how to lead and how to submit; two qualities of the first importance to a missionary.

During the extreme heat of that very hot summer of 1877, Dr. Binney was accustomed for the sake of retirement and because he found it cooler, to spend a great deal of time in a very large unoccupied outbuilding, a short distance from the house. He had it fitted up a little, and said that it was more like his Burman home than any other place; he could have plenty of air and no direct drafts upon him. A few days after the reception of Dr. Murdock's letter, Mrs. Binney, thinking he had been alone long enough, went out and found him walking back and forth, looking greatly depressed. She had hardly joined him, when he took from his pocket a letter to the Secretary, and putting it into her hand, said:

" If you can copy this for me soon, I will send it by this evening's mail."

The purport of the letter was, that under the peculiar circumstances of the case he had finally decided to remain at home and abandon further expectation of returning to Burmah. One extract will show the views which prompted his desire to return, and the spirit in which he nevertheless decided to remain.

I thought that my last days, however few, might be spent usefully for the cause, and that it was worth the risk and expense, but I have learned to leave all in the hands of him, for the love of whom I have more than once given up all that was dear to me in my professional life in this country.

After a careful reading of the letter, it was very evident to her who knew him so well, that this was to be a sore disappointment; and, that though he was then improving, yet when the hope which was buoying him up was removed, his health would probably decline at once. It looked like a very formidable undertaking to her, to start on such a voyage under the circumstances ; but not to go seemed more formidable still. They freely talked the whole matter over again; and she suggested among the reasons against his going, the probability that he might die suddenly, and therefore might die at sea.

"Yes," he replied, "I have not been unmindful of that; that would not be so pleasant—for you."

No allusion was ever again made to a burial at sea. The letter was not sent.

For a few days there was no further conversation on the subject of going back to Burmah. At length one day he was found again, walking backward and forward, but now with a countenance beaming with happiness.

"Well, dear," he said, "I have made up my mind not to notice any further what some of the Committee thought. Their objection, it seems, was finally removed, and so I will let it pass. This, I think is my final decision; I have reconsidered the whole matter."

He had embodied his decision in the following letter to Dr. Murdock, the Corresponding Secretary, dated Warsaw, Wyoming County, New York, July 21st, 1877.

MY DEAR BROTHER.—Your very kind letter of the 9th inst. was not received here till the 12th. I have delayed to answer, feeling it due to the Executive Committee and to myself to review the whole question of my return to Burmah. When I proposed to go out again, I thought it would enable me to spend my last days, however few, in finishing up the work of my missionary life, for which I have more than once given up what was so dear to me in my professional engagements in this country—to finish, if God be willing, in a comparatively short time, what no young man could do for some years. It would involve some expense, and some risk of my dying without accomplishing the work; but I thought the object was worth all the expense, and justified the risk. My review of the question confirms me in my first view. I have therefore concluded to accept the vote of the Executive Committee, with thanks for their kind feeling. In proposing to return to Burmah, I have no thought of ever coming again to this country. When my work is done, I hope through grace to go to the home of my Father in heaven. I cannot think it wise or Christian to chase around the world for the sake of a few more years in this life. In my last return, I neither sought nor wished it. I had little hope of getting able to work again, and wished to die quietly where I had done my best work. It was at the repeated request of others that I came, and one of those who urged it paid the bill, *all of it*, so that my passage home, at least, was not at the expense of the Mission. I am greatly indebted to you, my dear brother, for your kindness in this matter, as in all your intercourse with me.

As ever, affectionately your brother,

J. G. BINNEY.

Preparations for departure were cheerfully commenced, and nearly completed with comparative ease, when a storm of wind and rain came on, which lasted several days. He took a severe cold, inflammatory rheumatism ensued, and it looked for a time as if the Lord in his providence had ordered otherwise; the physician, however, succeeded in giving great relief, and advised that he should leave the place as soon as possible, as that climate was very unfavorable for rheumatism. He, therefore, hurried on to New York two weeks before the steamer was to sail; a physician there, who had been highly recommended, was called; and all that was possible was done for him. Much benefit was hoped from the sea voyage. It had always acted like a charm upon him, when ill; and every one recommended his going at the appointed time. Other symptoms were more favorable, but the rheumatism gave him little rest. On the day of departure the seeing of many old friends and the kind farewells were very trying; but he kept up till the steamer left the wharf, when he retired at once to his berth. On the voyage he had seasons of relief, so that he came out sometimes to the table, but was never really better. A physician of note was, on his arrival in Glasgow, called to visit him. He too thought that when the region of milder weather was reached he would experience great relief. They sailed from Glasgow, hoping that, as they moved southward, the relief would come; but it was not so ordered, and the disease finally affected the vital organs, and his sufferings were intense. An extract from a letter written by Mrs. Binney will finish the narrative. It was dated on the Steamship Amarapoora, Indian Ocean, November 27th, 1877.

To the Sisters and Relatives of my precious Husband.

DEAR ONES.—I know that you will hear from other sources of the decease of our dearly beloved, and will look with painful anxiety for such intelligence as I only can give you. I wish to

31

spare you this solicitude, and therefore nerve myself to write at once, fearing that, after so much fatigue and distress, there may be such a re-action that I shall not be able to have a letter ready to mail on our arrival at Rangoon, which will be in about a week.

Only yesterday morning, at about half-past nine o'clock, my dear one left me, and at four o'clock, the same evening, we committed his body to the bosom of the great deep. With what agony I did so, only He who knows and pities us in all our sorrows can ever understand.

After we saw that there was no further ground for hope of his recovery, and little even of alleviation of suffering, I still hoped he would live to reach Rangoon, that I might bury him in the Mission Cemetery, by the side of his beloved co-workers there. This, indeed, was the burden of my prayer for a few days, and so I ventured to tell him. He looked me earnestly in the face and said :

" I do think you should pray—that the time may be shortened. Ask the Lord, rather, to take me speedily to himself." ·

"Oh !" I said, "I can never do that. The Lord's time must be the best time. Let us try to wait patiently on him."

"All right ; so we will," he replied, and so he did.

But I soon was constrained to do the very thing I had thought impossible, and my prayer was that the Lord would take him to himself, where there would be no more pain or sorrow. And the Lord heard my prayer, and took him sooner than we had expected.

About ten days before his departure he had a turn of coughing which lasted over three hours. In my distress, having tried every means for his relief in vain, I said to him :

" The Lord hears prayer. Let us ask Brother Harris to come in and pray with us ; pray that you may be relieved."

He nodded assent ; I called Brother Harris, but before I could tell him what I wanted him to pray for, my husband said :

" Brother Harris, pray that the Lord's will may be done. I have believed my self to be his. I trust him. I desire to have no will of my own, but that he will dispose of me as he sees best."

Though he did not ask for relief, soon, from sheer exhaustion, he fell asleep. We then discovered that there was a partial paralysis of the throat, and I avoided so great suffering again by giving him only the most carefully prepared liquids. His sufferings were very great from the very day we left New York till it pleased the Lord to take him, and he bore them all with great fortitude. But I will not dwell further upon these painful details. During the whole way he clung to me with such love and trust as was wonderful. The only way I ever obtained his consent to my leaving him for a moment was by reminding him, that unless I got a little rest, I might be compelled to leave him altogether. Indeed, this feeling of dependence had been growing upon him for months. During two or three of the last weeks he would not allow me to sit for a moment where he could not see my face. This required of me an unremitted effort to appear cheerful. I once said, on leaving him for an hour, to sleep:

"Brother Harris will do everything for you."

"Oh, it is not that. I want *you* by me to think with me, to sympathize with me, to pray with me. I can't do without you."

This rendered it difficult for others to relieve me as they desired, but Brethren Harris and Stevens were very kind, doing all in their power, so that, after we reached the Bay of Biscay, I managed to get a little sleep every night; but I can never forget the joy he always showed when I returned. Had I known that he would be called so soon, I think I could not have left him so often as I did; but I thought I must spare myself a little for his sake. He always expressed the most perfect trust and confidence, but he said one day:

"I had hoped, as dear Dr. Wade did, to have shouted 'Hallelujah!' once before crossing over."

I think he did leave joyfully; for just before he ceased to converse, I, supposing him even then unconscious, was attending upon him, and turned around to reach a handkerchief, when one standing by asked me what I was looking for. I, not wishing to talk, replied, "nothing." He instantly opened his eyes, beaming as with joyful anticipation, upon me, and said:

"*I* am looking for something."

"What are you looking for, darling?"

"I am looking for the speedy coming of my Lord and Saviour Jesus Christ, God over all, blessed forever."

The latter part was uttered with a loud, firm voice, which might well be called a "Hallelujah." I do not think he spoke an entire sentence after that, but he called my name to almost his last breath. He often prayed audibly for me, using the pronoun "us" very generally. He spoke during the last two days several times of having desired to do a little more work, but said, as the Lord did not permit him, there must have been a good reason.

I know you will all feel very sad about his having been buried at sea. At first, the thought was very painful to me, but only one short day and night has made me feel quite differently. It is the utter loneliness and desolation of heart that distresses me, not that his dear remains are committed to the deep. The ocean does not seem hard and cruel that it has swallowed them up; but rather, like a great, loving friend, has opened her kind arms to receive my treasure, which she will safely keep until called upon to "give up her dead," when she will promptly obey the summons. We committed him tenderly to the Indian Ocean, whose waters lave the land of his adoption, and connect and mingle with those that wash the shores of the land of his birth and of the whole world. It seems to me to be fit that he, whose sympathies and prayers and labors were for the universal brotherhood of man, should thus be buried. When I arose this morning, instead of shrinking from looking out upon a "vast and dreary waste of waters," as I might have done, I looked from the window of my desolate cabin upon the grand old ocean, with a yearning tenderness and calm such as I never have felt before, and such as I think I never could have felt towards any little spot of earth, however highly decorated or beautifully situated.

There was no display at his burial. I had him suitably dressed, and he did not look emaciated or haggard, as he had done for the few preceding days; but his noble presence commanded respect, as it had in life. They covered him with the British flag, expressing regret that there was no American flag on board to add to it. After about seven hours the ship's bell tolled, and all on board assembled on the deck. The first and last two verses of that beautiful hymn, "Servant of God, well done," were sung. Brother Harris read a few passages of Scripture, selected from the fifteenth chapter of First Corinthians, and the twenty-first of Revelation, and engaged in prayer. The ship was then stopped a while; the officers lowered the body gently down; and, after a few moments' solemn pause, the ship went on her way. All last evening and to-day a subdued, quiet demeanor everywhere prevails. The whole occasion seemed so sincere, so devoid of all affectation or parade, so in harmony with the character of our beloved, that I could not but feel that the loving Father had ordered it all.

There will be great disappointment when I reach Rangoon *alone.* The Karens will feel it deeply; but the Lord has ordered it, and it is best as it is. I will only add that my dear husband never for a moment regretted having "offered," as he said, "a little more service to the Lord." He was sure he had done right in coming back to the Karens. Just before leaving Scotland, after the luggage had been sent off and we were all ready to go to the steamer, he locked the door, and we had a few moments of prayer together. He was very ill, and told the Lord, with the simplicity of a child, all about it. I can never forget that prayer. He renewedly dedicated us to the Lord; living or dying, we would be his; prayed for grace to honor him in suffering or in service; prayed for the coming of his kingdom; and I felt then that we were all right, come what might. God has been pleased to verify his promise toward me. My strength has been equal to my day. I have not been really sick an hour since I left New York. I have often been so weary and sleepy that I would lie down without undressing, or even throwing over me a cover; but an hour's sleep would generally so rest me that I would soon be at the side of my dear one, ready to serve him. I know you will all pity me and pray for me. I now feel as if life will be very desolate, but if the Lord has anything more for me to do, he will give me strength to do it.

With true love, ever yours,

J. P. BINNEY.

31*

CHAPTER XXIII.

MEMORIAL SERVICES AT RANGOON.

1877.

MEMORIAL services were held, the first Lord's Day after the ship's arrival, in the beautiful little Chapel of the Theological Seminary, which he had two years before dedicated, and in which he preached his last sermon. The principal part of the report, prepared by Rev. D. A. W. Smith, is here inserted.

THE MEMORIAL SERVICE.

Dr. Binney died on board the Steamship "Amarapoora," November 26th, 1877, latitude 80° 32′ north, and longitude 67° 54′ east, and was buried at sea about three days' sail west of the island of Ceylon. The first tidings which greeted us as, on Wednesday, December 5th, we hastened on board the steamer to welcome the long-expected party of missionaries, new and old, was that Dr. Binney was no more. On the following Lord's Day appropriate memorial services were held in the Chapel of the Karen Theological Seminary, conducted by Rev. D. A. W. Smith, Dr. Binney's successor in the School. The Chapel was filled with the students of the Seminary and College, and a good attendance of other Karens, who had known and honored Dr. Binney in life, and wished to share in these last sad memorial services. All the Karen missionaries were present, with the exception of Rev. D. L. Brayton, who was prevented by illness.

364

There were several also from the out-stations, who were glad to be present to show their respect for the departed, and to mourn with the bereaved widow. The pulpit, behind which Dr. Binney had stood so often, was suitably draped; and an excellent photograph of Dr. Binney, heavily bordered with crape, stood on the communion table, in front of the pulpit.

The services were all in Karen. An opening hymn, which had been a favorite of the deceased, was sung, after which appropriate selections of Scripture were read, and Mr. Harris led the congregation in prayer. The hymn "Nearer, my God, to thee" was then sung, when Mr. Smith spoke as follows:

"Last Lord's Day, as we left the Chapel, after evening service, we said among ourselves, 'Next Lord's Day the missionary party will have arrived, and perhaps Dr. Binney will preach to us in this Chapel. If he cannot preach, he will surely say something to us; if unable to do as much as that, we shall at least look upon his face and rejoice in his presence.' But to-day how different is all this from our anticipations! We are not permitted even to look upon his face. This place, that knew him for so many years, shall know him no more. He is gone; and nought is left for us to-day, excepting the remembrance of him. But *this* is no small boon; we are glad to have known him. We are grateful that it was ours to be associated with him in work; to listen to his counsel, to receive his instructions, to have familiar intercourse with him, to see him at work, and to see his work. This recollection of personal relations between ourselves and the departed teacher gives us joy on this day of sorrow.

"Dr. Binney was a man on whom to lean. He could be relied on. His yea was yea, and his nay was nay. He was genial in domestic and social intercourse. He was a wise counsellor, true and honorable in his friendships, uncompromising in his principles; a man to whom one would go, and not in vain, for advice and sympathy in trouble." * * *

"His body lies beneath the waves. We cannot erect a monument over his grave, on which to record the virtues, and with which to keep alive the memory, of the dead. But he can well dispense with such a memorial. This Theological Seminary, founded by him, and to which he gave the best years of his life; and the long roll of native pastors, teachers, and evangelists—who were trained by him for their sacred work,—are his abiding memorials, living stones of remembrance which can never perish."

Rev. Sau Tay then arose and said: "Our revered and beloved Teacher Binney came to us the second time, after an absence of several years, in the month of May, 1859, when I immediately attached myself to him in his work. I studied and recited under him, and at the same time assisted him in teaching and in every way in my power, up to the very day of his final return to his native land. I have been with him as large a portion of my life as I have spent with my own father; and most happy have I been with him. I knew him better, perhaps, than I knew my own dear father. I was with him in my maturer years; and my heart yearns for him even as for a father.

" He had been absent from us nearly nine years, when he returned, as I have mentioned, and we thought he had probably nearly forgotten our language. He arrived on Friday night, and on the Lord's Day preached to us with great freedom and power. His first address, especially to the students of the Seminary, was founded on these words, 'The joy of the Lord is your strength.' At that time the students of Maulmain were obliged to leave their pleasant accommodations and come to Kemendine, Rangoon. They were very homesick; their hearts yearned for 'Teacher and Mamma Wade.' They had no comfortable houses, either for sleeping or studying; they were mostly strangers to Teacher Binney and to their associate pupils; but when they heard that sermon they were comforted and encouraged.

"At that time I was young and unable to help him much, and he was obliged to do almost all the teaching himself. Besides teaching three or four hours daily, he had charge of the church, and preached often on week evenings, once on Sunday mornings in Karen, and on Sunday evenings in English. He also had a Bible class on the Lord's Day; and this went on for more than two years, when I was able to relieve him a good deal, and as his own strength was failing, he lessened his work a little.

"Our revered Teacher, though a man of the very best feelings, was never very familiar. He guarded well his lips. But though he did not speak at random, he talked much when he had anything important to say; and people remembered his words; and it was well to do so. He was both wise and truthful. If he said a thing, we never doubted him ; and if, by his promise, he led us to expect anything, it was to us as if already fulfilled. We always implicitly trusted in him. He was also a man of large heart; and his sympathies and plans were by no means confined to the Karens. Among his last acts he devised plans for the good of Burmans as well. His pupils were accustomed to call him 'a just and true man;' and even the heathen Burmans, who had a great deal of intercourse with him in working for him, were accustomed to call him by that appellation.

"Our Teacher has no grave. In this respect he is like Elias and Moses and Judson. We can not understand God's purposes, but we know he makes no mistakes. Is it that too much respect might have been paid to the grave? Perhaps so. But there was probably a better reason. I think the Lord permitted him to become an example for us, who have been his pupils and children, even in his death. Our teacher followed Christ's example to the last, and did not count his life dear unto himself. Shall we not imitate this example? If he did not shrink from duty to save life, shall we allow anything to come between us and a faithful doing of our Master's work?

"And these labors and self-denials of our beloved Teacher were greatly approved and blessed of God. Multitudes of preachers and teachers have been raised up in consequence. His work will never die. These are his living epistles in every part of our country. They are the pillars of our churches throughout Burmah. In this we rejoice greatly."

Rev. E. B. Cross, D. D., next arose and said : " The occasion on which we are assembled here would seem to be one for lamentation and tears. Why then do we not weep and show tokens of grief? The reason is that we can not think of him who has gone as in a place of tears or grief. We think of him as dwelling now in a place of glory and of joy, and for him we cannot grieve.

"You have heard that he was expected here, and that in a few days you would see him in your Chapel and in your midst. But he did not come, and his grave is not with us. There is no headstone of marble to record his name and deeds. But he has a better and more enduring record than can be fixed on the headstone of a grave; for you are his epistles, known and read of all men. We can visit no place in Burmah where his living epistles are not found. We go to Tavoy, and we find them there. We go to Maulmain and Bassein, and his epistles are many. In every place we find his work written in living lines, not with ink, nor upon tablets of stone, but on the fleshly tablets of many hearts; and they cannot die or perish.

"We are not here to praise a Teacher, nor to praise any man; yet there are those now, as in the days of the apostle Paul, whose names are known and whose praise is in all the churches. God, in his own way, has distinguished some men from others, and has made their lives, their history, and special events in their history, monuments, or at least marks, of his own special acts of providence. In our mission in this land, God seems to have chosen Dr. Judson to introduce the gospel—the simple message of salvation by the cross of Christ; and in the same way he seems to have chosen Dr. Binney to introduce the School of Theology to the Karens; and both Dr. Judson and Dr. Binney have been buried in the sea. We do not know the reason, but we know the fact. This may be a better monument. We may never forget these men because of this providence and the coincidence itself; a coincidence which forces itself upon our minds.

"The perishing flesh of our brother and teacher is not here. His body is not before us. We do not see his face, but we shall see it. It is our part to imitate his example, and, as teachers, to be like him; to follow him as he followed Christ."

Rev. Norman Harris, who sailed with Dr. Binney, and was with him when he died, then spoke as follows: "How can I tell you of Teacher Binney's sickness and death? I saw the Teacher before he left you for America, and we talked together about our work, as being nearly done. After he left you, several asked me whether Teacher Binney would ever come back. I replied:

" ' We have no ground to hope he will be able to return.'

" When I was in America, the question was repeatedly asked:

" ' Will Dr. Binney ever go back to Burmah ?'

" ' No,' I replied; ' he is too old and feeble to go out again.'

" When the time drew near for me to sail, I was surprised to hear that Dr. Binney was to be one of the party; and when I met him on the steamer in New York, I said to him:

" ' I thought you would never go again to Burmah.'

" ' I have a little work,' he replied, ' which I wish to do there.'

" I said, ' Burmah is a good place to work in.'

" ' Yes,' he replied; ' and a good place to die in.'

" The Teacher suffered much in crossing the ocean, and in Scotland. While there he called a physician, who told him that place was bad for him, and by all means to go on, and when he arrived at the Mediterranean Sea he would be better. We came on, and when sailing over that sea perhaps he suffered less pain, but his strength gradually failed. After several days he told me his throat was bad, and said, ' This is a new disease, unlike anything which I have had before.' It became difficult for him to eat or drink, and sometimes he coughed badly. One day he said :

" ' Brother Harris, I think I am the Lord's ; I trust him. Pray that the will of the Lord may be done, either for life or death. I have no will but his.'

" He did not ask me to pray that he might be well again, but that the will of the Lord might be done.

" Your Teacher trusted in that same power which I, with great pleasure, have heard him preach to others. He was not afraid to die, because Christ has taken away the sting of death for believers. Dr. Judson was buried east of the island of Ceylon, and Dr. Binney about seven hundred miles west of that island."

Next they sang, with deep feeling, the translation of the hymn—

"Asleep in Jesus, blessed sleep,
From which none ever wake to weep."

Mr. Harris closed with prayer, and the benediction.

CHAPTER XXIV.

TRIBUTES TO THE MEMORY OF DR. BINNEY.

SOON after the intelligence of Dr. Binney's decease was received in England and America, and at the various mission stations in Burmah and India, more than one hundred letters of condolence and sympathy were received by the bereaved companion of his life's voyage. A remarkable fact, and one which it is presumed very rarely in similar circumstances occurs, deserves record:—Not one of all those letters lacked that nice and tender discrimination, the want of which so often causes to bleed afresh, wounds, which, according to the merciful ordering of our natural constitutions, time does more or less serve to heal. Many of them were beautifully simple and touching; but they were mostly of so personal a character, and so connected with the bereaved, that, while they have awakened the liveliest gratitude, they were permitted to serve the simple purpose intended, to soothe and comfort. Two or three extracts or entire letters are given a place here, not because they were written with any other end in view than the others, but because of the peculiar relation sustained by the writers; or because, for other reasons, they are testimonies of great worth to the character of the deceased.

FROM J. N. MURDOCK, D. D., TO MRS. BINNEY.

BOSTON, MASSACHUSETTS, January 25th, 1878.

MY DEAR MRS. BINNEY,—The mail brought us on Monday the sad news of the death of your honored husband. I cannot say that it surprised me after what I saw of him in New York and heard of him in Glasgow; but I am none the less afflicted. He was so anxious to do a little more for the spiritual welfare of his loved Karens, and I knew there was so much need of what no one could do so well as he, I was fain to hope that he would be spared to see his books through the press. But the Lord, who knows all about what is needed, and how it is to be effected, has taken him from his cherished work to his heavenly reward. But, my dear friend, his work is not an unfinished work. He has been taken away from it, but it is complete, because it is as the Lord has ordained. The plan of his life was of the Lord; and how loyally, faithfully, and truly he pursued it till the day when the Lord took him! His course was finished, his work was done, and his crown is secure.

In writing to you, as I must, in terms of condolence and sympathy, I cannot refrain from congratulating you that your life has been so largely cast in relations of closest and most endeared intimacy with such a man as Dr. Binney. His intellectual, moral, and social qualities were of the rarest order. His intellectual grasp and breadth, his dignity of bearing, his gentleness, his integrity, his high sense of honor, his devotion to duty, combined to stamp his character with a heroic mould. I never met a man who more fully commanded respect and veneration. I shall miss his always considerate and kind expressions, and his always judicious views of matters which we here are obliged to take on the credit of other understandings. I grieve with you over this great loss.

Accept, my dear friend, my sincere sympathy in this hour of your trial. While you comfort yourself with the contemplation of the exalted character and incomparable worth of your lamented husband, you have the higher consolation of knowing that he is in heaven with his God.

"Now our Lord Jesus Christ himself, and God, even our Father, who hath loved us and hath given us everlasting consolation and good hope through grace, comfort your heart and establish you in every good word and work."

Yours with sincere commiseration,

J. N. MURDOCH.

S. F. SMITH, D. D., TO MRS. BINNEY.

NEWTON CENTRE, MASSACHUSETTS, January 28, 1878.

MY DEAR MRS. BINNEY,—Among the sad, but precious testimonials which you are doubtless receiving from sympathizing friends in this country, I claim it as a privilege to add my witness. You know how long I have known your incomparable husband, and how highly I have esteemed him. I feel that in his departure " a great man is fallen in Israel." He filled in his lifetime a sphere of lone conspicuity, having done what no man ever did for the Karens, or can do. As the originator of the Theological Seminary, and moulding it wisely from the beginning into form and shape according to the pattern in his own mind, he conferred a priceless boon on the people and their ministry for all time. Whatever subsequent teachers may do, his work lay as the corner-stone on which the building has been fitly framed together. I am aware that he had much to struggle against in his protracted work in Burmah. But none can doubt his faithfulness, his energy, his wisdom, his zeal, his entire consecration. The blessings of thousands will come upon him, and you as his helper, companion, and joy.

You will have had ere this innumerable words of sympathy and consolation from your many friends; and I am sure those consolations have been sealed and intensified by those of the Divine Paraclete, speaking in them and above them. What more is needed than Christ's own words of sympathy, "The Comforter, which is the Holy Ghost, whom the Father will send in my name." There you have, in one verse, the three Persons of the Divine Trinity speaking peace—all there is of God. Could you have more?

I am glad your dear husband took Rome on his way to the New Jerusalem. Methinks it will aid his intercourse with the Apostle Paul in glory, and add to his capacity to comprehend him, to remember that he, too, was in the Eternal City and saw the Coliseum, the Tiber, and perhaps the Ghetto, and the site of Paul's "own hired house." The associations of earth will surely make heaven the sweeter, and the memory of the "City of the Seven Hills" will illustrate and endear the city having everlasting foundations. How the grand missionary of the first century and the younger but noble missionary of the nineteenth will enjoy together the intercourse with the believers to whom that wonderful eighth chapter of the Epistle was addressed.

Let me assure you of my congratulations for him who now looks back on a finished life of usefulness and honor; my congratulations to yourself, connected so intimately, so dearly, so helpfully, and so lovingly, as well as so long, with such a servant of God, and my sympathy, and prayers that you may be divinely sustained and grandly sanctified by this bereavement. If you have less to love on earth, you have more in heaven.

With highest Christian regard,

I am very sincerely yours,

S. F. SMITH.

FROM J. G. WARREN, D. D.

MY DEAR MRS. BINNEY.—Though I was Dr. Binney's junior by a few years, my acquaintance with him dates back nearly to the time when he entered on public life, his first settlement being at West Boylston, in Worcester County, Massachusetts— my native county, and my home till maturity. While he was there I came into his presence a few times at the general meetings of the Baptists, and gained some idea of the sources of his power, and of the promise he gave of future usefulnesss

From that time till the day of his death and burial in the Indian Ocean—fitting receptacle for such a treasure—I followed him; first through the medium of his letters, as published in the *Baptist Magazine*, afterwards by social intercourse, while he was in this country, and by listening a few times to his sermons and addresses, and most of all by the correspondence which went before his re-appointment to the position of Theological Teacher to the Karens, and the many letters I received from him while I was Corresponding Secretary of the Missionary Union. * * *

If any ask for a portrait of your husband, I should say that in stature he was of medium height, standing erect, every limb exquisitely formed and performing promptly its part, while the whole frame work, compacted and knit together, executed promptly and well the tasks assigned it by the ruling powers within. The head, for such a trunk, was large; the eye keen and penetrating, yet benignant; the face manly and noble, its entire expression being generous and kind, while firm and determined. In mind he was self-centred, self-poised, self-reliant; and, I do him no harm when I say, self-filled. In other form of words, he had a mind of his own, the gift of God, to be and remain his, by original right and possession, and to be employed in working out the end which himself approved, and hence he never "borrowed leave to be" from any mortal; always had opinions, faiths, sentiments, and corresponding practices of his own.

He was a born disciplinarian and teacher, whether amongst Americans or Karens, fully grown men or children. All instinctively felt his sway—a sway sent abroad in the very atmosphere around him, without any set purpose of his own, but by the spontaneous out-go of his being. All gathered at his feet as voluntary, humble, and receptive pupils, to take on, take in, and assimilate whatever he might impart, and so they gradually grew up into him and became conformed to his image. His children are scattered all over Burmah. Herein is the real prerogative and true glory of an instructor. Hence, I have often said, it is worth more to me to come into casual and involuntary contact with some minds than to sit whole ages under the formal teachings of others. In the first instance, I should receive an inspiration that would thrill in me forever, lifting me up and impelling me forward. In the other, I should become loaded down with lumber on the outside, a dead weight to impair every step, while within would be lodged not one particle of creative energy.

I do not think I should do justice to Brother Binney if I attributed to him a massive intellect after the model of the late Dr. Wayland, which at moments was slow, not to say heavy. His mind was, however, of an uncommon order, with all the parts well developed, and each ready at call to leap forth and perform at its very best the assigned task. Few men ever had the intellectual powers all under so complete discipline, and fewer still could make such power do his bidding with such consummate skill. This was evinced both in the class-room and in the pulpit. In the last named position alone had I an opportunity personally to observe it.

His very presence in the pulpit, as he rose to speak, captivated an assembly, and all eyes were turned on him, expecting to receive something from him; nor were they destined to disappointment. The moment he opened his lips, words of grace proceeded out of his mouth, and on and still on he went in a simple, direct, incisive. all-persuasive utterance, unaided by manuscript, but not without the most painstaking preparation, by reading, by protracted thought, and often by writing and re-writing, yet never committing verbally to memory. This preaching cost him something. All his hearers craved more from the same source.

I seem to hear some one asking, "Was Dr. Binney the only full-grown man we ever had in Burmah?" My answer is ready. He was only one among many fully developed men—men of superior excellence of character, each on a model peculiar to himself, as originally designed by the God of Missions, and wrought out by him.

To these also is appended a tribute, published in the *Examiner and Chronicle*, soon after his decease, from the pen of A. J. Huntington, D. D., who was a beloved co-worker, with him, while in Columbian College, Washington, D. C.

The testimony of the Senior Professor in Columbian College, the late Wm. Ruggles, LL.D., has been given from time to time in this narrative, in a manner that could not admit doubt of his sincere esteem for Dr. Binney and his hearty interest in the work to which his life was devoted. It will suffice to say that at various times he gave more than twenty thousand dollars towards the support of the educational work, with which Dr. Binney was connected, so that the names of Binney and Ruggles are closely allied in it.

FROM A. J. HUNTINGTON, D. D.

DR. BINNEY AS AN EXAMPLE.

So far as our Baptist churches are concerned, a star of the first magnitude has just set; and we do well again and again to turn our eyes upon its lingering radiance. Admirable tributes to the memory of Dr. Binney have just appeared in these columns from Dr. W. T. Brantly and Dr. S. S. Cutting. My only apology for adding to what they have so well said, is my intimate connection with him during his Presidency of Columbian College, and the high regard which then and ever afterwards I had for him.

To his intellectual qualities, to his remarkable power as a preacher, to his decided success as a pastor, to his eminent ability as a College President and Professor,—it is unnecessary to refer, since his rare talents were acknowledged by all who knew him in these different spheres of action. But it is my purpose rather to point to some of those prominent features in his religious character which make him an example worthy of the imitation of every Christian.

1. He is an illustration of *the power of a strong faith*—of that faith which the Bible signalizes in the worthies of old—in Enoch and Noah and Abraham and Moses and David and Samuel and the prophets—of that faith which is the cardinal grace of the New Dispensation, and without which no one has been, and no one can be, a successful worker in the vineyard of the Lord. Dr. Binney, as he professed to believe, so did really believe with the simplicity of a child, in that holy God whom the Bible

reveals as the Rewarder of the righteous and the Punisher of the wicked ; and he so believed that he looked, as it were, into the eternal world, saw the judgment seat, before which he and all men must appear, and heard, as it were, the welcome, "Come, ye blessed," and the doom, "Depart, ye cursed." He really believed that Jesus, by his blood, obtained eternal redemption for all who accept him. He really believed, as if he had received the command from his own lips, that his Lord had commissioned him to tell to ruined men the news of this great salvation ; and he believed that this message, if faithfully delivered, would, with the promised aid of the Spirit, arrest the attention of men and turn them to God. He believed, and therefore spake in words of earnestness and power. He believed, and therefore, as a herald of the cross, braved again and again the dangers of the deep and the smitings of the tropical sun. It was because he had this faith in him who is invisible, that he endured, fearing not, faltering not, desponding not, and finished his course triumphantly, exclaiming, "I am looking for the coming of my Lord and Saviour Jesus Christ, God over all, blessed forever." Now this is the faith that the Bible inculcates, but which we greatly fear is dying in the church. But just such a reasonable, simple, Scriptural faith must we have if we would please God, conquer sin in our hearts, and win men to Christ. This faith alone can feed the flame of our love when it grows cold, urge us on when we loiter, strengthen us when we faint, and by giving us a view of the outshining recompense of the reward, help us to turn off our eyes from the world. Lord, increase *our* faith.

2. Dr. Binney furnishes us an example of *Christian consecration.* Where there is this vigorous faith, there will be a hearty consecration. No one could have known him well without perceiving that his piety was not formal, but was a living principle, animating his whole being ; that he had not chosen the ministry as a profession, but had entered it because he had heard the voice of God calling him to it ; and that he discharged his duties as a Christian and as a Christian laborer, not in a perfunctory way, but because he felt that his beloved Lord had imposed them upon him, and because it was his meat and his drink to do

his will. It was easy to see that he had not nominally, but cordially and unreservedly, given to Christ his whole body and soul —all that he was, all that he had, and all that he could do ;—that he felt he was not his own, but was simply the servant of Jesus, bought with his precious blood ;—that he recognized his Lord's complete ownership of him and absolute right to use him as he pleased, and his own duty to glorify him in all that he did—to go and come at his bidding, to live where and as his Master might bid him to live, and to die where and as he might bid him die. Hence, while his health and that of his wife permitted him to labor for Christ in Burmah, he there did with his might the work which was there assigned him ; and when it became necessary for him to leave the East, he devoted himself with like earnestness and fidelity to the duties of preacher and pastor in his own land ; and when an affection of the voice compelled him to withdraw in a measure from the pulpit, he still continued with the same zeal and energy in his Master's service, first as President of the Columbian College, and in his second sojourn in this country as a teacher for a time in a colored Seminary at Richmond, Virginia. In every place, in every sphere, he seemed to live not unto himself, but unto him that died for him. If all the professed followers of Jesus were real soldiers, thus devoted to their Leader, the strongholds of Satan would speedily give way before the rushing onset of the sacramental host. A cavilling world would not then talk of Christianity as an effete and waning system. And who will say that even this apostle to the Karens had all the consecration to which such a Lord and Saviour is entitled ?

*　　*　　*　　*　　*　　*　　*　　*　　*

Not to mention other prominent traits of his character, as his *strict conscientiousness*, his *incorruptible integrity*, his *firm adhesion to the right*, I pray God that the contemplation of those to which I have referred, may tend to arouse us from our apathy and self-indulgence and neglect of Christian duty, and to stimulate us to cultivate the virtues of this valiant soldier of the cross and to follow him as he followed his Lord.

FROM GEORGE DANA ·BOARDMAN, D. D.

The winter of 1854–1855 I spent in Augusta and its vicinity. Accordingly, it was my privilege to attend Dr. Binney's ministry, and, as his health was precarious, to render him occasional assistance.

Dr. Binney's figure was rather spare, but lithe; his complexion fair; his brow ample; his eyes benignant; his smile genial; his voice cheery; his manner dignified, but hearty. His intellectual qualities were strongly marked, but well balanced. He had the faculties of observing minutely, gathering and arranging his data discriminatingly, planning broadly, watching details patiently, reasoning accurately, deciding slowly, but sagaciously and firmly. In a word, he had tact. He was specially gifted with the educational instinct; a born instructor, his influence over young men was stimulating, broadening, and healthful. His moral nature was profound. He was courteous, without insincerity; affectionate, without effeminacy; conscientious, without perversity; generous, without recklessness; catholic, without laxity; genial, without frivolity; grave, without primness; brave, without boastfulness; self-denying, without asceticism; flexible, without feebleness; conservative, without obstinacy; prompt, without rashness; decisive, without dogmatism; self-reliant, without self-conceit; ready to take responsibility, without either courting it or obtruding it. He was a patriotic American, a cosmopolitan philanthropist, a broad scholar, a sound theologian, a powerful preacher, a conspicuously able teacher, a wise counsellor, a steadfast friend, a devoted husband, a heroic missionary. The casket in which once shone that precious jewel now lies enshrined in one of the coral crypts of ocean. But in the day when the sea shall give up its dead, both great and small, it shall be seen that among its many rendered trophies not the least important will be he whose name on earth was

JOSEPH GETCHELL BINNEY.

INDEX.

9 781334 935039